WATCH HER
Thrive

Copyright © 2013 Kimberly Riggins and The Watch Her Thrive Project

ISBN: 978-0-9848130-2-5
ISBN: 0984813020

All Rights Reserved. No part of this publication may be reproduced, stored in a retrieval system, or transmitted in any form or by any means, electronic, mechanical, photocopying, recording, or otherwise without the written permission of the publisher.
All product names are copyrights and trademarks of their respective owners.

The contributing authors retain the copyright to their entry or entries.

The Naked Book Press

Cover design by Lucinda Kinch

WATCH HER THRIVE

Stories of Hope, Courage and Strength

Kimberly Riggins

&

82 Powerful Change Initiators

DEDICATION

For every woman who fights fear on a daily basis…there's always a way out.

For my son Grayson: as soon as you entered the world, I thought the love I felt for you would burst. You have forever changed my life.

"Never doubt that a small group of thoughtful, committed citizens can change the world. Indeed, it is the only thing that ever has."

— *Margaret Mead*

CONTENTS

FOREWORD	xvii
HOPE	1
Watch Her *Lydia Criss Mays*	3
Why Hope is Part Choice, Part Action *Anne Samoilov*	7
Hope Returns *Share Ross*	11
Opportunity in Disguise *Ande Lyons*	15
All Roads Lead to Your Mojo *Deborah Kagan*	21
It Only Has to Work Out Once *Nicole Burley*	27
On Bus Stations and Baby Tigresses with Invisible Stripes.... *Linda Eaves*	33
Hope *Holli Thompson*	35
Women on a Mission: Five Soulful Steps to Become Unstoppable *Stephanie McWilliams*	41
The Anatomy of Hope *Susan Mathison*	49

Even in the Struggle   53
Tara Mohr

The Key to a Life of Bliss Lies within the Messages of
Your Inner Voice   55
Kate Muker

And Then   61
Victoria Prozan McGlinn

Follow the Breadcrumbs   65
Amber McCue

The Hope of Love   69
Candace Smyth

I Wanted to Quit but Hope Whispered Hold On   75
Catrice M. Jackson

Reflection into My Darkness   81
Giusep Michelle Vitale

Looking Down at the Bonfire   85
Lucinda Kinch

The Magic Formula: Three Steps to Thrive   91
Marci Shimoff

The Start of a Revolution   97
Micaela Bubola

My Mistake was Actually a Miracle   101
Nichole Kellerman

The Cards We Are Dealt   105
Rachel Luna

Hope is Still in the Jar   109
Cigdem Kobu

Give a Brick   113
El Edwards

I Am Part of the Freedom Story   117
Kristi Griem

Beyond Expectations   121
Megan Potter

Never Throw Away Your Rose-Colored Glasses   125
Jacqueline Fairbrass

COURAGE   131

Remembering When I Woke Up   133
Erin Giles

The Fireball Known as Courage   139
Sarah Burns

The Lioness Within   145
Alexa Fischer

The Day I Stopped Lying to Myself   149
Andrea Owen

When You've Got Nothing Left to Lose But Weight   153
Rosie Battista

How Learning to Ride a Bike Gave Me the Courage to Live   159
Melissa Cassera

Lean into the Unknown, Lusciously   163
Allana Pratt

Taking the Leap   167
Amy Scott

Fear Less, Moxie More   171
Danielle Dowling

Twenty Five Cents for Freedom   177
Denise Barry

Courage is for the Crazy at Heart   183
Hillary Rubin

Courage Cred *Jenn Burton*	187
Turning Toward Love *Alana Sheeren*	191
Panacea Love *Jennifer Louden*	195
The Rock *Leah Shapiro*	201
My Truth, The Real Truth *Lisa Consiglio Ryan*	205
Pleasure Saves the Day *LiYana Silver*	209
You Are All You Ever Need to Be *Marlee Ward*	215
Making Fear Your Bitch *Michelle Leath*	219
Learning to Show Up as Me *Nicole Mangina*	225
Courage: F-It, We'll Never Know Unless We Try *Sheila Viers*	229
From Destructive to Dazzling *Goddess Star Monroe*	233
The Most Courageous Thing You'll Ever Do… Just Be YOU *Stephenie Zamora*	239
Remind Me *Sue Ann Gleason*	245
You Were Born to Shine *Tracey Selingo*	251

Everything You Want is on the Other Side of Fear *Liz Dennery Sanders*	255
Qualification: Pain *Vanessa Katsoolis*	259
Live in Courage and Thrive *Debra Oakland*	265

STRENGTH   269

Shame Helped Me Find Strength *Charly Emery*	271
Beautifully Broken: Finding Strength Through Loss *Amy E. Smith*	275
Being Bendi *Kristin McGee (the bendigirl)*	279
To Be Fully Self-Expressed *Allison Braun*	283
Challenge Accepted *Amanda Howell*	287
You Were Born With It *Baeth Davis*	291
Strength Over Fear *Danielle Diamond*	295
The Soul of Safety *Dara McKinley*	299
Redefining Success for Strong, Powerful Women *Denise Duffield-Thomas*	303
Find Yourself *Jenelle Montilone*	307
The Accidental Parent *Jessica Kupferman*	309

Strength: In Numbers of Tears *Sally Hope*	315
Let Love Be Your Fuel *Shenee Howard*	319
The Secret Gateway to Strength *Tracy Matthews*	323
The Courage to Be Me *Andie Graff*	327
Kindling *Casey Addinsall*	333
The Gift of Not Enough *Cassandra Herbert*	337
Seize the Moment – There's So Much More to Life than Happy Endings *Cathy Presland*	343
The Strength that Comes Through Dark Spaces *Lisa Grace Byrne*	349
Strength in the Tenderest Places *Grace Quantock*	353
My Recipe for Success *Tracey Ceurvels*	357
Why is Being Yourself so Damn Hard *Molly Mahar*	361
Breaking Down the Walls *Amanda Krill*	365
Tuning the Musical Instrument of You *Mahalia Michaels*	369
Wisdom is Strength *Kimberely Arana*	375

Dancing into Joy *Lela Barker*	381
Sisterhood of Strength *Jessika Hepburn*	387
The War Against Myself *Kimberly Riggins*	391
Acknowledgments	395
About The Watch Her Thrive Project	397
About Founder Kimberly Riggins	399
How You Can Help	401

FOREWORD

We live in a beautiful world where, unfortunately, horrific things happen.

Women across the globe are being silenced by violence. They are subjected to rape, domestic abuse, mutilation, human sex trafficking, and more.

Many of these women are unaware of their rights; they lack the resources to change their circumstances, and they are left feeling defeated.

Many others face social exclusion and must fight daily for their survival, struggling to provide their families with the most basic necessities, such as shelter, food, and water.

After learning this, I knew I had to DO something.

Women should NOT be punished for their demographics.

So I set out on a mission to help these women by providing them with opportunities they might never be exposed to and by giving them the space to not only thrive but to rebuild their lives.

It was Desmond Tutu who said, "If we are going to see real development in the world, then our best investment is women."

And I couldn't agree more. But if women are the cornerstone to improving the world, then we must collectively stand up for EVERY woman on the planet.

We need a voice—one that is loud and irrefutable.

Help me be that voice.

Join me and the other eighty-two amazing change initiators. Over the course of eighty-three essays, you will find insights, stories, tips, and heartfelt emotions from unique women who have already found their own power, including best-selling authors, entrepreneurs making change in their industries, and visionaries whose missions revolve around serving others. However you found this book, my desire is that it inspires you to BE the change you want to see in the world. I believe with hope, courage, and strength we all have the power to THRIVE—to move mountains.

Let's Change the World. One Woman at a Time.

xo Kimberly

Founder of The Watch Her Thrive Project

Proceeds from this book will go directly to Women for Women International, a charity working with socially excluded women in countries where war and conflict have devastated lives and communities.

HOPE

*"When the world says, "give up," Hope whispers,
"Try it one more time."*

— Unknown

WATCH HER
Lydia Criss Mays

Watch a young infant as she explores the world during her first breaths on earth. To family and friends, the sound of her breathing instantly makes the world a more beautiful place. In seconds, she has brought more love into the world than those who love her knew could ever exist. Watch the way her presence in the world makes it a better place.

Watch a young toddler as she expands her understanding of the world during her first few years. The way she loves others is brilliantly untarnished by pop culture's definitions of what does or does not matter. Everyone and everything is a friend and all are unabashedly loved. Watch the way her innocent actions teach adults how to love more deeply. Watch the way her presence in the world makes it a better place.

Watch a young teenager as she navigates the world bombarding her with expectations as a woman—to look, eat, speak, react, dress, and love in a certain way. The way she thinks is malleable, and yet she is her own. She is left to make decisions that are all her own, and society does play a role. She determines the role. Watch the way she executes her power to think and decide for herself. Watch the way her presence in the world makes it a better place.

Watch a woman as she steps out on her own for the first time. The way she grows is inspiring. Her decision-making takes on a life of its own as she provides for herself and the decisions she makes impact the world. Choosing a road—less traveled or not—is a choice she deserves. She is ready for the journey that is all her own. Watch the way she embodies the empowering responsibility of womanhood. Watch the way her presence in the world makes it a better place.

Watch a woman as she finds her groove. The way she moves through the day reflects a role model for others. People of all ages observe her skilled actions, conversations, and relationships as lessons to better understand their own interactions with others and the world. Her groove is unlike anyone else's as she comes to find a whole new self: herself redefined and strengthened again and again. Watch the peacefulness that permeates her being as she does what she does best. Watch the way her presence in the world makes it a better place.

Watch a woman as she reflects on life. Each breath donated to the world since birth has invited more love into the lives of uncountable people. Daily exploration of the world has provided her with a perception of how best to negotiate pop culture and society's ideals with her own. Her groove of life has offered unmatchable learning opportunities for others. No one could contribute to the world the unique gifts that she has. Watch her.

She has everything to offer the world. She did from the second she was born. She offers an indefinable, world-changing love by simply breathing. She offers greater understanding of the world by simply wondering. She offers a unique strength to be observed by others by simply thinking. And she offers an expertise paralleled by none by simply doing her thing.

People love her.

People are inspired by her.

People find her one of a kind.

People give more because of her.

People try harder due to knowing her.

People love more because she's in their lives.

People's lives are enriched because she is in them.

Watch her.

You are her.

You are her.

You are her.

Her = You

That woman is you.

You make the world a more beautiful place by simply being in it. You offer something no one else can to the entire world. Your smile can light up another's life, and your love can change the world.

How often do you watch her? How often do you see how strong, beautiful, loving, giving, and kind you are? How often do you give yourself permission to search your past for all the good that's planted there? How often do you give yourself permission to celebrate the You who's unlike anyone else on earth? How often do you give yourself permission to look into the future and dream about all the goodness you'll have to offer others? It's time to watch her.

We're watching you—not because we expect you to change the world, but because you change the world. You have since your first breath, and you will continue to do so well beyond your last.

Thank you for the gift you are to the world. Watching you invites us all to see more beautiful.

Lydia Criss Mays, PhD, is the president and CEO of See Beautiful™, an organization committed to empowering girls and women to see the beauty they inherently possess and empowering all to see more beautiful in the world. A former elementary school teacher, Lydia is also an assistant professor at Georgia State University in the Early Childhood Education department. Among Mays's published research articles and book chapters, she is also a children's book author of an award-winning coauthored book, *The Long and The Short of It: A Tale About Hair.* Learn more about Lydia at SeeBeautiful.com.

WHY HOPE IS PART CHOICE, PART ACTION

Anne Samoilov

I get told a lot how positive I am. That I always look on the bright side.

The truth is I'm not as filled with hope and cheery goodness as you might think.

I walk around looking at the world and am saddened by much of what I see. But for me it's not a simple passing—oh, that's so sad. I take it in—feel actual sorrow and often allow it to overwhelm me.

What can any of us do to help people struggling?

We have our own problems, right?

We have our own struggles?

Who says WE have to be the ones to fight for them?

When you reach your hand out to help someone, it's a choice, plain and simple.

So I ask you today, why can't hope be a choice too?

Hope isn't about being unrealistic or filling your head with unattainable dreams.

It's about making a simple choice to see the world as it can and should be.

So, how do I choose hope in my everyday life?

Here's a little of what I do. Some of it may be relevant to you, some may not. Hope hits every part of my day.

I choose to support creative entrepreneurs as they bring their ideas and dreams into the world. I have hope for them when they do not, because I know it can happen. I know they can do that project or take on that new path if they just stick to it.

I choose to give people a chance even when others have written them off. I have hope in individuals that other people just cast aside. Maybe it's naive, but I believe there's always a chance for greatness.

I choose hope each day I bring my daughter to school and put my trust in teachers who care for her while I'm at home working. I hope that she is being taught how to be a better human being. And I hope that I've chosen correctly.

I have hope and faith that I make the right decisions at every turn of my day; some are more visible choices than others.

What motivates you to activate hope?

OK, so here's the deal. Even though you have to decide to have hope—to live with hope as your primary filter for everything you do—it still takes a little effort to activate it. To make your decision real. Concrete.

Here's what I do to "remind" and activate hope. These are super simple strategies that I come back to whenever I'm not feeling it. I go back to these simple exercises whenever I am feeling downtrodden, hopeless, or simply depressed.

Look for the Corner

No matter how far down the hole you feel—if you lose your job, you or someone you care about gets injured, or you experience some other type of life upset—there's a corner you'll need to turn in order to come back from it. Look ahead and ask yourself, "Where's the corner? What's my turning point? What would it take for someone else to find it? Can I apply that to myself?" We all have a turning point—a corner. Find it—make finding that corner your goal. It doesn't solve everything, but once you find it, start to walk toward it, and you'll see hope slip into your life effortlessly.

Stop Complaining

Even if you feel like crap, don't talk about feeling like crap. I don't mean you have to be super over-the-top positive here; just stop complaining. So your job sucks, your husband never listens to you, you stubbed your big toe this morning...When you catch yourself complaining, zip it. It's actually really interesting how fast you'll start feeling better. Try it.

Get Outside or Get Active

Activity, movement, exercise—they are all amazing activators that renew confidence in yourself, your life, and other people, and by being active you'll generally be a happier person. Choosing to take care of yourself is so tied to hope; it means you have hope and you value yourself enough to start that hope with yourself.

One last note. Hope is a way of life—if you choose it and take action, you will live it.

Anne Samoilov is a mom to one growing, changing, and challenging daughter. She's also the creator of Fearless Launching, a unique online program teaching women entrepreneurs how to pull off their first launch, and The White Space Solution, a digital guide to simplifying and living your best life. Anne's happiest when she's hanging out with her husband and daughter at their home near Seattle, WA. To learn more about Anne, visit AnneSamoilov.com.

HOPE RETURNS
Share Ross

Without it:

Every breath is a struggle.

It's hard to wake up in the morning and get out of bed.

Nothing looks shiny and possible.

Life just feels…hard. Unfair. Painful.

With it…

Everything is possible

Everyone is lovable.

You are filled with a sense of grace and strength.

Hope.

Hope is the thread that ties us together. Even in tragedy.

I was sitting in my friend's house in Beverly Hills when I got a call from my brother John's wife, Diane.

"Share, there's no easy way to say this. Your brother Mike died."

"What? What happened?"

"Your dad found him in the garage. He died from accidental carbon monoxide poisoning."

I stared at the people around me who were trying to figure out what was going on based on my reactions. I simply felt empty. I felt like someone had shot me and I couldn't feel the bullet wound yet.

My brother Mike and I had always been close, but in recent years, we had become best phone buddies, swapping stories of our failed relationships and giving each other encouragement to pursue our dreams. I had recently driven from LA to Minnesota where he had fixed my 1970 Mustang Coupe. (He was a mechanic.) And he had just turned forty.

Diane was apologizing. "I'm sorry John didn't call you or your parents. They are really struggling right now so I offered to be the one to call you."

Poor Diane. I probably swore at her and quite possibly called her names. I have no recollection. I was furious at the world. I vaguely recall taking frustration out on the kitchen cupboards in my friend's house.

In a fog, I booked a flight back to Minnesota. At the funeral I saw my father break down and sob like I'd never seen him do before. It was terrifying to witness my powerful, all-knowing, six-foot father shaking and shuddering with grief. Mike's youngest daughter, Katie, reached up and put her little ten-year-old arm on his shoulder to comfort him. It was strangely sad and hopeful at the same time.

I slept in Mike's old room and played Neil Young's *Harvest Moon* album repeatedly. Katie would creep into the room late at night and lie on the bed next to me. Neither of us said a word as we listened to Neil Young sing. We just lay there and soaked in the soothing sounds.

It was May when he died, and as summer crept in my dad turned to his usual routine of gardening. My parents lived on two and a half acres of land, and even though my dad was a corporate man with a ton of responsibilities, he had always enjoyed growing his own organic vegetables. I helped him plant tomatoes, swiss chard, and green beans along with loads of other delicious foods. Together we pulled weeds. Together we dug our hands into the soil and gave our hearts a lovely distraction. We appreciated each other more than before. Under the hot Minnesota sun, he asked questions about my life he'd never asked. I answered more gently than I used to. I answered with more patience and understanding of where he was coming from.

I can't begin to imagine what it's like to lose an adult child. My mom was well-known for her bouncy personality and big smile, which had been replaced by a frown and sudden outbursts of tears. On some mornings as I walked into the kitchen, she would grab me and hug me like her life depended on it. She often tried to hide her tear-filled eyes and would get busy making food. She was the hub of our entire extended family. All the aunts, uncles, cousins, nephews, and nieces depended on her. They constantly called her on the phone with all their problems, and she always knew what to say. But now things were reversed and even that was upsetting to her. Sitting down at the piano together we played duets for hours. Playing the passionate romantics of classical music, we learned to laugh again.

As summer came to a close, I knew I had to fly back to my rock 'n' roll life in LA. Seeing my parents rise from their grief and eventually face each day with a smile gave me an inner knowing of how powerful the human spirit is. Suddenly my worries over petty details in my life seemed ridiculous. I knew that if my mom and dad were that strong, that fearless in their attitude toward life, then I could be as well.

Hope always returns.

Even after tragedy.

Even when it seems like there is nothing to hang on to.

I always remember…

If I move with grace and patience in my heart, hope will always return.

Share Ross is a video coach, CEO of Video Rockstar University, and artist coach. Share uses her past experience as a rockstar (bassist in platinum all femme rock band Vixen), adventurer, knitting book author (*Punk Knits*), options trader, and more to guide you on the adventure that is your life. "It's all about communication. What stories do you tell yourself and others? Those stories shape your destiny." To learn more, visit ShareRoss.com.

OPPORTUNITY IN DISGUISE
Ande Lyons

"Every adversity, every failure, every heartache carries with it the seed of an equal or greater benefit." – Napoleon Hill

Adversity is a wonderful teacher and personal trainer for thriving through life's journey. While we're in the midst of a perfect storm of adversity, all hands are on deck, and it can be hard to understand the learning and the knowing of such a difficult time. But adversity builds very important muscles...guaranteed to come in handy during every stage of your life. Adversity really is opportunity in disguise.

As I look back on the early days of my life, I see a lot of valuable lessons provided by Coach Adversity. While I was scrambling to keep my boat afloat, I didn't realize at the time how learning to navigate these murky waters prepared me for the hope, faith, courage, resilience, and tenacity I would need to thrive through bringing two beautiful boys into the world.

My husband and I had been together for six years when we decided it was time to start a family. He was forty, I was thirty-five, and we felt ready for the excitement and responsibility of raising children. Many of our family members and friends had started their families, and it seemed like a straightforward process: get pregnant, prepare the baby's room, give birth, and bring the healthy baby home.

In the summer of 1991, I got pregnant the first time; we were so excited. I had a little morning sickness...and a lot of spotting.

The doctor assured me there was no reason to be concerned about the spotting—the baby's heartbeat was strong—so we began preparing for the big day. At twenty weeks the spotting became heavier...cramping began...and I went into premature delivery.

Seven long hours later we gave birth to a fully formed beautiful baby girl who would not be able to live outside my body. The doctor and midwife kindly guided us in taking important steps for the moment...to have a name ready for the baby...and helping us begin the grief and loss process. Baby Marcy was alive a short time...long enough to give each of our fingers a squeeze with her precious tiny hands...before she rested her sweet cheek on her pressed palms and passed on. Although we were in shock and our pain and sorrow almost unbearable, we knew an angel had blessed us.

We later learned I had a fibroid the size of two grapefruits embedded in the wall of my uterus, creating a difficult environment for Baby Marcy. Six months later I had the fibroid removed; another six months of recovery and we were able to restart the baby-making process.

In the summer of 1993, I once again became pregnant. This time the morning sickness kicked in something fierce. Every day, all day it felt like I was on a deep-sea voyage without Dramamine. When I lay down, it would feel like the bed and the room were spinning. I had to find a solution. I read the book *What to Eat When You Have Morning Sickness* and learned how one could 'manage' morning sickness with an eating plan...barely.

An ultrasound at twenty weeks showed we were having a baby boy. We named him Jack and chatted with him daily, so excited about his arrival in a few short months. Everything was going smoothly until twenty-eight weeks into the pregnancy, when I woke up one morning and knew something was wrong. All movement had stopped. We rushed to the hospital where we had our worst fears confirmed. Baby Jack had died.

When a baby dies inside the womb, you are given Pitocin to induce labor. The process went fairly smoothly, and I delivered

Baby Jack's body within a few hours. When asked if I wanted to hold him, I declined. I just could not have that visual memory in my mind. His precious soul was with his sister...That's all that mattered to me. My husband held Baby Jack for an hour, rocking him in the birthing room's rocking chair. This provided him with the time and closure he needed.

Unfortunately, my placenta would not detach, and I spent the next four hours in surgery where several doctors had their arms up to their elbows trying to get the placenta out. It was a crisis situation...They ran out of nitroglycerin and had to run over to the neighboring hospital to get some; however, it didn't work to dislodge the placenta. I almost lost my uterus, and my hematocrit dropped to one number away from needing a transfusion. I remember lying there on the table, drugged and feeling no pain, yet sensing the urgency and panic going on in the room. After three hours of chaos, in walked the 'Silverback' of the baby delivering jungle. A hush came over the room, and everyone stepped back. He looked at me and said, "Don't worry. I'll take care of you." And sure enough, he reached inside and within seconds the placenta detached, my uterus was saved, and the drama ended. Whew!

We had a beautiful memorial service for Baby Jack. Many friends arrived to support us during this time of grief and loss. It's hard to describe the empty arms and empty cradle syndrome...So many hopes and dreams die with a child of any age, but especially sweet, innocent babies. Baby Jack was cremated and laid to rest next to his great grandmother where we knew he'd be in good hands.

Five months later I got pregnant again. Yay! This time I had no morning sickness and felt fabulous. Still feeling great at thirteen weeks, a good friend suggested I see her close friend who was the head radiologist for the neonatal unit at Boston's top teaching hospital. Carol took an ultrasound and sadly reported I had a blighted ovum. (A what?) This is when an empty egg gets fertilized by the sperm and takes on the characteristics of a viable embryo, but it isn't. Usually one miscarries in the six- to eight-week period, but mine was at the three-month mark. Off I went to surgery for a D and C...and home to tell my husband the bad news.

Needless to say, at this point we were wondering if having a biological baby was in the cards for us. My younger sister, a mother of two wonderful kids, offered to carry a baby for us...She's an amazing woman! We gave that option as well as adoption a lot of thought. The prize for us was being a parent however it happened: biological, adoption, or surrogate mother.

While we were processing what to do next, my husband's mom died suddenly. What a stressful time! Within a nine-month period we had experienced three huge losses, and all we could do was put one foot in front of the other, not even thinking about pregnancy, adoption, or a surrogate mother.

During this difficult period I got pregnant again! Carol the radiologist confirmed the pregnancy and referred us to a fabulous high-risk doctor. The morning sickness kicked in right on schedule too. Awful! At four months the amnio told us we were having a healthy baby boy, and we named him Hunter Noble Lyons.

Carol was available day and night to support us through this pregnancy, which was especially helpful at five months along when I thought for sure Hunter was dead. I called Carol at six that Saturday evening panicked and crying. She met us at the hospital thirty minutes later, and a quick ultrasound showed a healthy baby. Whew—what a relief!

At thirty-eight weeks, Hunter arrived kicking and roaring like a lion, healthy and strong, weighing almost nine pounds. We had a crowd in the recovery room...Dear friends and family HAD to see for themselves we'd actually had a 'successful outcome!' We were beyond ecstatic. I was amazed the poor kid wasn't biting his nails and pulling on his hair because that's what I'd been doing for the last seven and a half months!

A few years later Matthew Alexander arrived to join his older brother. We are so blessed to have two wonderful boys, and everything we went through was worth it to bring these two precious treasures into the world.

We didn't just survive during this time…we thrived. We not only had the 'muscles' to thrive, we also reached out for support along the way. A relationship counselor kept our marriage thriving, eating well and exercising kept our health thriving, and listening to daily inspirational messengers kept our sense of purpose thriving.

I share this sad but triumphant story with you to illustrate how important it is to keep your eyes on the prize and get the support you need to thrive in life. Don't let adversity stop you from living the life of your dreams. Everything we learned from 'birthing babies' we applied to future 'potholes' of our wild and wonderful journey together. Life is filled with opportunities in disguise…I encourage you to use tenacity, resilience, trust, faith, and courage to thrive through your struggles in life while keeping your eyes on the prize. It is worth it.

Ande Lyons is an experienced and enthusiastic entrepreneur with an MBA and several successful companies to her credit. Ande is the founder and chief passion curator for Bring Back Desire, where she shares tips, tools, and resources with women who want more intimacy, sensuality, and sexual excitement in their lives. To learn more about Ande, go to BringBackDesire.com.

ALL ROADS LEAD TO YOUR MOJO
Deborah Kagan

My parents' marriage wasn't working. They divorced when I was six and a half. And then they did what any good parents would do: they sent ME to therapy. Once a week I was dropped off at Dr. Tulipan's office—a sizable room with a couch along the back wall, wooden coffee table in front of it, and side chair to the side—all swathed in browns. Very blah. Like the doctor. I vaguely remember his face, slightly pudgy with sagging skin, glasses containing eyes that made me uneasy. There was a creepy factor to the doctor. Not full-on lecherous, but creepy. Mom picked me up from sessions with the same conversation in the car every time.

"Did you have a nice time, Doodle?"

"It was OK."

"What did you do?"

"We played card games."

Dr. T and I sat around the coffee table and played Go Fish. It was his main form of therapy. Even at six and a half I already knew this guy was a fraud.

After Dr. T, there was the therapist I haphazardly relied on in grade school. Come freshman year in high school our in-person sessions morphed into phone sessions when I went away to boarding school.

There my friends and school advisor quickly became my therapy, pushing the desire for this traditional method out the door. Never one to follow convention, I also decided to try some alternative therapies. Freshman year initiated me into the joys of alcohol therapy. A weekender-size suitcase in brown tweed, much like Dr. Tulipan's couch, housed "the bar." Baileys, Kahlua, Peppermint Schnapps, and multiple bottles of Pompov vodka talked me through teenage angst and my mom's second divorce. By my senior year, my boyfriend, who slept with everyone else under the sun including my best friend, sent me to cocaine therapy. I was under its spell for a two-year term, which nearly ended me. Throughout it all, I inhaled and exhaled nicotine therapy.

Freshman year of college, in an attempt to heal my lovesick heart, I added marijuana therapy, which led to Dunkin' Donut therapy. And then, I got a shove from above—the first of a series of epiphanies in my life. A sense of something bigger than me slapped a psychic Post-It on my consciousness. It said: there's more to it—this life—than what you perceive. To a just-turned nineteen-year-old this didn't make much sense. However, some part of me knew there was sense to be made.

At NYU's Tisch School of the Arts, I found deep therapy in the roll of artist, most especially in Martha Kimbrell's acting class. An older woman, she exuded actor from every pore. She was militant and motherlove. She preached the gospel of Lee Strasberg's method acting. Working out scenes in the loft-like classroom at 721 Broadway with the pigeon choir outside the windows facing the airshaft was heaven. Unrequited love scenes with Carlo made all the heartbreak I carried OK. Thelma and Louise scenes with Tanya gave voice to feminine fears and dreams. Improv exercises made space for spontaneity, trust, and joy.

Los Angeles came calling when New York refused to make a job for me after college. As much as my fierce New Yorker resisted LaLaLand, my true self felt accepted and more understood by the left coast. No one balked at me not eating meat or digging on crystals or talking about esoteric things. They were into it—even more so than me. In New York, toxins were a way of life: coffee, greasy burgers, urine-infested subways, and fresh bus exhaust on every corner. But in LA, wheatgrass, wheat-free gluten-free everything, and bee pollen were all the rage. It was there that I learned about fasting therapy—cleansing the body for short periods of time to release built up toxins. Fasting therapy's partner, colon hydrotherapy, also became a regular on my therapy scene. Because really, how can being less shitty be bad?

One of my other forms of therapy is yoga. I found it in LA. It grabbed me at first because I thought the teacher, Tony, was hot. Then I cried in every class for six months. It started in pigeon pose, moved to triangle, and then savasana. I silently cried out wounds and pain I didn't even know I carried. I cried inexplicable tears. However, at the end of every class I felt stronger and more equipped physically and emotionally. Yoga became an addiction of sorts. I had to go. Fifteen years, dozens of teachers, a bushel of retreats, one teacher training, and countless workshops later, yoga remains my steady therapy of choice.

These days meditation; kava kava ceremonies (where you drink a funky-tasting but highly potent elixir); San Pedro cactus ceremonies with shamans in Peru; annual pilgrimages based on astrology (I've been everywhere from Alaska to Ecuador to Tucson); Feng Shui (need more info? www.sacredinteriors.com); Aboriginal, Native American, and Brazilian healers; kirtan chanting (singing Sanskrit chants with lots of hippies); sessions with psychics, channelers, and mediums; shaktipat (where you get whacked with peacock feathers); and African dancing, trance dancing, and others are some of the alternative modalities I've dabbled in since the Go Fish days with Dr. T. I realize they're not for everyone.

What gives me pause is that each and every one of these therapies made me who I am today. They're each a piece of the life puzzle coloring my personality, wisdom, and heart. Without the initial shove from above opening the door to thousands more, I would never have known how important it is to cultivate a healthy mindset—what I call these days the Life Above the Neck. Without the yoga, cleansing, and various other body practices, I would never have known how crucial is it to be embodied—what I call these days the Life Below the Neck. Without acting class, career shifts, and countless relationships, I would have never known how much potential lives within us—what I call these days our Role Play. And without growing up in abusive households, traveling around the world, and experiencing my parents' divorces and then my own, I would have never have known how much our environment affects every aspect of our lives (especially how we feel about ourselves)—what I call these days our Environment Mojo.

If you take any piece away, the brilliance and fortitude that's unquestionably me would be less so. And I know for a fact it's the same for you. Because each and every experience you've had informed the unique tapestry that's so unquestionably you. Your life is a series of trophies. Sure, the shiny ones get more societal acknowledgement. But the tarnished ones—well, those, my friend, those are pure gold.

My hope is that you make peace with your path and recognize all the steps (the good, the bad, and ugly ones) have made you YOU. And no matter where you are, no matter what you want, there's a way to get there because all the steps until now have led you to exactly where you need to be. At this point, you'll know without a shadow of doubt what you are made of—pure mojo.

Deborah Kagan is a sensual lifestyle specialist with years of practice being a turned-on woman. Her careers and experiences as a high-end Feng Shui consultant, writer, speaker, coach, producer, dancer, yoga teacher, healer, artist, and, most importantly, a woman have led her to create programs that lead other women into their most delicious and authentic lives. Deborah is the author of *Find Your ME Spot: 52 Ways to Reclaim Your Confidence, Feel Good in Your Own Skin and Live a Turned On Life* and the forthcoming *The Sensually Empowered Woman*. To learn more about Deborah, visit Deborah-Kagan.com.

IT ONLY HAS TO WORK OUT ONCE
Nicole Burley

"These can't be my only options."

I stared at the four dating profiles of potential husbands that had been selected for me by the matchmaking website.

One of the guys wasn't tall enough for me.

One of them lived in Connecticut. (I'm in NYC and, for New Yorkers, even living across the park is considered "too far".)

One of them used poor grammar—and the other one didn't offer a picture.

These were all cardinal sins in my book.

And so another batch of candidates was disqualified before we'd even met.

I was thirty-four years old, which felt ancient to me at the time. I had been single for the past three years, after finally finding the pride to end a two-year "relationship" that could have qualified me for the Olympics in crying.

After three years spent recovering from THAT whole mess, and going on more first dates than I could count, I was ready to find a good relationship. Not because I "needed" a man to feel complete, but because I wanted a partner to share in my life.

I was a financially independent, successful young woman who owned her apartment. I wasn't looking for Prince Charming; I just didn't want to cry anymore because of a Prince Not-So Charming. The nausea and butterflies that came from wondering, "Is he going to call?" didn't seem fun anymore. I wanted to be with someone who didn't make me wonder.

"You should really be writing all of this down!" my coupled friends would tell me, as I shared the shock-and-awe tales from my terrible first dates.

"I can't believe all these lousy men you're finding. They shouldn't be allowed out of the house!" others would say.

Yes. It's true. There are men out there in the dating wild who are callous, ill-mannered, insensitive, poorly groomed, rude, obnoxious—and only looking for one thing.

It's also true that I was choosing them.

I was a bright, pretty, funny, well-educated young woman—and I seemed to be exclusively picking men who failed to appreciate any of it. And I blamed the men for this.

Oh, yes, it was always much, much easier to be frustrated and disappointed in the pool of available men than it was to accept that I seemed to have terrible judgment and kept pinning my hopes on the wrong kind of guys.

You see, I had an idea, criteria, and a model in my brain of who I thought I wanted as my mate and how he would present himself to me. Some would call it a "list." I thought of it as the "obvious minimum requirements."

The Man Of My Dreams would have swagger. He would have charisma. He would have charm and sophistication—and a really cool job. He would dress well and know cool, underground, insider kinds of things. He would sweep me off my feet with his coolness, and together we would live a really cool, jet-setty kind of life. Essentially, I was looking for a cross between George Clooney, Mr. Big, and James Bond.

And with those fantasies as my only guiding principles, I had unleashed myself into the dating pool. Is it any wonder that it wasn't really going my way?

There were countless flirty Wall Street guys who would promise the world—and then never call.

There were the super-busy, "work hard, play hard" guys who would talk about themselves all night long.

And then there were the very seductive, mystery men who would express their ardent interest in me over the phone...but then never show up for our planned dinner dates. This happened more than twice. Stood up! Were they married? Pathological? I may never know...

Yes—horrible, terrible, insincere cads. And I found every last one of them it seemed. I was like a terribly misguided moth drawn to a game-playing flame. Ouch.

Hard to know which was worse: the fact that there were men out there who behave that way or the fact that I seemed to be drawn to them, in spite of my protestations to the contrary.

"Why is this so difficult? I just want to find a good guy!" I would cry out. But my choices and my weird list of requirements seemed to say the opposite.

In truth, there were plenty of wonderful men out there. I just wasn't actually looking for them. I was too busy staring at the phone waiting for Pierce Brosnan to call.

When I think of how shortsighted and rigid my "criteria" was for whom I would date, it still makes me shudder. The things that I thought mattered—cool job, swagger, no more than four years older than me, millionaire, hip "insider"—were all keeping me in self-imposed pain, loneliness, and frustration.

"But I want what I want!" I would say. "How come everyone else gets to have their perfect match and yet I'm supposed to compromise?!" It just didn't seem fair.

Of course, what I didn't realize at the time was that I had already compromised—on all the wrong things.

I had perfected the art of the first date. I had lots of cute outfits, I was bubbly and lighthearted, and I spent a lot of time on my hair and makeup. I said all the "right" things. I could put on a great show, playing the role of The Perfectly Appropriate Girl.

But my performance was just as hollow as those flirty, seductive men who talked a good game but then never showed up for our dates. It wasn't real. It was a show.

I was more concerned with being "charming" than I was with being ME. No wonder there was never a connection with anyone. I wasn't really there! And no wonder I was drawn to men who were, in their own way, also putting on a big, fake, empty show. That much we did have in common.

I had just been dumped by someone I'd dated for two weeks when the matchmaking website sent me a "potential match" who seemed completely wrong and off base. He was ten years older than me (too old), his picture was in black and white (possibly misleading), and he had a "boring" job (not sexy). But his spelling was good and, even though the picture was black and white, he still looked handsome, so I agreed to go out with him, just to get back in the saddle after my dumpage.

I'd had an emergency root canal that week, and I was on antibiotics so I couldn't drink. It was a Tuesday night in the winter and, honestly, I just wanted to stay home. After the trauma of the root canal, plus the upset stomach from the antibiotics, I had no energy to put on my usual "show" for this first date. I didn't have high hopes for it anyway, considering all the strikes this guy already had against him in my ridiculously limited book. My expectations were as low as they had ever been on a first date. I don't think I even wore eyeliner.

Perhaps needless to say, I ended up marrying this man.

With no energy left to be anyone other than who I am, I was more present and comfortable in my skin than I had ever been.

I just couldn't do "the show" that night. And so I was myself. And it was enough!

I didn't pour my energy into saying "the right thing." I just said what I felt and shared what I believed. And, with my guard down and my true self in the room, I was able to see that the person in front of me actually shared many of my values. We believed a lot of the same things and shared a world view. I immediately stopped caring about his "boring" job—because it didn't matter, as long as HE was the man doing it. The connection we made over the things that truly matter in a relationship—shared values, beliefs, sense of humor—were all the swagger I needed. He also kinda looked like James Bond.

We met and that was it. I still can't believe it. After all my stubbornness and unwillingness to compromise, I ended up with someone who is nothing at all like what I insisted I wanted. But he couldn't be more perfect for me. He's better than my "fantasy"—because he's real.

I'm still amazed that after all those horrible dates it finally worked out with somebody. But, as my husband always says, "It only has to work out once."

Nicole Burley, MEd, is a certified life coach and health coach, with a specialty in plant-based nutrition. Guided by her philosophy, "Health is fun. Diets are not," Nicole helps her clients stay motivated as they get healthy, lose weight, and turn on the lights in their lives. Nicole is the author of *Proud Not Perfect: A Practical Guide To Healthy Habits—No Dieting Or Deprivation Allowed.* For more information about Nicole, visit NicoleBurley.com

ON BUS STATIONS AND BABY TIGRESSES WITH INVISIBLE STRIPES...

Linda Eaves

I picked up my beloved stuffed tiger at a gift shop in a Greyhound bus station as Mom and I waited for the route 306.

I vividly remember that first gift shop sighting of my pal then imprinting on him (Linus and his security blanket had nothing on me) because I was a tigress too—a bus terminal tigress exploring a jungle with concrete steps, vending machines, and coin-operated TVs.

There were many opportunities for epic six-year-old adventures in the stretched moments and minutes as we waited for our coach to roll in and take us the twenty odd miles up north to Everett, WA.

When we'd get to the end of our passage, Mom or I would go to the phone booth, drop a quarter in, and ring up Dad to pick us up at the Texaco on Hwy 99 a mile from our house. If the day was nice or we couldn't reach Dad, Mom and I would walk on home.

Tig and I went everywhere together—a bonded pair of two-toned kitties. Being two-toned was something I knew well as a mixed-race kid in the early sixties when it wasn't seen quite so much. Tig was gold and black. I was black and white—and no longer alone.

It was painfully obvious how different I looked from my white mom who was unsure how to manage my wild curls. Honestly, I wasn't sure how to manage the curious looks and questions about my dad: "Where's he at?" "What does he look like?" "You've got some black in you, right?"

My presence was public domain—me with my little girl exoticness self.

People didn't know what to think, and by simply being born I was a reluctant representative for biracial babies everywhere.

I didn't know what to say to these people! So Tig came to me at the perfect time to help the world make sense and stop wishing I was one or the other. Black or white. There was finally room for me to be the "and" child. Another choice. Tigress with invisible stripes.

Linda Eaves is a lover of curves, food, shopping, and irreverent humor. She loves to talk to women ready to reclaim what it feels like to BE in their body, at whatever size they are right now, with an emphasis on healing the body, soul, and relationship with food, self, others, and the world through the process of weight loss or obesity management. To learn more about Linda, visit LindaEaves.com.

HOPE
Holli Thompson

I wrote a blog post the other day about discovering your nutritional style through your food, and a woman wrote me, saying, "Great advice, but how can you understand how I feel? I'll bet you've never been overweight or depressed."

She could not have been more wrong.

Several years ago, I was lying in bed with the drapes drawn and the air-conditioning blasting, even though it was a perfect spring day. My husband walked in to check on me, and I was pressed deep into the mattress, holding my head in my hand, wishing for sleep or oblivion of some kind. He looked down and asked if I needed anything.

"I'm worried," I said. "I think there might be something really wrong. What's wrong with me?"

"I don't know, Holli. Let's wait until the migraine passes; we'll figure this out. You'll figure this out."

My husband knew that my secret passion was health and nutrition; I'd spent the years before meeting him vacationing at spas and reading everything about nutrition I could get my hands on.

Two years before, I'd lost three pregnancies. I'd gone through two IVF cycles. I'd gotten depressed after being pregnant for almost nine months and not having a baby at the end.

I was still sad and fighting my body. In fact, symptoms of autoimmune issues had presented themselves, a sign that my body was actually fighting itself.

I had seven sinus infections that year, all requiring antibiotics, and my "gut health," as I realize today, was shot. I felt good on antibiotics, and I felt my energy began to go downhill within two weeks of going off them. Migraines struck at random, and the lethargy and deep-down tired feeling that accompanied all of this was depressing in itself.

I'd put on weight, and I was tired all the time. I was on an emotional roller coaster, and I was struggling to get through the day most days.

What my husband knew when he made that comment was that he'd seen me tackle things before. I remained hopeful after each miscarriage, until finally we decided that the guarantee of a baby through adoption was for us and we flew to Russia for our son. We both knew that adoption was our path. We were right and we brought home our true son.

I reached a place that year, as I lay in my bed, where I was afraid, and I knew that the medicines, which were by now a handful of pills, weren't helping. I was living on allergy pills, migraine pills, antidepressants, antibiotics, sinus pills, anti-inflammatory pills, and nasal sprays.

This couldn't possibly be my life. I hoped and trusted that this was not my path and that I'd find my way back. My husband did too. I was frustrated, afraid, annoyed, angry, sad, desperate, exhausted, and overweight, but I was never, ever hopeless.

Hopelessness was not an option. I was young and happily married, with a new baby that I loved. I had things to do and a boy to raise. I had a lifetime to fill, and deep inside, deep down beneath the pain and weight, and my tired, achy, fibromyalgia body, was excitement. Life was exciting. Life was wonderful. I loved my life, but my body wasn't supporting me, and it was affecting everything.

HOPE

My situation had to change. My husband was right to trust in that.

Later that summer, after another sinus infection hit, another round of antibiotics, and at least a couple of migraines, I emerged. Going out after a migraine, after being sick in bed again with an infection, I felt tender. I was sensitive, and almost fearful. What if I wasn't ready? What if I begin to feel badly?

We attended a dinner hosted by a friend to benefit a green initiative in our community. I had to jump in and help, and I was enjoying being among friends. One of my friends leaned over to me with a look of concern. How are you feeling? You're sick all the time.

Really? "Hmm, well, I feel great." The last thing I wanted to be known as was sickly.

"Have you considered that your immunity is seriously compromised?" There was something about the way she said it that scared me. It hit me between the eyes. No, I hadn't considered that, thank you. But I sure did then.

The next day I made a list of holistic practitioners I'd heard about—a nutritionist, an acupuncturist, colon hydrotherapy, live blood analysis, my gynecologist, and more. I got out my calendar, and I made appointments. I joined a CSA, a local community supported agriculture program that I had once loved and let slide.

I pored through my library of nutrition books and cookbooks. I entered the kitchen, early in the day, and I began my journey.

The hope and vision of what my life was meant to look like was calling me. I was walking slowly, but purposefully, into the river of my life. I was tired of lying by the shore.

The following year I had only one sinus infection, and my migraines came fewer and farther between. I realized that I was intolerant to dairy products and that the resulting inflammation was one of the root causes of many of the symptoms I'd experienced.

In late spring, I celebrated that my seasonal allergies never came that year and I'd lost over fifteen pounds. I continued my "program" the following year, gradually increasing movement, adding in good foods, and taking out ones that didn't serve me well.

I weaned myself off of all the medications, with my doctor's approval, and within the next year I lost over forty pounds. My doctor called one day asking if I was OK it had been so long since he'd seen me.

Four years later, I couldn't remember my last sinus infection, cold, flu, or migraine. I realized I'd never needed an antidepressant. I realized that removing my extra weight and weaning myself off of the medications, while adding in lots of movement, was my path to happiness. Yoga, walking, juicing, and lots of leafy greens were my new meds.

Today, I regularly plan my TV show appearances and head over to the studio with delicious healthy food, most of it made in my kitchen. I work on my book, I run down my road, or I go to a Barre class. I plan and shop for organic foods, and I do my best to keep my now twelve-year-old son healthy and happy.

I meet with clients by phone or in person, and I help them figure out their nutrition. I analyze what they're doing like a sleuth, searching for the pieces of the puzzle that don't feed them well. Just like I did for myself, I now do for others. I teach classes, and I speak to women, and I try to share my story as much as I can.

I was where you are, I wrote her. I do understand. How can I help you?

Holli Thompson is the founder of Nutritional Style. She has helped hundreds of women around the world lose weight, increase their energy, and find their glow. Holli has been profiled in *More Magazine* and featured in *More's* "Reinvent Yourself" TV special. She appears on CBS, ABC, and FX networks as a nutrition and food expert and speaks to women's groups and national organizations, including the American Heart Association. To learn more about Holli, visit NutritionalStyle.com.

WOMEN ON A MISSION: FIVE SOULFUL STEPS TO BECOME UNSTOPPABLE

Stephanie McWilliams

I don't have to be psychic to know one thing:

You're a woman on a MISSION.

A woman who's got a big calling way deep down inside.

You've got an itch to make a big difference. Maybe you want to change the world, be of service, or help others in a big, bold way.

So how do YOU follow in the footsteps of other great and earth-shaking women? (Because you know in your bones you're capable of doing it too…if you only knew how.)

It's not an easy question. It's an even less easy answer…

Life can look messy, challenging, painful, and outright annoying sometimes. I know firsthand—I've been there myself.

I used to be seventy pounds overweight, clinically depressed, and totally OCD. I went bankrupt, my best friend committed suicide, and my father was diagnosed with terminal cancer—TWICE! (Luckily he's stubborn and is still around fifteen years later). I've been through hell and back. Had zero self-esteem. Had decades of lousy love relationships. And I felt hopeless more times than

I care to admit. (And trust me, this list could go on, and on, and on, and on…)

Basically, I was the poster child for what NOT to do.

But once I figured out some pretty powerful insights along the way, everything changed. Dramatically.

I've ended up having my own popular TV show on HGTV called *Fun Shui*, running a thriving six-figure mentoring business for female entrepreneurs called Unstoppable You, and living in San Diego paradise with my amazing sweetie of seven-plus years and our two diva cats.

Best of all, I'm ridiculously happy much of the time.

So how did I go from THAT big ol' giant mess to this 360-degree spin in the opposite direction?

It wasn't easy. And it didn't happen overnight. But there are five factors that are important if you want to live out your life's mission:

1. TRUST YOUR LIFE—ALL OF IT!

Some days it's easy to think you've stumbled onto a bad B-movie set…where it sure feels like life would be SO much better… if only X, Y and Z would change, gosh darn it!

I get it. I fought life tooth and nail myself for many, many years.

But what I've come to realize is that we resist those things that are our biggest GIFTS—those hidden opportunities divinely handed to us on a mysterious silver platter. They are the VERY situations needed to teach you a thing or two, crack you wide open, shove you in a whole new direction, or give you some serious skills for the cool things to come.

Sure, most people will commiserate when things look REALLY bad. They'll think this "trust life" theory is pie-in-the-sky wishful thinking!

But what if you could have hindsight WHILE something challenging was taking place? What if you could float above it to get a God's-eye glimpse at the meaning of it all?

Looking back…my bankruptcy taught me that money was easy to replace. It helped me clean up my limited thinking around moola and taught me everything I needed to know in order to hit that six-figure mark.

Looking back…my best friend's suicide taught me to live every day like it matters. It showed me that love never dies and that death is just a transition, never an ending.

Looking back…my father's cancer inspired me to heal our relationship. I saw with my own two eyes that healing miracles were possible and got proof that mind is most definitely over matter.

So let's play "What if?" for a moment:

WHAT IF…you actually CHOSE the life you've got?

WHAT IF…lousy stuff actually helped you give birth to your big dreams?

WHAT IF…your biggest enemies were merely God-in-drag?

It's time to start living life like you CHOSE it—if nothing more than for the sheer awesome fact that you'll feel unstoppable when you do! Then you may discover what I've come to know: what I used to think was oh-so-wrong might, in fact, be oh-so-very right.

2. NEVER EVER BELIEVE YOUR BRAIN

Think about it:

Everything you know was taught to you by some seriously unenlightened (well-meaning) adults. Oy.

"My name is Stephanie = Check!"

"The sky is blue = Check!"

"Good little girls 'behave' = Check!"

After downloading millions of thoughts, you start to believe them as if they're true—drug around like a puppet by your very own goofy brain.

But the brain don't know squat.

It tells you you're screwed up at your core. You're not doing life "right." You're not pretty enough. Thin enough. You should be farther ahead. And you should get more done.

It's a slave driver, pure and simple.

Now don't get me wrong: brains aren't bad! They keep you from being eaten by bears or walking in front of fast-moving cars. They're great for holding your fork, brushing your teeth, and tying your shoes. But if you use it to steer your life's mission, it will most definitely muck things up…

Why? Because of this simple truth:

ALL suffering stems from believing your thinking (especially when it says something, or someone, should be different than it is).

Serious as taxes.

Find one example to the contrary, and I'll pay you a million bucks…

Your goal is to let your frontal lobe chitchat away like a never-ending white noise machine in the background of your life—just don't take it personally, and definitely don't EVER believe it!!!

When you are no longer a slave to your thinking, then and ONLY then can something else speak through you—and that is precisely the moment when your MISSION begins…

3. LOVE UP YOUR MOST UNLOVABLE PARTS

I used to believe that I was a diamond in the rough. But I spent years trying to heal, fix, and tweak my other undesirable parts. I thought my core was pure goodness—and if I could just get rid of the glop, things would be fine…

But nothing could be farther from the truth. And nothing could be more impossible!

HOPE

EVERYONE is angry, jealous, doubting, and sad...sometimes (just in case you hadn't noticed). To fight that oh-so-obvious fact is one seriously hopeless cause. And when I finally started to embrace my humanness—with all its quirks, oddities, and (seeming) flaws—life forever changed.

So if you want to live your mission you've got to learn to love it all—especially the parts you tend to love the least...Only when you fall madly in love with yourself can you ever expect others to do the same, or ever truly love another unconditionally.

4. FOLLOW YOUR INNER GPS

Did you know that you come fully equipped with your very own internal GPS. system?

You access it by simply paying attention to your passions—what lights you up? Moves you forward? Cracks open your heart? Or grabs your attention?

Some call it intuition. Others, gut instincts. But whatever you call it, call on it OFTEN! These signals are the green-light indicators that you're headed in the right direction. It's the only trustworthy advice you can count on—the only thing on this planet that will never ever steer you wrong. Thing is, we're brought up NOT to trust it. And therein lies the problem.

Everyone told me I was NUTS to become an artist. But I followed my calling—and I made a great living being creative.

I was told I was CRAZY when I left my day job to pursue Feng Shui. But I took the leap—and had a TV show land smack in my lap.

Society told me that TERRIBLE things happened when you went bankrupt. But I followed my gut—and everything's been uphill ever since.

So even if friends disagree, no one understands, or family doesn't cheer you on, follow your calling! No one can know what's best for your soul's highest good but Y-O-U. And maybe, just maybe, things will work out better than you could have ever imagined...

5. KEEP MOVING FORWARD, NO MATTER WHAT

When it comes to following your mission, there's one thing to be sure of: following your inner "Call to Greatness" will scare the bejeezus out of you. Guaranteed.

Truth be told, I almost sabotaged my TV show because I had sheer terror pulsing through my veins—and under those circumstances, it's pretty tough to resist the wild urge to cut-and-run!!!

The closer you get to the dreams you cherish most, the more your brain will throw some serious temper tantrums and try its best to seduce you back into the ho-hum status quo. So whether you end up peeing your pants, tossing your cookies, or thinking you're going to die, you have to learn to keep moving, one baby step after the other.

Fear is normal. We all have it. Even the rich, famous, and ubersuccessful feel its grip. The only difference between you and them is that they keep moving anyway…

…And now, so will YOU!

You've just got to feel the fear and do it anyway.

Fear only goes away when you face your biggest roadblocks and live to tell the tale. And there, shining bright, on the other side of fear, stands what you desire most: the feeling of total, utter, outrageous unstoppability! Once you've faced what you once thought would crush you, you feel (and know) that you can take on the world.

And that's precisely when you DO.

So I hope this gives you a jolt and jump-start toward YOUR unstoppable mission. And while these five steps ARE simple, they are in no way EASY. You may spend a lifetime becoming an expert in each.

But having the wisdom to know what works and know what doesn't gets you a great running start.

Because I want you to know that miracles DO happen.

It is what life looks like when you let go, trust, and show up at your unique 100 percent.

…Here's to your Unstoppability!!!

Founder of Unstoppable You and former host of a HGTV's popular design show *Fun Shui*, Stephanie McWilliams is an intuitive business mentor for female coaches, healers, and purpose-driven service professionals—women who want to change the world AND make an awesome living doing what they love. Stephanie's surprising mix of practical business savvy plus spiritual sass gives women a rare and refreshing experience as they remove lifelong hidden blocks and build up unstoppable momentum so they can live out their divine purpose in the world. To learn more about Stephanie, visit JoinTheUnstoppables.com.

THE ANATOMY OF HOPE
Susan Mathison

I love mornings. And what is it that gets me out of bed in the mornings? I think it is always hope: that today will be a wonderful day, full of promise and possibility with interesting experiences and even a few magical moments. And in my work as a physician, I try to be a messenger of hope as well. I prescribe action steps even before medications or treatments to help my patients' live happier, healthier, and more beautiful lives.

Norman Vincent Peale writes: "Have you ever stopped to wonder what it is that keeps you going from one day to another? What lies behind your ability to fight your way through periods of discouragement or depression? What makes you believe that sooner or later bad times will get better? It's a little, four-letter word that has enormous power. Power to bring failures back to success. Power to bring the sick back to health. Power to bring the weak back to strength. It's hope."

Hope: How do we get it and keep it? I think the message is contained within the word itself.

Heart **O**ptimism **P**urpose **E**nergy

Just like the Lion in *The Wizard of Oz*, having heart gives us courage to face our challenges and fears. It is the force that guides the baby bird to flutter out of the nest and strengthens the cancer patient to endure painful but life-saving treatments.

Thankfully, we are hardwired for optimism, research in neuroscience and social science shows. Despite natural disasters of epic proportion, economic downturn, violent crime, systemic poverty, professional crisis, disease, and divorce, we believe, across every race, region, and income bracket, that the future will be better than the past. While optimism without a dash of realism can be risky, leading to bad investments or bad partners, a positive attitude has clear health benefits, minimizing stress and soothing our minds and enhancing positive behaviors. Researchers found that heart disease patients who were optimists did a better job taking care of themselves by exercising, eating well, and taking vitamins. A study of young cancer patients (under the age of sixty) found that pessimistic patients were more likely to die within eight months than optimistic patients who shared similar cancer stage, overall health, and age.

Eighteenth-century British poet and songwriter Isaac Watts offered this insight on the purpose of hope: "Hope thinks nothing is difficult; despair tells us that difficulty is insurmountable." Purpose helps us imagine a better reality and gives us the motivation to pursue our goals and the belief that we can achieve them. Hopeful purpose will cure cancer, eliminate hunger, and solve a myriad of societal and personal problems.

Hope gives us energy to achieve our purposeful goals and even economic success. I read of a great example of this. Esther Duflo, an economist at the Massachusetts Institute of Technology, is known for her data-driven analysis of poverty. She and her colleagues studied a program in the Indian state of West Bengal, where people considered extremely poor were given a small productive asset—a cow, a couple of goats or some chickens, and a small stipend to reduce the temptation to eat or sell the asset immediately, as well as weekly teaching sessions teaching them how to tend the animals and manage their households. The goal was that there would be a small increase in income from selling the products of the farm animals provided and that people would become more adept at managing their own finances. The results were far more impressive than originally hoped.

Long after the financial help and hand-holding had stopped, the families of those who had been randomly chosen for the program were eating 15 percent more and earning 20 percent more each month than people in a comparison group. They were also saving. The effects were so dramatic that they could not be attributed to the direct effects of the grants: people could not have sold enough milk, eggs, or meat to explain the income gains. Further analysis by Dr. Duflo and her colleagues showed that recipients worked 28 percent more hours, but mostly on activities not directly related to the assets they were given. They found that participants' mental health improved dramatically. It was as if the very poor were given an infusion of hope for more than mere survival.

When in a rut or even crisis, I retire to my bed at night. I resolve to look at my problem with a different lens. How can this problem be a possibility? John Homer Miller wrote: "Your living is determined not so much by what life brings to you as by the attitude you bring to life; not so much by what happens to you as by the way your mind looks at what happens. Circumstances and situations do color life, but you have been given the mind to choose what the color shall be." I reflect on past actions and plan for the future with greater knowledge. I choose the colors of heart, optimism, purpose, and energy to help me live my best life.

"Everything that is done in the world is done by the hopeful," Martin Luther said. Age, circumstances, or financial wealth do not matter.

Without hope, nothing is possible. With hope, possibilities are endless. And each morning sunrise reminds me of this.

As a holistic cosmetic surgeon, double-board certified physician, and founder of the Catalyst Medical Center, Susan Mathison is fascinated by the power of the integration of medical science, cosmetic artistry, and sacred self-care. She created POSITIVELY BEAUTIFUL to serve as a sanctuary of support, information, and resources for women who long to know their true beauty both inside and out for the first time in years—or for the first time in their lives. To learn more about Susan, visit PositivelyBeautiful.com.

EVEN IN THE STRUGGLE
Tara Mohr

Even in the struggle, you are loved.

You are being loved not only in spite of the hardship, but through it.

The very thing you perceive as wrenching, intolerable— a far cry from your plans the thing you see as life's attack on you, is an expression of love.

There is the part of us that fears and protects and defends and has a story of the way it is supposed to turn out.

That part clenches in fear, feels cursed and abandoned.

There is another part, resting at the floor of the well within, that understands: this is how I am being graced, called, refined, by fire.

The secret is, it's all love. It's all doorways into truth It's all opportunity to merge with what is.

Most of us don't step through the doorframe. We stay on the known side. We fight the door, we fight the frame, we scream and hang on.

On the other side, you are one with earth, like the mountain. You hum with life, like the moss.

On the other side, you are more beautiful— wholeness in your bones, wisdom in your gaze.

The sage-self and the surrendered heart, alive.

Tara Sophia Mohr is an expert on women's leadership and well-being. She is the creator of the global Playing Big training program for women and the author of *Your Other Names: Poems for Wise Living*. To learn more about Tara, visit TaraMohr.com.

THE KEY TO A LIFE OF BLISS LIES WITHIN THE MESSAGES OF YOUR INNER VOICE

Kate Muker

When I was twenty-four, everything appeared to be going great. I made a lot of money working as an account manager for a strategic communications company. I bought myself a new car, lived in a downtown condo with my best friend, and partied almost every weekend. I worked hard and played hard. I looked ambitious: I strove constantly for the next promotion and raise, even taking night courses to further my education and become a better candidate for those plum jobs.

I'm still ambitious today—but the forces behind my ambition and the energy that fuels my dreams are much different.

In my twenties, all those seemingly ambitious moves I made were motivated by a lack of self-worth, my need to be acknowledged, and my endless quest to find inner fulfillment through outside things: my job title, the clothes I wore, the neighborhood I lived in. I didn't feel confident in who I was. I never felt that being me was good enough, and I tried to act the way I thought would make people like me. I used alcohol and drugs for liquid courage; I thought I could only be fun (and have fun) when I dropped my inhibitions. Drugs and alcohol certainly provided some highs in my life—but with every artificial high comes a serious low in the days that follow. The incongruence between who I was while intoxicated and who I was at my essence was eating me up inside.

One of the biggest challenges I faced at the time—and what I would later realize was a deep blessing—was that my inner voice kept telling me there was another way. Despite all the trappings of my seemingly fun and successful life, I couldn't disconnect from that deep calling within to seek my path of truth.

Personal growth and spirituality intrigued me in my early twenties, even before I really understood what those things meant.

Yes, I felt that inner voice—but my deep inspiration didn't bubble to the surface right away. It wasn't until the pain of staying on that path got so uncomfortable that I started searching for new ideas. Growing up in east Vancouver (a low-income neighborhood), I'd never heard of someone seeing a psychologist. Even in my twenties, no one I knew saw one or admitted to seeing one. Still, I felt called to seek one. I remember Googling and landing on a page with words that felt like they were written for me: feeling lost, empty within, seeking answers of inner truth. I was nodding my head yes with every sentence.

I remember telling my best friend and boyfriend at the time that I was seeing a psychologist—and feeling ashamed. But despite my misguided embarrassment and the commitment of $150 an hour once a week (which is a lot of money for a twenty-four-year-old with no medical benefits), my desire for my life to change was much stronger.

This was the first step on my path toward self-worth and self-love. When I look back now, I realize that this step was fundamental in building a sense of belief and trust within myself.

My life didn't transform overnight. But finally, I didn't expect it to. I no longer looked to a better job title or a cuter car for instant "happiness." In the six months that I saw my psychologist,

I began to clear a new path for my life. Within a few months, I ended my relationship, quit my job, and decided to travel Europe for three months by myself.

The most powerful guidance I felt in all these experiences came from listening to my inner voice. Even when I felt ashamed, even when I chose to leave a good job with a high salary, even when the people around me thought I was crazy—listening to my inner voice taught me an incredible lesson.

Traveling alone for three months provided me the perfect opportunity to cultivate my relationship with my inner voice and my self-confidence. Each morning I woke and had to decide what I wanted to do and where I wanted to go; I had no close friends to lean on for help in making those decisions.

During my adventures, I became more and more interested in following a spiritual path. I read books about personal growth and was very attracted to people who were on their own spiritual paths—but I didn't yet have a clear understanding of what spirituality meant to me. I remember thinking I was going to find one book that was going to teach me what spirituality was, as if there were a single definition for it.

When I returned home, I became more and more clear about the life I wanted to live and the decisions I would need to make to continue on that path. I often felt tempted to feed my ego, and I'd occasionally slip back into old patterns—seeking attention through drugs, alcohol, and negative relationships. But each time I indulged, the pain I felt in the days that followed was intolerable. I would dread getting out of bed. I felt ashamed because those experiences were so far out of integrity with myself. Simply put, I felt yucky and really low. I knew I was worth more than how I was treating myself.

Although I experienced sometimes painful ups and downs throughout my shifts, when I look back now I can see that I was always moving in a positive direction. Things didn't change overnight, but within a couple years I saw a significant difference in who I was, how I was living my life, and what I was attracting into my life. Over time, the small changes added up to become big changes—and they were all the result of being willing to explore something different from my present reality and making continuous baby steps of learning and growth.

I started to feel fuller from within. I stopped craving negative relationships. My health became a high priority. I was confident in who I was and what I valued.

I stopped seeking things on the outside to feed my happiness and started seeking things that were fueling me on the inside, like running, meditation, and reading. These were all forms of self-love; the more I did things that demonstrated self-love, the less I wanted to choose things like drugs, alcohol, and negative relationships.

By twenty-six my life had taken an obvious turn in a new direction. I started to grow away from my friends of thirteen years. While it was difficult to let them go, we no longer had the same interests or values.

A few months after my twenty-sixth birthday, I met the man of my dreams: my best friend, my soul mate, and now my husband. We shared similar values; we were both open-minded, thirsty for life, and committed to personal growth. There was an instant connection. I felt at home with him from the very first time we spoke on the phone.

What I learned is the deeper the connection I developed with myself determined the depth of magic I could experience in my life.

It all started by listening to the subtle nudges from my inner voice, believing there was another way and taking action. There was no magic potion. No secret. No single way.

If you want to experience the beauty and magic that lives within you, take small steps—even baby steps—each day to cultivate a relationship with your inner voice.

The gift of life is that the true essence of each and every one of us is LOVE. Our job is to remove the barriers that block us from experiencing that shining love within ourselves.

Kate Muker is the CEO and founder of Conscious Divas, a company that creates community for conscious women both on and offline. Conscious Divas inspires and empowers women to be the best versions of themselves by connecting deeply, discovering one's authentic path, living passionately, and being fabulous. To learn more about Kate or Conscious Divas, go to ConsciousDivas.com.

AND THEN
Victoria Prozan McGlinn

Urgh.

It's so frustrating. Two steps forward, one step back. Or is it one step forward, two steps back? Depends on the day, I suppose. No matter how many steps are taken, in any direction, the slam of life crashing into the wall repeats. Over and over, as I shake my tiny fist at the sky. But whaddya gonna do?

Once upon a time, in a land not far away at all, I had lost hope that people could change. That I could change. You know, change-change. Like in big expansive ways that altered lives forever. Removing monkeys from backs. Rebuilding a life from the ground up, the inside out, with little to no resources. Seeing past limitations and out into the rambling wilderness of betterment.

Well.

I did think it was possible, but only for superhumans with tenacity us regular folks were just not born with. Hope Heroes. They are like Olympic athletes of emotional growth in my head. They're out there, but not in everyday life. Only on Oprah or the *New York Times* Bestseller List or a feel-good story on the evening news would true evidence of epic hope be found. The rest of us should just strive for the little bits of hope and change our lives could bear. I mean come on, right?

So.

It was a great way to keep myself off the hook. The hook of wanting and striving for more in my own life. I had it pretty good. A Midwest, middle-class roof over my head. Fresh, affordable food not a ten-minute drive from my front door. Family and friends who love me, even if there are plenty of times they don't quite understand me. To strive for too much else would just be greedy, right?

But.

Deep inside, under the layers of social conditioning, scars of living, physical addictions, and thick self-doubts, hope was fueling a little tiny flame that there was more I could be experiencing in my time on this planet. The warm burn I allowed myself to feel now and again didn't seem greedy. It felt good. Right. In sync.

But.

I still doubted how this pilot light could heat my whole life. I wanted proof, dammit. No one else seemed to have their shit together, so why would I be any different? I had tried (or so I thought) and I'd seen others try too. But we all seemed to sink eventually. So I clung to my excuses and stopped tending that lingering flame.

And then.

My life ripped open. A loved one fell. Down. Hard. As painful as it was to watch, it still didn't come as a shock. I confess my hopes for him reorienting the priorities in life had faded so many years ago that it didn't even seem like losing hope. It seemed more like a fact. Suffering day in and day out was his path. Despite support, love, and friendship, nothing made a difference as he ran straight into the addiction abyss.

And then.

His years of free fall ended. Thankfully his life did not. Strangely, miraculously, and hopefully, he made a commitment to himself. But not like all the other times before. His instinct for survival seemed to kick in and override all the other crap. Big time. With nothing left but hope, he stood up. And stayed standing. The only thing that remained the same in his life was his existence. And the people who loved him. The rest of the accouterments were swapped out. And the new versions were each filled with shiny hope.

And then.

He went from screwed up beyond comprehension to the other end of the spectrum. He led at work. He made a difference in his community. He displayed discipline that kept him healthy, grounded, and sane. He went from twenty years of being one paycheck away from living under the overpass to having a flush savings account. He had turned his life around. He had changed. Like change-changed. He became my Hope Hero.

But.

Where did this leave me? My excuses of deep-change-is-not-possible were exposed like the wizard behind the curtain. Now I have to own up to my own bullshit.

Urgh.

But wait, if this kind of superhuman feat can be accomplished by those in my very own midst, was I also up to the task? Maybe that little hope I kept toting around all these years knew better than me. Holy moly. What if? What if those around me who have given up aren't as captive as they think they are? What if Marianne Williamson was right? We're powerful beyond measure? That's not a tiny flame of hope; that's a million suns of blinding power to charge my entire existence.

Well.

I guess I got some shit to do.

Victoria Prozan McGlinn is on a mission to unleash your imagination into the four corners of your business. As the creator of The Superluxe Naming Experience, she teaches client to take their business vision and turn it into potent, stand-above-the-fray language that generates heat everywhere it goes. Victoria draws on her professional experiences in client relations, customer service, and graphic design to offer creative insights and uncommon perspectives that make your brand pop and your clients swoon. Visit her at VictoriaPM.com.

FOLLOW THE BREADCRUMBS
Amber McCue

From student body president to knocked up at the age of seventeen. It's like a bad Lifetime movie. Picture it—prom queen hiding a secret from everyone who stares on as she gets crowned. One would think that prom queen hiding the secret of her pregnancy might be headed down the road to nowhere.

In fact, statistics would argue that I had a 60 percent chance of living below the poverty line. Forty percent of teenage mothers report still being below the poverty line at the age of twenty-seven and have lower-than-average earning potential for the rest of their lives.

In our small town of five hundred, where everybody knows your name, news spreads like wildfire. People were surprised and baffled that this well-organized, upbeat high school student, who was on her way to college in the fall, went and got herself knocked up. Mine wasn't the first teen pregnancy in our small town, but it never ceased to amaze and shock and give people something to talk about.

Gossip was expected—that was probably the worst of it. Any decision I would make from that point forward would be known by everyone in town. Judgment was doled out as made evident by the whispers and stares I would receive as news got out.

Embarrassment and shame reigned supreme.

Those near and dear to me were concerned and poured out their love as I went forward to make some of the biggest decisions I had ever faced. Abortion or no abortion? Give the baby up for adoption or keep the little love bug? Go away to college as planned? Live at home and go to the local community college? Skip college all together…?

I was seventeen years old.

Everybody had a point of view. What I heard loudest were the words of one person: "You can do this. You've got this, Amber. You will be a good mom."

You've got this.

He reminded me of what I knew all along—I've got this.

You've got this.

My confidence that I could be a success was verified. Shame and embarrassment vanished.

That one person reminded me of what I wanted for my life. I knew where I was going.

Sometimes things get thrown your way that you wouldn't expect—cancer, financial hardship, car accidents, the loss of a job. Sometimes the things thrown at you are so unimaginable that you can't help but ask why—cancer of a young child, the loss of a mother at a young age. Sometimes you do things to yourself that you can't blame on anyone or anything.

The thing about life is you don't get to pick what is thrown your way.

You choose how you react to those challenges.

Choice.

This is your power. Your strength.

The way you choose to accept and respond to these challenges defines who you are and who you will be.

For me, there was no doubt in my mind that I could have this baby—love this baby—and still do exactly what I had planned.

Crazy?

Maybe.

Crazy wins.

I had already been accepted to Marquette University in Milwaukee, Wisconsin. I would have my baby and take her to college with me.

I saw no other way. There was no other option.

How exactly would it work out?

No clue. But it was a done deal.

I could see it, and I envisioned it working.

Vision is queen.

I decided it would happen. I saw it happening. I believed it would work. I followed the breadcrumbs and took steps to make it happen.

Done deal.

Opportunities are presented. You rise to meet them. People challenge you. Question you. Think you are crazy. You know there is no other way. You put one foot in front of the other. You follow the breadcrumbs, challenge status quo, and create your own destiny.

On December 22, 1998—Christmas break of my freshman year of college—my daughter was born.

I returned to school in January 1999 with my daughter by my side. We joke that she was the youngest person to ever attend Marquette University.

We graduated in four years. Student loans. Yeah, I'm still paying them off.

I immediately went on to find the job I dreamed possible.

My daughter?

She started high school this week.

High school.

She is smart, thriving, and enjoying the freedom that comes with being loved, supported, and allowed to be her own person. She is creating her own story.

The echoes of conversations that happened behind my back as my daughter was born remind me that courage is about following the breadcrumbs and believing that crazy dreams happen.

Trust yourself—especially when it seems crazy. It's those breadcrumbs that show the way.

Decide.

See it.

Believe.

Take action.

Repeat the steps above and change course as needed.

Amber McCue's mission is to help entrepreneurial superstars and leverage their righteous potential as savvy business owners. Amber doesn't just want entrepreneurs to HAVE a business; she wants them to OWN it. Her specialty is helping entrepreneurs develop leadership strategies that will propel their business into the big time. To learn more about Amber, visit AmberMcCue.com.

THE HOPE OF LOVE
Candace Smyth

"What keeps us alive, what allows us to endure? I think it is the hope of loving, or being loved." – Meister Eckhart, late medieval German mystic

It was six years ago. My daughter, Kate, was a few months from her second birthday. It was February and really cold that year in DC. A new full-time federal government job had just leapt into my lap. I was still adjusting to the work and the time—the job was taking me away from Kate a couple hours more each day. My husband and I had just hired a nanny (who was loving and perfect for Kate), but I was feeling an intense longing to have more time with my daughter. (I even bought a domain name to try and help work it out: www.moretimewithkate.com.)

I was also feeling really unhappy in my marriage, very alone and not connected to either my husband or myself.

That February, Kate and I flew to Alabama for a cousin's weddings. I still don't remember exactly why, but my husband didn't come along with us. It was part of a growing separateness.

When Kate and I returned, things seemed even more out of sorts at home. He was even more distant, and I felt just mean. I didn't find out why until later. Finally, my sister, after hearing my complaints about his frequent late nights, prompted me by saying, "He is having an affair, Candace!" I searched our home computer. I figured out his password and tapped into his Gmail account.

And, there it was. I later found out about the Washington blizzard and fun in the snow the two of them had while Kate and I danced under the beams of a beautifully decorated Alabama barn with the new bride and groom.

I lost it. I read his e-mail to her about how good she looked in those tight jeans. I printed out the e-mails so frantically I broke the printer. He had been working late that night, so I called him to confront him in the craziness of my frenzied self. Mind chaos? Breakdown? I thought I knew how that felt; I thought I could handle it. Not. I felt so alone and panicked. I called his brother. I called his best friend's wife. I called two of my friends, and they came over (thank God). When he finally did call me, it was from a bar. I confronted him on the phone. He denied it. I confronted him outside our home in the woods across the street from our apartment, beneath a cold, dark sky.

He denied it. I did not believe him. I had seen the proof. Yet, I was the one who seemed to be losing my mind. Chaos, grief, loneliness, isolation fueled my freaking-the-eff-out mode of "What do I do now?" I cried, I screamed, I railed at him. I even ripped his T-shirt one night. He finally did admit it, but he still maintained he did nothing wrong. And me? I was not in my "right" mind. I wasn't living from my head—it was all heart and true fear. For weeks, I just felt anger and resentment and more anger and true isolation. I called every friend I could. I took Kate away to Kansas City to visit my closest uncle and aunt and stayed in a bathrobe all weekend.

My diaphragm seized, and I felt a constant intense pain that wouldn't let up. I tried to stay sane for Kate, who was not yet two years old, when she was awake. (It really is about sanity when you are there writhing on the floor for hours.) And I would let it all go at night when she was asleep.

I begged him to go to counseling with me. I did not want our marriage, in no small part for our growing daughter's sake, to fall apart. After two months of counseling, although admitting his affair, he could neither apologize nor ask for reconciliation. Finally, three months after discovering his e-mails, I said, "OK, that's it." I asked him to leave. He moved out.

The truth is I was already a mess quite independently of him.

My mom had died in a car accident when I was twenty-two. I grew up in a sweet but conservative and ever-watchful, small Alabama town, and my mom, who grew up poor to marry a rich man on the other side of town, tried to control my every word, my every action. My dad was more approachable but distant in his own way too. Every Sunday I sat in those straight-backed wooden pews of a Southern Baptist church and learned how women and children should be happy in their subservience.

When Mom died, I was lost. But, I also felt like I could rebel and not be punished anymore. At the time, I was in my first marriage to my high school sweetheart. A year later, I decided that being married was too restricting. I was in my first year of law school in DC. I told my husband it was over and soon met a charismatic human rights attorney. My husband at the time moved back to the South and we quietly divorced.

I struck out into a new land of rebellion from promiscuity to leftist legal activism, what I told myself was a fiercely "free" lifestyle. I was my own woman who finally had control over herself, or so I believed. I had one relationship or hook-up after another. I took a soul-sucking corporate law firm job, betraying the principles I had only recently embraced.

I was driven by fear—of being alone, of being unloved, of being unwanted. I jumped headfirst into a relationship that I knew—or so I thought—I could control. We got married about a year later, and I clung to him for dear life.

Several years and one beautiful baby girl later, he was the one who could not take it anymore. His affair brought down not only our marriage, but every other self-deceit that I had been telling myself for years. I was in pain, pain, pain but determined not to feel it.

I was on my own. I immersed myself in yoga. I read Pema Chodron (*When Things Fall Apart, Start Where You Are*) on the bus through the city on the way into work, began my own weekly therapy sessions, and meditated every evening once Kate was in bed. Certainly, there was a glass of wine thrown in there from time to time as well, but I really started to care for myself. I truthfully faced what I had been hiding from, forgave myself for as much of it as I could at the time, and began to love me for me (something I never learned and probably had never really done since childhood). I discovered that it is only through love that we find hope.

In early summer, I attended a hip opener workshop where I stretched out in pigeon pose for fifteen minutes and wrote on the piece of paper in front of me "I forgive him." But also I felt something else. It was my aha moment. It was not just his behavior. I was as much to blame, and I needed to forgive myself too.

I had to take responsibility for my part in our failed marriage and relationship and take steps toward forgiving myself and him.

So, I started to look deeper. I finally saw my own controlling behavior in the relationship—how I had left him and the marriage both emotionally and physically and, to be honest, how bitchy I had been to him. And, I realized something else. I had been relying on him to bring me happiness and security. Any time that he did not or could not provide that for me, or anytime that I simply for whatever reason didn't feel happy or secure, I found something about him to complain about. No, he was by no means perfect. But I could no longer deny that in the beginning of our relationship I had accepted the things I now abhorred.

I had to be honest about my own shortcomings, honest and forgiving.

Later that summer, feeling calm, secure, and open-hearted, I called an old friend to just talk. I found out he too meditated and had been focused on his own healing. We took a day trip to the beach and fell madly in love. (To be honest, I had fallen for him years before when I was in law school and he with me, but circumstances prevented our coming together intimately.) Almost three years ago, he became my husband and Dad "number two" to Kate.

I am by no means "healed" today nor have it all together. I have learned a lot, and my experiences have helped me to shape what is today my present. I love being Kate's mom and seeing her grow and experience her own strength, wisdom, and joy. I work on myself constantly and have a partner who does the same. It isn't always easy, but every hurdle informs us for our next and brings us all closer together. We don't hide behind blame or try very hard to catch it when we try to. I also really work at being the best co-parent I can be with Kate's dad and am grateful every day for our relationship as it is today.

With every fear, I now look inward for the strength, the love, the knowing that all is as it is supposed to be and know I must pay attention and not hide. Right now, this moment.

Candace Smyth is an attorney and family mediator in Washington, DC. After going through her own painful divorce and feeling unsupported by the traditional process, she decided to open a divorce mediation and divorce process coaching practice to help couples mindfully and holistically get through the divorce process. Candace provides both online and in-person North Star Sessions™ workshops across the country focusing on restorative yoga, breathwork, and Ayurveda analysis, nonviolent communication techniques, and practical support so that clients are supported and empowered to take affirmative, self-made movement forward in the divorce process and in life. To learn more, visit CandaceSmyth.com.

I WANTED TO QUIT BUT HOPE WHISPERED HOLD ON
Catrice M. Jackson

"Hope is believing in the possibility of something that will fulfill you in a deep, soulful way. Hold on to the whisper of hope, for you cannot thrive without it." – Catrice M. Jackson

You may be feeling like you want to quit because there's too much pain and struggle in your journey. Don't quit...hang on. I bet you've heard the whisper of those words more times than you can count, right? Me too; it's the voice of hope. It's the voice of your soul telling you to hang on just one more moment, one more day. Deep down inside you believe and know there is something more for you, something better waiting to appear in your life; yet the reality of your current circumstances tells you loud and clear to just quit!

Quitting may feel like the right thing to do, and all the evidence in your life right now may affirm your desire to quit. But...don't quit, hang on! I distinctly remember a plaque my late and favorite aunt used to have hanging on her wall. I never knew what it meant, and when I asked her she tried to explain to me what it meant when I was about nine years old, but it never made sense. For some reason the message on her wall always stuck with me. The plaque read "When you get to the end of your rope, tie a knot and hang on." –Franklin D. Roosevelt. I've heard that quote many times in my adult life, but it wasn't until recently that

I understood its true meaning at a soul level because I was at the end of my rope.

One of the biggest teachers in my life has been the journey of entrepreneurship. I knew at the age of eighteen that I would one day be my own boss. In 2008, I took an uncalculated leap of faith into the world of entrepreneurship after experiencing a life-changing moment where my soul spoke loud and clear: "It's time to answer the calling in your soul." I was so excited and eager to be free from the captivity of a job that I quit my job right at the beginning of the 2008 recession.

Truthfully, I didn't know we were entering in the recession, and frankly it probably wouldn't have made me stay employed; I was desperately ready to be free and finally live my dream.

Over the past five years, there have been so many times I have wanted to just quit! Even though I've accomplished many wonderful, notable things, such as authoring three books, receiving the entrepreneur of the year award, coauthoring an international best-selling book, and the list goes on, I wanted to quit because I wasn't making the money I wanted, I didn't know how to get more clients, my relationships were changing, my only son left for college, and I was emotionally devastated, and too many other life challenges to list. It always seemed easier to quit, and on occasion I did quit. I quit in the moment. I quit for a day or several days. I quit for a week or two, but I could never really quit being an entrepreneur; hope wouldn't let me, and I knew there was more for me than just surviving in life and business.

Being an entrepreneur has taught me more about myself than anything else I've ever experienced. I've successfully raised my only son, obtained the highest degree you can get, been with the same man for eighteen years, and been married for years, and all the other monumental and emotionally challenging situations of my life still have not taught me what entrepreneurship has taught me about me. Those chapters in my life included other people whom I could blame or celebrate for my experiences and outcomes. I keep emphasizing the word "being" because *being* an entrepreneur is not something you do; it's who you are from the top of your head to the soles of your feet.

The biggest surprise of my journey has been the realization that entrepreneurship is a spiritual experience, a walk and test of my faith. It was easy to put myself, my lifestyle, my family, and my financial stability in the hands of an employer and a weekly check. When I chose to be free from employment, I consciously chose to put it all in my hands. That was the biggest mistake of my life, and the lesson to come would teach me to put it all in the hands of God, to stand confidently in my faith and hold on to hope.

When business was good, I was proud. When money came in, I felt secure. When I was in the spotlight, I was confident. When I experienced business success, I was elated. When it all went away or barely trickled in...I was embarrassed and afraid, hiding and disappointed. For one full year, business seemed to have dried up. I was losing confidence, feeling alone in the dark, and grasping for something to believe in, to hold on to—something to lift me out of survival mode to fully thriving in every aspect of my life. It was in the darkness that I saw the light of truth and reconnected to it. You see, I thought I was the business. I believed I was in control and that my business, my soul-gift, was outside of me, and it wasn't until I was faced with the reality of loss on many levels in my life that I realized that I always had it all. Instead of just hearing the voice of hope, one day not too long ago I decided to listen to it with my heart.

In my dark, humbling experience it finally clicked that it's not business, it is personal. I had to lose it all to regain my connection to the source of all things. I thought God had forgotten about me, but I realized my previous choices led me to a front row seat in what I call God University. At the end of my rope, I tied a knot and held on for dear life, took my seat with gratitude, turned on my tape recorder, and awaited divine instruction. The lessons of humility, love, and appreciation lasted a whole year, and I learned that I am not a business, I am a servant. I learned that I can have the desires of my heart when my intention is anchored in serving instead of selling. I learned to always remain in-spirit and connected to the source of abundance and be humbly grateful for everything, even in the moments when I want to quit. The most important thing I learned is that being an entrepreneur is a spiritual honor, a privilege and an opportunity to serve the world as the gift of me in a way that I could never do by working a job.

Entrepreneurship is not a job; it's a journey. It's not work; it's living out what you were created to do. It's more than selling yourself or a product; it's more about serving the world from your heart and with your gifts.

No one told me how tough, frustrating, lonely, and challenging entrepreneurship would be. I had no idea how many times my ego would die and rise again on this journey. Prior to this entrepreneurial journey I never imagined I would crave quitting as much as I did, but every time I wanted to turn out the lights, put the closed sign on the door, and never look back, I heard the whisper of hope say, "Don't quit." It wouldn't go away, and I am so grateful that it kept and keeps speaking to me. I've learned how to be and live my truth, to serve with spiritual intention, and to say yes to thriving instead of surviving. Thanks to entrepreneurship, divine guidance, and my tenacity to hold on to hope, there's more joy in the journey, and I am cocreating my dreams instead of dreaming about them and loving life.

If the whisper of hope is speaking, even if you feel like quitting, stop and hear it now; tie a tight knot and hold on. If you believe deep down in your soul you were created to do more than work a job or thrive instead of survive, turn up the volume on that whisper of hope until it guides you into unwavering faith. Hope believes in something, but faith is knowing and trusting in something; that something is you and the Spirit. Step confidently into your faith and keep taking steps even in the dark. Don't give up! You've come too far, and the whisper of hope will light the path of your desired destiny.

If life is trying to teach you a lesson, take a front row seat, get the divine lesson, reconnect to the source of your abundance and desires, and say yes to your spiritual assignment because that is the real business of entrepreneurship. I didn't give up. I didn't quit, and neither can you. I refused to just survive, and hope kept my dreams alive. Today I thrive from the inside out because I didn't allow my circumstances to dictate my destiny. The gift of you is your business and it is personal. Open yourself up for the world to experience; be spiritually led; serve, don't sell; and watch yourself thrive!

Catrice M. Jackson, MS, LMHP, LPC, The Voice Whisperer believes every woman's voice needs to be heard. Catrice is the global visionary leader of the GetNAKED Movement and founder of the Awakened Conscious Shift and PINK Elephant Conversations. Catrice uses her voice to awaken, liberate, inspire, and empower the lives of women worldwide. To learn more about Catrice, visit Catriceology.com.

REFLECTION INTO MY DARKNESS
Giusep Michelle Vitale

A new friend has been dropping in and out of my life for the past few months. A kind soul. Yet, her visits have been bittersweet cycles. At the start of each visit her soothing companionship brings me joy; then somehow that soothing sentiment shifts into discomfort.

During the sweetness realm, we share of ourselves pleasantly, uncovering mutual interests. Suddenly, as she listens and asks lots of questions about me—what I have done and where I want to go—I begin to understand that there stands a dysfunction toward others. Through my deep breaths I accepted an invitation to dance. She quickly measures herself in comparison to me to judge the rightness of her own actions: "Oh good. I am glad you did that then; that means I am on track," she happily replies at times. This is when I enter the discomfort realm. I visualize her treading water, desperately reaching her arms up for guidance, willing to take on any direction, failing to turn inward for self-discovery. I judge her as immature and unsure, all the while failing to turn inward myself and leaving my discomfort unexamined.

Coincidently, aimless wanderings amid the vastness of cyberspace led me to words of wisdom. Perhaps this was divine guidance in disguise. These words reminded me that deep within the whirlwind of happenstance, there is meaning: what unsettles me in another reveals something yet unresolved in my own being.

As these words of wisdom simmered, I began to understand that this discomfort was bitterness that bubbled up inside of me because I feel threatened: I fear that my friend will create a road map to follow along down the path I have planned for myself, without even asking me if I want company. I fear her disempowering me by overtaking the essence of my uniqueness. I fear her morphing into a better version of who I want to be. I feel jealousy.

Why do I feel threatened? Because I am not grounded in my own uniqueness. Because I do not trust the authenticity of the light that shines within me and how it is connected to the light that shines within her and to the light that shines within the universe.

Beyond a friend this being was an angel reflecting myself back to me. This reflection shined with darkness, revealing an ugly part of me. When she reflected my darkness onto me, I saw the malignant vision—that false expectation appearing real (fear). I feared it; I turned away from it, choosing instead to judge her. With that unfair judgment, I pretended the war was over and the land clear for a fresh start.

But there is an ugly darkness within me. One which no light can overshadow. This angel visit reminded me of my polarized nature—of light and darkness. It reminded me that there are cracks all over me, each containing a story of unresolved shadows, itching my skin for attention.

The recognition of my polarity—of the light and dark within me—is the birthplace of healing; for healing does not necessitate destruction. I recognize this ugly darkness sitting within me: I lack trust of my own authenticity. By acknowledging it, I begin to caress it, stroke it gently, slowly shifting my relationship with it into a space of appreciation and love, accepting that my light necessitates my darkness.

Finding these dried-up, loveless spots within myself presents the miracle of opportunity to water and tend to the grotesque within me. For to love myself, I need to wander through the depths of me to recognize and accept all of me, even that which is grotesque. This is the process of letting myself heal into the beautiful uniqueness of my own truth, into a realm where I feel empowered by my authenticity.

This angel dropped in again just a few days ago. This time around, armed with a warm teacup of self-love and compassion cookies, I greeted the angel with a perspective of abundance ready to celebrate whatever path she chooses, without feeling threatened, but instead filled with the wisdom that the light that shines within her shines within me, shines within the universe.

This angel showed me where to plant another seed of love within me. It will take a while for the love to grow. But I already feel it. It has already changed me, ever so slightly. I have come to feel the darkness of judgment arising within me at times—as I feel my authenticity weakened and threatened—but I can name the experience for its dark qualities. I remind myself that this is part of the darkness of my being that is a necessary companion to my light. I recognize that I am devaluing my authenticity. I feel this and then I release it, trusting that love can live even in the darkness.

I am grateful to be able to put these thoughts into words, releasing shame through vulnerability. I am grateful to be on the path to trusting more and more my authenticity, recognizing that the light that shines within me shines within the universe.

Giusep Vitale is a Venezuelan living in Boston where she shares yoga with kids and grown-ups and studies counseling psychology. She is a lover of laughter; it is her preferred medicine right next to dancing and dark chocolate. You can find out more about Giusep at GiusepVitale.com.

LOOKING DOWN AT THE BONFIRE
Lucinda Kinch

I've always been able, sometimes against my own will, to see the good in others. I've been labeled a hopeless romantic and a dreamer. An astrologist once told me my "north node" positioning blesses me with the ability to see the wounded child in a murderer.

Most of the time, my so-called rose-tinted shades give me a lovely perspective on things. My natural view of the world as a beneficent, trustworthy place gives me hope for humanity and lost souls. But there has been a big chunk of my life—almost a third now—during which my default mode of seeing the good in others, despite their behavior, became a bitter curse.

My hardest lesson began when I decided to play healer to a brilliant, charismatic man who I thought was the most wonderful person on the planet. He was perfect for me in every way, although very damaged and hurt by life. I believed then that I could fix his problems and make him whole. But despite my best efforts, he gradually revealed himself to be a control-obsessed, pathologically insecure abuser. For reasons that have only recently become clear to me through a lot of inner work, I gave away my power to that man for ten years. That's a year for every finger on my hands that will never return—a decade that I long to redo for my children's sake so I could be present in their early childhood years, rather than being consumed by concern for our basic survival.

It's hard to imagine now, and perhaps someone looking at my life from the outside would wonder how I could think this, but I somehow thought that if I could only love him enough, be gentle enough, lighten his load enough, and bring some ease to the furrow in his brow, he would love me back and all would be right in our little world.

But what I got in return for my efforts—in fact, it seemed the harder I tried the worse it got—was years of psychological and sometimes physical abuse. I've had my heart shattered over and over, been to hell and back in my own head, allowed myself to be used as a doormat, and been spit on, undermined, and degraded. I love the magic and the light in my life and would prefer to dwell there entirely, but because of this man I have dived deep into my soul's own velvet shadows of darkness.

I recall in particular one instance in which I found myself abandoning my own personal power and integrity just to keep a fragile equilibrium. One night while my newly born son was sleeping, the man I loved and the father of that child threw me across the room. I had been trying to make peace after another argument and was appalled to witness something in his eyes suddenly shift. He seemed to go away somehow and slid into an instant mindless rage. As I recall it now, my descent to the floor happened in slow motion. As my head slammed on his desk and I fell, he cursed and left the room. I began to panic but managed fumblingly to collect myself and dial 9-1-1.

As the first ring came, I quickly hung up. I had just then remembered something he'd told me months before—that his previous wife had had him arrested twice. The clincher for me in that information: he'd told me that he "could never love her the same after those calls." I realized in that moment that if I summoned help, he'd never love me the same, either.

I panicked anew then, since his care for me and our child was paramount. I believed that I couldn't allow anything to threaten that, even if I was hurt in the process. His acceptance and approval of me meant everything. When the 9-1-1 operator called back, he answered the phone in the other room and used his considerable powers of persuasion to turn the tables on me. He accused me of assaulting him and said I was the one at fault. While speaking to the officer in the dark outside our house shortly afterward, I took full blame, frozen with fear.

The officer wrote me a harassment ticket as the side of my head throbbed in red-hot pain, but my fear and shock kept tears at bay. Later, he accused me of staging the incident so I could charge him with abuse.

This marked the beginning of a long, downward spiral for my spirit. I learned how to keep my head down, literally and figuratively, and put a tight lid on the big, passionate spirit that I am. I became entirely submissive, except for the rare times I erupted in rage when I got fed up with being baited like a bear tied to a stake. I lived constantly ready to fight or run. I allowed this man to isolate me, as the conditions for his love—the rules of the game, as it were—grew ever more complex and hard to follow. Without even knowing it consciously, I completely gave my power away.

My spirit wandered lost, bereaved. I had unwittingly shut down my powerful intuitive connection to the divine, to my Source, and allowed this small, sad, and fearful man to become my All.

And yet one day, at last, in a burst of righteous fury, I found the courage to protect myself and my children. He countered with malicious slander in the court systems, extreme and disturbing efforts to alienate my boys from me, and continued emotional and psychological abuse in any form he could manage from a distance. However, I could see more clearly by then—thanks to my own inner work, support from a renewed circle of friends, and a wonderful, healthy new man in my life—that I had to withstand my ex's assaults for my sake and my children's.

When we experience what I call "intimate terrorism" in our lives—a toxic relationship with someone we have strong life ties to, such as the parent of your children or your own parent or a family member—it can be superbly difficult to extricate ourselves. We are attached to them and have hope that it will get better, or that the person will work on themselves and experience a breakthrough that will resolve the impasse. It's not like a coworker we can report or an acquaintance we can ignore. It's very personal, and we often get stuck working through it with them to whatever degree we allow interaction.

But I've come to understand that it's our birthright and natural ability to rise from the ashes, dust off the soot, and mend our charred hearts.

Despite everything I've experienced, I still believe deep within myself that somehow, on some level, we call to us our greatest challenges and the most difficult people in our lives. Through these encounters, if we choose, we learn to expand our light beyond the hell and heartache to heal the wounds with our own inner strength.

Violence is never OK. Whether emotional or physical, abuse is hateful and wrong. It is the act of someone who deeply loathes himself or herself and who has no inner resources to allow resolution of that self-hatred. And the victim of such abuse has a choice: keep being abused, keep shutting yourself off from your own shining connection with the Source, or rise up like the legendary phoenix bird and soar out of the smoldering ashes of your bright expectations, crushed hopes, and stillborn dreams.

If we open ourselves to it, there is a treasure deep within those cinders: a faith born of hardship that we are strong; we are divine; we are whole, good, and worthy of love. At our shimmering cores, there is perfection and untarnished and unimaginable power. It's up to us whether we accept and use that power to become the best human beings we can be.

May all beings awaken to the light of their true nature!

May peace reign deeply among us.

Lucinda Kinch is a visionary fine and graphic artist. She empowers women with Inner Goddess Portraits as powerful personal totems. Lucinda is currently writing her memoir, which she hopes will inspire experiencers of abuse to remember their divine, empowered, and whole selves. Learn more at LucindaKinch.com.

THE MAGIC FORMULA: THREE STEPS TO THRIVE
Marci Shimoff

For the first thirty-six years of my life, I had been very achievement-driven. I worked hard, pushed myself, and was crystal clear about what I wanted. But, I wasn't very good at letting go, relaxing, and opening to receive what the universe brought me.

Early in my career, I'd learned a wonderful formula for manifesting anything in life from Bill Levacy, one of my life coaches. The formula consists of three rhyming steps:

Intention: Be very clear about what you want.

Attention: Focus your attention on what you desire. Make sure your thoughts, words, feelings, and your actions are in alignment with your intention.

No tension: Relax, let go, be in a state of ease and open to receive from the universe.

While I was really good at those first two steps—intention and attention—I had a hard time with the "no tension" step, even though the most wonderful miracles have come to me when I've been able to let go into "no tension." Perhaps the most dramatic example of this relates to my biggest career breakthrough. Let me share the story with you:

I was thirteen when I attended my first event featuring an inspirational speaker, Zig Ziglar. As I saw him walking the stage, passionately giving his speech and moving the entire audience, I said to myself, "*That's* what I'm supposed to do here on this planet." I had a very clear intention and vision. I saw myself traveling around the world inspiring millions of people to live their best lives possible. At that young age, my intention was clearly set.

My attention was also strong. For years, I did everything I could to support that intention happening. Eventually, I got an MBA in training and development (the closest degree I could find to match my intention), started my career as a corporate training consultant, and taught seminars on stress management and communication skills in Fortune 500 companies across the United States. I read every self-help book I found, attended every self-help seminar I could, studied other speakers' delivery styles, learned every self-development technique out there, and followed the success principles I'd discovered in order to make my dream a reality.

I was fortunate to have an amazing mentor in Jack Canfield—years before the *Chicken Soup for the Soul* books had even been conceived. He taught me (and many others) how to deliver self-esteem training programs. Soon after I attended his "Train the Trainer course," I began teaching those programs to women's audiences. Though I was having some success working for a seminar company teaching one-day training programs, I was frustrated because I wasn't having the big success I'd dreamed of.

On top of that, I was exhausted. I felt like a road warrior, traveling two hundred days a year. I would speak all day long (in high heels), then get in a car at 5:30 p.m. and drive three to four hours to the next city, fall fast asleep, and wake up early the next morning so I could be in the training room by 7:00 a.m. ready to do that routine all over again. I did that day in and day out.

And while I knew in my heart that inspiring people was what I was supposed to be doing, I sensed that there was something bigger that was supposed to happen. My vision was to reach more

HOPE

people worldwide, but I couldn't seem to break through to the next level in my career. I'd hit a wall.

Tired, confused, and drained, I started doubting my future: what was next and how could I get there?

As grace would have it, my dear friend, Janet Atwood, took me by the hand one day and said, "Marci, you're coming with me. You're burned out. You need a break. We're going on a seven-day silent meditation retreat." Shocked, I answered, "No way. I haven't been silent for more than two hours in my life! I can't imagine seven days of silence. Impossible." But Janet was insistent, so off we went to a week of what I thought would be silent torture.

The first few days were really challenging, but I finally settled in to the silence and started enjoying the ease that came with it. On the fourth day, in the middle of a meditation, a lightbulb went off in my head, and I saw the words "Chicken Soup for the Woman's Soul." As soon as I had that vision, I knew exactly what I was to do next—write that book.

At the time, only the original *Chicken Soup for the Soul* book was published and nobody had thought of creating other specialty books. I just knew this was it—something that would touch many people and that was a calling for me! This was, I felt, a gift from the universe.

The only problem with the scenario was that I still had three more days of my silent retreat left. I'd just had the great epiphany of my life and I couldn't tell anybody!

So, as soon as the silence was over, I ran to the closest pay phone, called up Jack, and said, "Listen to this: Chicken Soup for the Woman's Soul." He said, "What a great idea! I can't believe nobody's thought of this before." He then called his publisher and said, "Chicken Soup for the Woman's Soul." To which the publisher replied, "What a great idea. I can't believe nobody thought of that."

Within a few months, I had a signed contract to coauthor the book with Jack, Mark Victor Hansen, and my business partner,

Jennifer Hawthorne. A year and a half later, *Chicken Soup for the Woman's Soul* was released and in its first week hit #1 on the *New York Times* best seller list. Since then, I've written a total of nine books that have sold fifteen million copies in thirty-three languages, and I've traveled around the world speaking about the messages in those books.

Relaxing into a deep state inside—the state of no tension—is what led to that pivotal "aha!" moment that transformed my career. It was proof to me that it's those three steps—intention, attention, and no tension—together that create magic in our lives.

Working on *Chicken Soup for the Woman's Soul* was more fulfilling than anything I'd ever done before in my career, as it was birthed out of pure inspiration. I could feel that I was moving in tune with the universe—that I had plugged into something bigger than me; I had just gotten on the train, and it was moving me forward.

After the book came out, I was quickly speaking to audiences one hundred times bigger than those I was used to speaking to—I was reaching ten thousand people instead of one hundred people at an event. And the best part was feeling like I was fulfilling my life purpose.

As time went on, I met amazing teachers who had been my idols in the transformational field. They were becoming my colleagues and friends, and I felt more empowered and more deeply fulfilled. I was getting to play in a bigger way.

Six years later I'd written six titles in the *Chicken Soup for the Soul* series, and I knew it was time to move on—I was full of Chicken Soup! So, I applied the same "magic formula" to my next step. I got clear on what I wanted, put my attention on it, and most of all, I relaxed and trusted. That's how *Happy for No Reason* and *Love for No Reason*, my two most recent books, were born. When I took some time to go inside and listen to my inner knowing, those projects were revealed to me. And they've been the most fulfilling work of my career.

I'm thrilled that they both became New York Times best sellers and that their messages of unconditional love and happiness have reached many people around the world. This is further proof that when I relax and let the universe flow through me, the benefits are infinitely profound.

Tips for No Tension

We often get discouraged from the circumstances of our lives—we look around us and we don't see how we can have what we truly want. We struggle, we work hard, but we overlook the power of relaxing and letting go.

These days, whenever I feel out of balance or stuck, I lean into that "no tension" step of my magic formula. That's what puts me back into the flow of creativity and love.

Since the art of letting go is still something I haven't mastered, I think of three words that help remind me how to relax into no tension. Perhaps they'll help you:

The first word is "trust." Trust yourself and trust life. Ask "What can I do to move into that state of ease? What's the next step for me? What expands me?" Then, trust your inner voice to move in that direction.

The second word is "courage." Have the courage to hang in there, get through the difficult times, and keep moving forward. No matter what it looks like on the outside, listen to your heart and have the courage to follow it.

The third word is "compassion." We need compassion, particularly with ourselves. Remember, in the midst of whatever challenge you may be facing, offer yourself care and understanding. Nurture and nourish yourself. You'll be able to get through anything if you can be gentle, loving, and compassionate with yourself.

People often ask me if taking care of themselves and focusing on their own inner happiness and love is selfish. Absolutely not. On the contrary, I believe it's the least selfish thing that you can do.

The more fulfilled you are, the more you're able to offer to the world. The world gets the benefit of your elevated energy.

That concept is reflected beautifully in my favorite Chinese proverb:

When there is light in the soul, there will be beauty in the person.

When there is beauty in the person, there will be harmony in the house.

When there is harmony in the house, there will be order in the nation.

And when there is order in the nation, there will be peace in the world.

My wish you for you is that you feel the love in your heart and the light in your soul. May we each experience that love and light so we can light up and transform this world.

Marci Shimoff is a #1 New York Times best-selling author, a world-renowned transformational teacher, and an expert on happiness, success, and unconditional love. Marci's books include the New York Times best sellers *Love for No Reason, Happy for No Reason,* and six titles in the phenomenally successful *Chicken Soup for the Woman's Soul* series. Her books have sold more than fifteen million copies worldwide in thirty-three languages. To learn more, visit HappyForNoReason.com.

THE START OF A REVOLUTION
Micaela Bubola

I was about fifteen to sixteen years old when I noticed a feeling of intense Love within me. I obviously felt Love for my family and friends, but at that age I became aware of the force and power of the Love I had inside.

I remember thinking to myself after seeing one of my best friends at the time go through a tough breakup with her boyfriend that I just could not understand how two people who had constantly and consistently told each other they loved each other and showed each other so much affection just all of a sudden could not love each other anymore or be mean and harsh to each other. This concept could not enter my being; for me once you told someone you loved them, it was FOREVER! There was no taking it back.

So I sat with my frustration and pondered and felt a deep desire to tell everyone on the planet that Love never ends, that you can't take Love back, and that all we can do is Love more moment to moment to moment. As a young teenager, I didn't really know what to do with it. I felt my feelings, remained confused, and continued with my life.

You know how life has its ways of showing you the way? Well, several years later, I experienced my own loss of Love, and it was more painful than I could have ever imagined. I had just moved from Florence, Italy, my hometown, to San Francisco, California, to go to college. And, six months into my stay, I got the phone call everyone dreads to receive. My aunt was on the other line, and I could hear it in her voice that something terrible had happened; my father had been in a horrible car accident in Bulgaria on his way back from a dinner meeting with his assistant: the assistant survived, but my father did not.

My world fell apart. My rock, my daddy was gone. I would never talk or see him ever again. I was devastated. I was a young girl (I considered myself still a child at that age) without her parents beside her in a new country, just learning to adjust to the difference in the culture and ways of life. And now I was in such pain that I could not function. I had to quit my job, and I flew back home. This was the start of the darkest period in my life. I had just lost Love. I was so mad at the world, at God, and at everybody. I started to retreat and developed my inner "bitch" to deal with the pain. I began to treat people very badly, until one day I saw myself from the outside looking in and did not like what I saw.

I thought to myself: "Who is this person? I don't know her. Why is she so mean? How do I get back to the happy, loving, innocent girl I once knew?" So my journey back to Love started with discovering who I really was inside—who was living inside after taking away the hurt and the pain, the disappointments and the sadness.

This journey took many detours and pit stops, as I endured a few more losses of Love (life is very good at that!) as I entered into relationships with men who used me, verbally abused me, and just took advantage of my good nature and generosity.

I was thirty-three, I had just become a mother, and I found myself discovering that the man I had fallen madly in love with was not who I thought he was. I gave him everything—my heart, my body, my time, and my money—only to be betrayed over and over and over again. I was put down, demeaned, made a fool of, and used like an old rag that wasn't needed anymore. I came out of that relationship broken, destroyed, with nothing left to give. My self-esteem and confidence were shot, and I had realized that

I had compromised myself for a false sense of belonging and connection. I had not upheld any boundaries, and I had gone against my principles out of fear and a desire to feel the Love I had so long ago lost.

This time I had someone else I was now responsible for, the only thing in my life that brought me joy, and that allowed me to feel the force of Love alive within me again. There was now something greater than myself, something worth fighting for, my beautiful daughter Arabella. She sparked a fire in me and helped me see who I was. She showed me that unconditional Love existed still, if I only allowed it in, and it started all from the inside out. The Love had been within me all along; I was just not willing to see it because I was so angry and hurt. Once I pulled the veil of suffering away from my eyes, my journey was over, and I had found myself and Love again…

I woke up to the fact that I had to learn to Love who I was first before I could truly Love from my overflow anyone else. Forgiving myself for bad decisions and accepting responsibility for those decisions was the first step. Then all I could do was be in awe of the true being I was: Loving, Passionate, Committed, Kind, Compassionate.

"Now what?" I thought. "Now what do I get to do with this immense force within?" I remembered my thoughts as a young teenager wanting so badly to tell the world about Love. An answer came to use my gifts and talents to show people that there is an immense amount of Love within and that loving who they are inside will allow them to then Love everyone around them, no matter what, without taking it back.

This was the start of the Love You Revolution.

Micaela Bubola Passeri is an inspirational fashion designer and self-love expert. She is on a mission to spread the message of Love through the purity of original style and is committed to helping women, men, and children love and accept who they are as they are, with their talents and gifts, their flaws and imperfections. She is also the founder of the Love You Revolution Movement through which she volunteers her time and resources delivering her workshops at no charge in domestic violence shelters, schools, and nonprofit organizations. Learn more at LoveYouRevolution.com or Bubbola.com.

MY MISTAKE WAS ACTUALLY A MIRACLE
Nichole Kellerman

Growing up there was a lot of partying going on in my house; I just thought that was normal. People were always over dancing to music, partying in the hot tub, laughing, just having nonstop fun until wee hours of the morning. I thought this must be how every family is—I stay in my room with my little brother; they party. This is normal.

Then, as I grew up, I realized this was far from the truth. At the end of my senior year of high school reality hit me over the head like a two-by-four. At that point, Mom and Dad had been divorced for a few years, and yet both of them still continued to party on a regular basis.

Weeks or even months would go by without hearing from Mom because she was off partying with her boyfriend of the week, and Dad would drink away his anger and sadness every night with a bottle of VO and Pepsi until he was drunk enough to fall asleep.

I was at a standstill; I had no idea how bad things really were until that point.

My parents were addicts in many areas of life: drugs, alcohol, work, depression. They were severe addicts who were on a path of total self-destruction.

I began to wonder if I even knew who my real parents were—my sober parents. They were never going to get better. They would never find sobriety. They would never be the parent, friend, grandparent, or support system that I would need as I began my life into adulthood.

I was in so much pain it was overwhelming. I started to get lost in a downward spiral of my own: an addiction with my body. I was obsessed with food, exercise, and calories. It was all I thought about:

"You disgust me. Get your fat ass to the gym!"

"You don't deserve to eat anything; you look like a cow!"

"Everything I wear just makes me look fat!"

"Only eat a little and work out for two hours today."

It was a great way to avoid reality, but over time it continued to get worse.

The abusive thoughts started to consume me, taking every essence of my being. I was drowning.

I soon turned to drugs and alcohol, trying to silence the thoughts of self-hatred, but it never worked. They would always come back louder and more abusive than the last.

Looking back on it now I realize I was trying to numb my feelings—numb the pain of no longer having my parents and never even knowing who they really were.

After two years of this self-destructive cycle of addiction, I hit my rock bottom. I was over being at war with myself. I saw a commercial for personal training school and figured since I was in the gym all the time anyway, I might as well get paid for it.

I started going to college and getting my life back on track; I wasn't about to follow in my parents' footsteps! I lost the weight, ditched the addictions, and the best part was I found my passion: health, fitness, and making other women feel as good as I did!

That was almost eight years ago, and I haven't looked back. I have the life beyond my wildest dreams. I live in one of the most majestic parts of the world, I have a boyfriend to die for, and I work from home motivating and guiding women into the body and the life they too deserve. Yep, I'm pretty darn lucky, but not without a fight.

I have done lots of healing since that time, and coming to terms with my reality was more heart-wrenching than I could have ever imagined. But, you know what? I don't regret it, and I would never wish for anything different. Truth of the matter is I wouldn't be who I am today or where I am today if it weren't for all those things.

When life drops a huge mountain right in front of us, we only have two options.

We can feel defeated and quit, or we can find the strength within ourselves to get back up and climb up that sucker, no matter how hard it will be.

When I was lost in my own addiction (which was really just a distraction), I felt defeated and I gave up. "How dare life curse me with this?" I let my parents' addictions not only destroy their lives, but mine as well. I let the death of their souls kill mine too.

There comes a time when we all need to take an honest look at our lives and ask ourselves, are we surrendering to one of life's mountains? Are we walking away with our tail between our legs because we don't think we are strong enough to take it on?

Believe me, I know how easy it is to just give up.

I have failed more times than you know. I have been curled up in a ball on the floor crying for days wondering if life would ever get better. BUT I found it in myself to get back up and try again, and again, aaaaaaaaand again, until success.

And you know what? The reward when you get to the other side is more liberating, freeing, and exhilarating than ANYTHING you have ever felt! ANYTHING!

If you are looking up at a mountain right now wondering why did this happen to me, how am I going to get over this, and teetering with the idea of giving up—DON'T.

You can do this. You can. You hold within you all the strength and energy you need to get over this…and if you didn't, life wouldn't have given you this mountain.

If I can do it, so can you.

I believe in you.

Sending you lots of love and strength.

Nichole Kellerman is a weight loss and lifestyle coach. Having struggled with her own weight and self-image in the past, she is bound and determined to help as many women as possible learn the RIGHT way to lose weight. Her mission is to show you how to put an end to the dieting torture and show you how to lose weight while having a BLAST. Learn more about her at NicholeKellerman.com.

THE CARDS WE ARE DEALT
Rachel Luna

One of my earliest childhood memories is of me as a three-year-old visiting my mother in the hospital. I remember someone picking me up and telling me to say good-bye. She removed her oxygen mask with her right hand and gave me a kiss. "Good-bye, Mommy," I said innocently. I didn't fully understand that this kiss would be the last kiss. It was the last time I saw her alive.

On Tuesday, January 17, 1984, Magda Dilva Gonzalez succumbed to AIDS-related pneumonia. With her last breath, my life was forever changed. The "battle for Rachel" began immediately following her demise. Aunts bickered over who would raise me, as my father, a former IV drug user, who was also HIV positive, struggled to make the decision. God bless him, he gave it a good run of raising me on his own, but less than a year later he realized there was no way he could successfully raise a toddler on his own in the ghettos of the Bronx.

The day he dropped me off at my godmother Carmen's house I remember crying and screaming for him. "Daddy, Daddy, don't go. Please, Daddy, don't go." It's amazing the memories a child will hold onto. At four years old, I experienced my very first heartbreak, and for years I would struggle with abandonment issues, feelings of inadequacy, and the insecurities of never having a father fully present in my life. This experience would be the first limiting belief to grip my future: men will always leave you. To his credit, my father made mediocre attempts to be a part of my life over the next fifteen years. I'd get an occasional phone call, a weekend visit two or three times a year, and on one very good Christmas a stolen Nintendo game system he had purchased from a junkie. His mediocrity as a father contributed to limiting belief number two: men are unreliable and will almost always let you down.

For years I had been told that my mother had died of "natural causes," and no one ever let on that my father was sick. It wasn't until I was about nine or ten that the truth came out. Right there, while sitting on the front stoop during one of my rare weekend visits, my father's then girlfriend blurted out to a neighbor, "Her mother died of AIDS."

"LIAR! LIAR! My mother died of natural causes," I yelled. "I have her death certificate, and it says natural causes. You just want to hurt me because you're jealous that my dad loved my mother more than he loves you." Tears of rage poured down my face as she challenged me, "Go ask your father. He's sick too."

My heart dropped to the floor. What? My father was going to die too? How could this be? What kind of world was this that I should lose my mother, rarely see my father, and now lose him too? It had to be a lie. I raced back into the house screaming at the top of my lungs, "Daaaaaaaaddy! Why did you lie to me?! My mother died of AIDS and you're gonna die too?" Sobbing uncontrollably, I flung myself at him. "Loi (his pet name for me), calm down. Who told you that?" he asked, trying to remain calm. "Your stupid girlfriend. She's outside telling the whole neighborhood that Mommy died of AIDS and you're gonna die too." It was one of the rare times I saw my father enraged.

At that same moment in walked his girlfriend, and the two began a heated screaming match. When it was all said and done, my father sat me down and explained that it was true—my mother had died of AIDS and he was going to die too. Now it all made sense why people always looked at me with pity in their eyes and why my older brothers would always make comments about how unfair our lives were. They knew the truth.

HOPE

And now that I knew the truth, my second heartbreak and a fresh, new limiting belief I would hang onto for years was born: trust no one; even the people you love are liars.

Life had dealt me a bad hand. I was the bastard child of two AIDS-infected people, a legal ward of the court, and an emotional orphan. As the years passed by, the struggles continued. I battled bulimia for several years, and when I overcame that struggle, I decided to join the Marine Corps Reserves. But my father's deteriorating health put a hold on my plans to go to boot camp. I simply could not leave and risk him dying while I was away. Nevertheless, the day I knew had been coming for fifteen years but still wasn't quite ready for had finally arrived. My father died.

I put on a brave face and threw myself into my studies and in the summer of '99 I went to boot camp. People kept asking me how I could get over my dad's death so easily because on the outside I looked tough. I smiled, I hung out, I studied. To look at me, you'd never guess I too was dying on the inside.

A year later, the pain, heartache, and grief I had suppressed all came to the surface. The final realization that I would never see or speak to my father again was more than I could bear, and for the next two years I was on a path of self-destruction. I drank heavily, skipped classes, and bounced from one bad relationship to another, all the while racking up a substantial amount of debt.

One day, while lying on the bathroom floor in a pool of my own vomit, I realized this was no way to live. If I kept going this way, I'd end up just like my parents. I had a choice to make. I could let my depression and pity party get the best of me, or I could take responsibility for my actions and turn my life around.

I knew I wanted more for myself. I knew I was capable of achieving more. I made the decision to, for the first time in my life, allow myself to be vulnerable and put down my "shield of strength" and ask for help. I met with my college guidance counselors to map out a plan to graduate on time, and most importantly, I worked my tail off. Thanks to the support of a lot of people, I was able to turn my life around. And it all started with me putting my pride aside and asking for help.

Despite the challenges, there were many rays of light in my life. My godmother, whom I began calling Mom soon after moving in with her, has been amazing. She's always made me feel like I was her very own. She made sacrifices to send me to private school, took me on vacations, and despite her own fear of the water took me to the pool every chance we got. She taught me then and still to this day teaches me the importance of working hard and making sacrifices and what it means to persevere.

The biggest lesson in my life has been the realization that allowing myself to be vulnerable has empowered me to receive more, do more, and be more! When we are vulnerable, when we can admit we need help—that we can't do it alone—others show up with loving, open arms ready to fill in the gap. Today, I have the most amazing life, a husband I adore, two beautiful daughters, a thriving business helping others, and the peace of mind of knowing that there is always hope when we remain hopeful, and there is always love when we remain open to receive it.

Founder and owner of The Tailor Made Life a full-service life and business coaching practice, Rachel Luna is passionate about helping women create inspired and fulfilled lives. She is an expert success coach and speaker with a proven track record for helping her clients get results. Rachel has been seen all around the web and was recently featured in the nationally published *Latina Magazine*. To learn more about Rachel, visit TheTailorMadeLife.com.

HOPE IS STILL IN THE JAR
Cigdem Kobu

I'm writing these lines to you the day after I lost the baby I've been joyfully expecting.

Loss.

Grief.

Huge grief...

And yet, had I been living in the eastern part of my country, miscarriage at eleven weeks would have been the least of my problems.

* * *

I come from a country where people believe the first woman was created from one of the ribs of the first man, and consequently, that women are lesser to men.

I come from a country where girls who have just reached puberty are forced to marry and have kids when they haven't fully enjoyed their own childhood yet.

I come from a land where women are beaten, harassed, and mistreated every day.

I come from a country where girls are raped by their cousins, uncles, and other male relatives and then executed because they were raped.

I come from a culture where many idioms degrading women are part of daily language, such as those that mean "half-witted," "bad luck bringer," "the lacking one," "the enemy of income," and "long hair, short wit."

I come from a land where the fundamentalist Islamic government in power today does everything to prevent girls from having education after elementary school, to have their heads covered, and to have anyone who has an abortion put on "the blacklist."

Yet, I am not one of those women.

* * *

There is a big divide in my culture when it comes to women—a chasm that is as deep as the Blue Bosphorus running through my beautiful hometown, separating the Asian side from the European side.

I was one of the lucky girls who was born into a family who lived in the biggest and most advanced city of the country and who valued education and equality for both boys and girls.

I was also fortunate because I belonged to a lineage of powerful, self-sufficient women.

I had the chance to go to a wonderful private school and to learn foreign languages that opened up entire new worlds in front of me.

I was able to go to college and study public relations and advertising and then switch to film studies. I was free to work since I was sixteen, even though a young girl pursuing part-time jobs before college was not common even in my urban community back then.

I belonged to the cultural minority. I must have been born under a lucky star.

I have always been aware of this and felt grateful every single day.

* * *

His Holiness the Dalai Lama made a famous proclamation at the Vancouver Peace Summit in 2009 and said, "The world will be saved by the Western woman."

It is true that Western women have the freedom of speech, the freedom of choice, easier access to high-quality education, and resources many non-Western women in the East do not have.

However, I choose to repeat the Dalai Lama's words with a slight change in the wording: "The world will be saved by Women."

Not just by Western women, but by women in general. The world will be saved and healed by the entire feminine conscious.

* * *

As the Greek myth goes, Elpis, the spirit of hope, was trapped along with the other daimones in a jar by Zeus and left to the care of the first woman called Pandora.

When Pandora opened the jar, all of the spirits escaped except for Elpis (Hope). Pandora immediately put the lid back on the jar while Elpis was still inside.

Hope remained in the vessel to comfort humankind.

* * *

"The Masculine" has brought us nothing but trouble. It has been leading us to collective calamity. It is about time as women that we start to heal each other and the wounds of our world.

It is about time that we awaken "the Feminine" in our husbands, partners, brothers, and sons.

It is us who will lead the world to peace, equality, and abundance.

And we have all the keys. We are the pioneers of possibility. We have the power, perception, and creativity to bring about a peaceful unity and give birth to a new world.

Elpis is still in the jar. If we awaken and empower each other, and ourselves, Hope promises to bestow on each of us the good things that are in our future as the entire humankind.

Cigdem Kobu is a business growth coach and catalyst who believes business is fun when it nourishes your heart first. She holds visionary conversations with gutsy, creative women about mindful living and sustainable business and she creates playgrounds where women solopreneurs learn, create, and prosper together. Cigdem is also the curator of A Year With Myself, the most comprehensive personal growth program for women who are ready to change their lives from the inside out. To learn more, visit WickedAwesomeLife.com.

GIVE A BRICK
El Edwards

Once upon a time there was a nightclub. You'd expect it to be in the middle of a busy city, but no, this nightclub was in a village—a village named after the prisoners who would walk through it on their way to prison. Charming and quaint, eh? Not quite.

In the very corner of a field, behind the nightclub, a church was built. Gifted to the community. Built with love. But now attended by so few. C'est la vie.

Except. This little church had a dream, a gift to give back to the community. A place where youth clubs could meet, children could play, and meals could be served to elderly neighbors. A place of love and hope in an area shrouded in so much darkness.

And so this story is about the time when one young mum's brain found itself in possession of an idea—an idea that could change the landscape of that village for generations to come.

An idea that could change the world.

All it would take was faith, hope, and love. And sure, the greatest of these is love. But you're here to hear a story about hope. And so this one is about the time when it all seemed impossible, but she never gave up.

Spoilers? Yep. But who doesn't love a happy ending?

Are you sitting comfortably? Good. Then I'll begin.

Or continue. Because you've met the church, in the village, behind a nightclub. And the vision, to create a place for the community. The church was small, so it would need to be extended and improved.

So having jumped through all the hoops that a building project presents, they were faced with the realization that the cheapest offer to build the extension was going to cost one hundred thousand pounds. (That's one hundred and sixty thousand of your US dollars.)

"One hundred thousand pounds? One hundred THOUSAND pounds?!? It might as well be a million! Where are we going to find one hundred thousand pounds??"

And that's when she had the idea.

"It's easy. All we need is one hundred thousand people to give us a pound."

But of course, neither she nor her mum or dad, or anyone else in the church, knew one hundred thousand people. But she did know computers. And this newfangled invention called the Internet. (I dare you to tell me that this wasn't perfect timing!)

"All we need is a website. And a way for people to give their pound online. And it'll be easy." (Easy? Ha! Thank goodness she didn't know the half of it!)

After tapping away at her keyboard for several nights, our young mum found out that yes, it was possible to give donations online. She even found a British bank that would let her do it for free, but only if the good cause was a UK-registered charity.

Bugger!

"OK, so what if we set up a charity? I mean, it's going to take some effort to get the one hundred thousand people to each give a pound. Having gone to all that effort, why stop there? Why not carry on and help other people make a difference in their communities?"

And that was the day that Give A Brick was born.

Within three months they had the registered charity status that they needed. Everything was moving quickly. Exciting times. Cue lots of celebration and smiles. Fab!

Except, as is so often the case in the very best stories, things didn't exactly go according to plan.

It was like a total blackout for two years. They had a website. They talked a lot about the stuff they could do. But nothing ever really seemed to happen. Three-quarters of the already small church congregation left. Disaster!

And then one evening, almost two years after having that first idea, our young mum happened across another charity website, powered by something called WordPress. She did some digging and decided to completely overhaul the Give A Brick website, set it up using WordPress, join Twitter, and see what could be done from there.

Like lots of people, she really didn't get Twitter. What was the point of sending a text message to a load of people she didn't know, telling them what she was having on her toast?!? It was all a bit bizarre.

But the more she played with it, the more she started to enjoy the conversations. And ever so slowly, little by little, people gave. Sometimes it was dollars rather than pounds. But that didn't matter, it could all be converted and used to buy actual bricks (well, concrete blocks) and get the foundations laid.

In the meantime, Give A Brick started to help smaller projects too. A local football team was given new kit, an unemployed but ambitious young dad was given money for a website so he could start his own business, a student from the US who wouldn't graduate because he couldn't pay his fees was given financial aid.

Suddenly it was no longer just one project in one small corner of South Wales. People on opposite sides of the globe were getting the help they needed.

As for the community center behind the nightclub, the roof goes on this week. Five years after Give A Brick was born and yes, it's still not finished. (Although, by the time this story goes to print, I'd love to hope that it will be!)

Everyone loves the story of an overnight success—the singer plucked from obscurity, the first-time author given the massive advance, the Olympic gold medalist who had never set foot in a boat before the previous games.

But behind every overnight success story there are years of hard work. The sleepless nights and setbacks aren't sexy. We leave those out of our stories because how fun is it to tell people that you kicked your heels for two years?

Sometimes, all you can do is dig in, grit your teeth, and just keep going. That's the real story behind every overnight success.

"Everything is possible for one who believes."

Jesus said that, and it's as true for you as it is for Give A Brick and the church behind the nightclub.

All you need is to believe. And never, ever, ever give up.

Because if one young mum from an obscure town in South Wales can set up a charity that impacts a generation, just think what you can do!

El Edwards is chief jester and director of fun at Pompoms Included and founder of UK charity Give A Brick. To learn more, visit PomsPomsIncluded.com or HeavenAndEl.com.

I AM PART OF THE FREEDOM STORY
Kristi Griem

She was taken at a young age away from her family, with the promise of a job and added income to send home. Tricked. Trapped. Traded.

Trafficked.

Millions of women and children are trafficked every day within countries and over borders. What has been called today's form of modern-day slavery is hard to stop because it is such a lucrative business. It is a common story: "promise of a job," or "freedom to run your life the way you want to," or "we'll take care of you the way he never has." And suddenly they are gone.

But there is hope. Around the world, in a massive global movement, thousands of organizations and law enforcement officials are working to end slavery in the sex trade, allowing children to have a childhood and live, thriving.

There is hope for girls like Neema: She was born in a small village, north of Calcutta, India. At eight years old she went blind in one eye from chicken pox, and because her family was too poor for medication or treatment, she has lived with her shriveled, useless eye for years.

At eighteen and with no hope of being married, her mother brought her to Sonagacchi, Calcutta's largest red light district. I guess the thinking was at least she could provide some income for the family through prostitution rather than being a burden.

The day after Neema arrived she stumbled on some of Freeset's staff. Freeset (www.freesetglobal.com) is a fair trade business that employs women out of the sex trade in Sonagacchi into jobs with dignity.

Women are able to move from being the product to making products. The next day one of Freeset's staff went to where Neema was staying and met with her and her mother. Having heard their story, Freeset's staff was immediately compelled to offer Neema a job on the spot; she hadn't yet begun working in the sex trade. Her mother began crying in the corner of the little room, tears of joy and hope because her little girl had gotten a chance of a future.

After further discussion, Neema's mother began to share about her younger daughter, fourteen years old, with no hope for a future either. Well, now there is. Freeset is working to open a second location, not far from where Neema is from. Many of the women who are traded, tricked, or trapped into the sex trade come from Neema's area.

There is courage. Freeset staff and (now) free women from that village will visit Neema's family and younger sister so that she is never brought to Sonagacchi in the first place.

Neema's been working for two weeks now and doing really well. Her smile is infectious, and Freeset is looking into a new cosmetic eye for her. She's beautiful and marriage now is definitely not out of the question.

Trafficking may seem like it is far away, too big of a problem, or too lucrative for someone like you or me to do anything about. After all, it likely doesn't affect you on a daily basis. What I am learning is that it does affect me on a daily basis, because the world is not so small anymore. I participate in slavery when I support companies that use slave labor; I enable traffickers when I turn my head the other way.

I help now with Freeset in a small capacity by doing what I can. I wanted to be part of something bigger than myself. I wanted to be able to look into my children's eyes and know I was advocating for children that had no voice. I help free women from human trafficking through my purchases. My kids' teachers get little gift bags from Freeset, a gift that matters, that means freedom, and changes lives for good. Every bag Freeset sells helps the business to be sustainable enough to train more women, training them in jobs with dignity, freeing them from the sex trade.

Why did I choose to help Freeset when there are thousands of great organizations out there? Freeset values women. As a woman myself, my heart soars to see another woman thrive, especially against the odds. At the end of the day, the women at Freeset want the same things I do: freedom, acceptance, healthy kids, loving family, and a roof over our heads. Every woman who works at Freeset has health insurance, retirement benefits, reading and writing classes, daycare for young children, medical care, and help with learning how to manage their finances. They value women so much so that they are committed to take care of the whole woman, recognizing that the cycle of poverty and lack of education cannot stop without first valuing the lives that walk through their doors.

There is strength. The more small changes we make in our lives, the more we are able to strengthen the numbers that advocate for change. There is strength in numbers. What can you do? I challenge you to purchase one fair trade item this year as gift instead of something that is mass produced. Check out the Fair Trade Federation for ideas of fair trade businesses (http://www.fairtradefederation.org/) or use funds you have already allocated to purchase teacher gifts and donate to a charity or organization that helps orphans, AIDS victims, trafficking, or cancer research on behalf of the recipient. Chances are they would welcome a note that says they "helped" someone else and extended their reach beyond themselves.

I invite you to become part of the freedom story. It is a part of my story now, and I know I can look back with no regrets. Reach out and extend hope to someone who needs it. Step up and be the one with courage to face down injustice. Gather friends around you to be a show of strength in your community, advocating for those with no voice. Join the journey and change your story for someone else's good.

Kristi Griem lives in the US with her husband and two young children. She is passionate about ending human trafficking and honored to be a part of the freedom story for Freeset women. Kristi is humbled to leave a legacy for her kids, in which she hopes she helped be a voice for those who had no voice. Visit her at KristiGriem.com.

BEYOND EXPECTATIONS
Megan Potter

"Well, we were expecting that," my uncle said casually as he went about washing his car. "It was bound to happen eventually." He could have been talking about my dog dying or a bad grade instead of to my desperately jangly announcement that I was pregnant.

At fifteen.

It's not that I was particularly bad, or even stupid. But my life had been the sort to date where teenage pregnancy was more a shame than a shock. Mine was the gossip where you shake your head and cluck your tongue and say, "Poor girl. Such a waste; what a shame." But not necessarily a surprise.

No intervention was held. There was no great sweep to save me. There was a simple causal shrug of the shoulders and then back to everyday life—for them. There was no disappointment, because they'd never bothered to have any expectations for me.

"She got herself into this. She can get herself out."

* * *

There's one thing my pregnancy very swiftly taught me: once you get yourself into a tough situation (like say, being the pregnant daughter of a single mother on welfare at only fifteen) there are no easy solutions.

There are what may look like the easy solutions, but none of them truly are.

Both adoption and abortion promised minimal material hardship but came with mental and emotional anguish, while keeping the baby was a path of inevitable physical and material hardship—at least eighteen years of it without let up. I wasn't naive; I knew that every single one of my options sucked the big one. But a choice had to be made.

There are some hard places that you can close your eyes to. You can turn yourself sideways and pretend you aren't jammed between a rock and that hard place for a bit and you can put off making that hard choice. For a little while.

Being pregnant isn't one of those situations. A baby is a pretty solid and inevitable consequence that can't be held back. Can't be delayed. Can't be—eyes squeezed shut—ignored (and turning sideways definitely won't help). Though, Lord knows, some women have tried.

A baby.

A baby. A baby. A little, crying, squealing baby.

Like the parting seas, being pregnant left me standing like a boulder alone on the barren ground with the ocean of rich life just a step to either side but inaccessible to me. My friends and family peeled away, leaving me standing alone—a tenth grader in the halls with a pile of binders, a ream of crackers, and a circle of emptiness around her.

The people who did stay in my life were dutifully kind. But they had an agenda: adoption.

Their campaign was swift and unrelenting.

"If you keep it, you won't finish high school."

"If you keep it, you'll never make anything of yourself..."

"No guy will want you if you have a child. Keep it and you'll be doomed to be alone..."

HOPE

"You might be able live with us, but not if you keep the baby. We wouldn't have room for two of you."

On and on I heard the promises of a life of hopeless, endless struggle; my only salvation would be to give my boy away.

And then I heard the stories of all the happily adopted people that they knew and how content and fulfilling that life would be compared to the life I could provide.

It was an unrelenting barrage designed to weaken and, eventually, break me, turning me to their plan for my life. But the still, small voice inside me had one clear clarion call. It beat within me as constant as my heart: No. No. No. No. Keep. Him. You. Need. To. Keep. Him. No. No. No.

I wasn't foolish. Or ignorant. I knew the chances were stacked against a baby and me. I knew the consequences, the limitations, but I also knew this was my truth. My path.

So, while everyone shook their heads and clicked their tongues, one week after my sixteenth birthday I brought my very real, bouncing baby boy home with me.

No one had any expectations for me, but my one hope was that I knew something they didn't: This difficult path was mine. It was meant for me, for us.

* * *

Hope is a funny thing, isn't it? It's like home or a lighthouse: When you are out at sea in life you can't see it and you rarely think of it. But in the darkest, most terrifying moments you remember it and it becomes your anchor, your destination, your guiding light.

My path was never easy: I lived through poverty, struggled through school, got married, raised a rambunctious boy, came to grips with infertility, cried, laughed, screamed, and loved. But always, always I knew this path was mine. Ours.

Today my boy is nineteen, and I just celebrated my fifteenth wedding anniversary, and I am the proud owner of an ever-expanding business where I empower women to hear that still, small voice within them and then to find the courage to walk their own paths—no matter how tumultuous they may look from here.

Today my life looks nothing like my former limitations had promised it would because I refused to accept those limits. I shattered expectations and went beyond limits. Because I knew I could.

Megan Potter is a Chinese face reader and Limitless Woman Extraordinaire. She's an earthy soul with just enough Fire thrown in to keep her fun, which is why you definitely want to come play with her! She LOVES working with women leaders who are eager to transcend their limits and is gifted in the art of immediately recognizing your patterns (and blocks) and then using Chinese face reading and the five elements (a tactic of Chinese medicine) to unleash the superhero in you. Visit her at LimitlessLiving.ca.

NEVER THROW AWAY YOUR ROSE-COLORED GLASSES

Jacqueline Fairbrass

"It's never too late to be who you might have been." – George Eliot

The little girl sat at the top of the stairs watching the adults' mill around in the hall. Something big and scary was happening. She made herself as small as possible and waited.

She looked down at her best shoes, white socks, and party dress. She was dressed for a party, but it didn't feel like a party was coming. There had been excitement as her grandmother had quickly dressed her and told her to be on her best behavior. The cloth used to scrub her face was scented with grandmother's soap. Didn't that make today special?

Finally grandmother called her downstairs. She took her by her arm and crouched down in front of her, looked her straight in the face, and told her, "Your mother has had the baby. But she is now very sick. The baby is sick. Your mum can't look after you anymore. You're a big girl now. You are going to have to look after your mum and the baby. It's time to grow up and be a big girl."

Little Jackie looked down at her shoes and thought how pretty they were. She looked up at her grandmother's red-painted mouth as she spouted words she didn't understand. She breathed in the smell of cigarettes and gin and felt queasy. All she knew was that being a little girl was over. It was time to grow up. She now had to look after her mum and her brother.

Jackie was three.

Jackie's mother continued to be "ill" all through her childhood, going from one mysterious condition to another. After an initial operation, the baby boy was fine, fit, and healthy. Her mother doted on him. Jackie was jealous but had no time for that. There was always work to be done.

By the time Jackie was four, she knew she didn't want to be like the women in her family. They were always sick. They were weak. They were bullies. She looked to men to be her role models. She emulated her father and tried to be one of the boys.

As her aunts had children, all boys, she became the caretaker of them too. Traipsing through the streets of London with a pack of boys to look after and care for, she became strong and bossy.

Life was work. Cleaning, caring for others, cooking. Her mother was violent and irrational. Often Jackie took a beating for not being good enough. "Wait till your father comes home" and another beating ensued. Life was work.

She lived in terror, walking on eggshells and struggling to be a "big girl." But there was one part of Jackie that couldn't be taken away: a little place inside her blossomed. She had her imagination. Jackie dreamed and dreamed and dreamed. In Jackie's head was a world of flying horses, pretty faeries, beautiful clothes, sparkly jewels, and happy families. On the outside, Jackie looked tough, doing her best to be a boy. On the inside, the inner Jackie lived in a gentle world of wonderful joy and magical moments.

By the time Jackie was four years old, she was aware of playing different roles in her life. There was nothing she could do to please her mother, but she kept trying. Her father liked both the meek girl who curled up in his lap and the tough girl who tried hard to be good at football and cricket. She learned determination.

Fast-forward to Jackie as a teenager and at thirteen her mother had her put on depression medication. With the onset of hormones, her emotions were all over the place. Her inner world was changing. How can a teenager growing up in a rough seaside town dream of winged horses and faeries? She turned to meds. Then came the alcohol.

Oh, the sweet bliss of oblivion. Promiscuity followed. When you've never had a life or body of your own, how do you say no? And with the alcohol and meds it all became such fun. By fifteen Jackie was addicted to alcohol and sex. What had happened to the pretty little girl who sat on the stairs waiting to hear if her mother had died?

The rich inner world was faint, but she still had her rose-colored glasses and found the beauty in life. She could lose herself drawing and painting or going to an acting class. Sometimes she dreamed of living life without her parents, without her family; she dreamed of a happy home, with laughing children, without sickness, violence, and anger. Her powerful imagination came to her rescue again. This time she'd find a prince charming.

Jackie at twenty-two: divorced, depressed, medicated, and back home again. A new phase began. Still looking to numb the pain, she became a workaholic. Still emulating the men in her life, Jackie began working two jobs and partying. By now, Jackie was on uppers in the morning and sleeping pills at night. She replaced sex and booze with work and pills. But Jackie still had her amazing imagination, dreaming of when things got better, dreaming of rescue from her sick mother and violent father.

Gradually, as Jackie woke each morning feeling groggy from pills and booze, she started to realize that her whole life was groggy. She was living from day to day; still looking after her sick mother; still playing different parts: a chameleon, blending in each part of life. Not standing out, but sitting still like the girl on the stairs. One day she threw all her meds in the loo and flushed.

Jackie started to work out. Still trying to be more like the men, her cousin the boxer taught her how to train. It was only 1978, but there was already a health food store in her town. She learned about herbs and vitamins and started to take supplements. The dreams and rosy-colored world of her imagination began to thrive and grow again. The more she dreamed, the more her outer world started to change.

Jackie's imagination and her life started to blend. She decided to change. But she still hadn't gotten life right. One night in 1980 Jackie got pregnant. Again, a new Jackie was needed. The beautiful little girl she gave birth to was not going to feel like she had to be a chameleon. She was not going to live life sitting on the stairs watching and waiting. She was going to feel safe to be a girl and she was going to be healthy.

Jackie talked to the faeries in her mind, rode on the winged horse in her mind, imagined the life she wanted to live, and looked after her little girl.

Her daughter grew up strong, brave, and always full of hope. She had a second daughter, who embraces life with strength, courage, and an inner knowing that hope and imagination can change your life. Jackie looks at her two granddaughters and sees the seeds of the beautiful, strong young women they will become. Hope lives on in all of us.

Jackie is now Jacqueline, Jacqui to her friends. She has given up addictive behavior and is grateful for her strength, courage, her ability to dream, and her persistent belief in hope.

I now know that my imagination was and continues to be my inner voice, my intuition speaking to me, guiding me with strength, courage, and most of all the hope of something better to come.

I know now that my mother has mental illnesses and cannot be the mother I dreamed of. I know that I became the mother and grandmother that I wanted. I live every day knowing that happiness is a choice and that abuse and depression can be overcome. I still dream, wish, laugh, and love. I take great joy in being a strong and courageous woman. I still see the world through rose-colored glasses, and I share my joy with everyone I meet.

Never throw away your rose-colored glasses. Even the darkest days will lighten. You will love and laugh again when you remember to dream.

I came through an abusive childhood. I have survived beatings, torture, and rape, mental and emotional horrors. I leave a legacy of lives I've touched through my holistic health and life coaching business. And I have given the world two wonderful young women.

Now at age fifty-five I have my Prince Charming. I never needed to be rescued; I needed to rescue myself. He's a lovely man who I choose to share my life and dreams with. He loves me for my strength, courage, and hope. And he loves that, at heart, I'm a little girl.

Jacqueline Fairbrass is the happiness coach and licensed hypnotherapist at Feeling Absolutely Fabulous. This now dazzling diva of Happiness was a young woman who grew up in a toxic and dysfunctional home, where she had low self-esteem and was withdrawn and depressed. Jacqueline turned her life around and for the past twenty years has been teaching others how to make healthy, holistic, and happy choices. To learn more about Jacqueline, go to JacquelineFairbrass.com.

COURAGE

"Above all, be the heroine of your life, not the victim."

– Nora Ephron

REMEMBERING WHEN I WOKE UP
Erin Giles

I remember following,
never leading
yet not feeling satisfied
with being agreeable.

I remember when everything in my world
revolved around getting attention...
finding a man,
making him happy,
and being numb
to my own dreams, desires, and passions.

I remember looking at the bruises,
and the holes in the walls,
after drinks and hits
and still not thinking
enough is enough.

I remember the things I did that made me numb...

they were never enough.

They weren't even surprising,

yet they hurt each and every time.

I remember when crying was an everyday occurrence,

and arguing was a part of my daily truth.

I remember how it felt to realize

for the first time

that I could leave,

let go,

move on,

be free.

I remember realizing that everything

I had believed for so long

wasn't true.

I was shocked,

full of excitement for a new journey,

yet...scared.

I remember coming to the truth of God's love

it wrapping me up,

holding me tight

and giving me the peace

to embrace what he had for me.

COURAGE

It felt like...

white light,

real love,

a fresh start

and real life.

I woke up.

On the outside it looked like I had everything all figured out and that my life was already kicking ass. I was the first woman in my family to get a degree and not get pregnant at an early age. Although I was proud of that, all of the other mess I was living in wouldn't allow me to thrive. I wasn't taught to go after my passion. I was taught to follow, not lead. So I got a degree in a major that a friend recommended because I couldn't make up my mind.

My life with men was the same. I followed; where the attention came from, I went. It led to abuse, drugs, and drinking. I was numb—numb to what I was purposed for and so numb that my happiness was something I didn't even dream of.

When I "woke up" I was twenty-four years old, and it felt like my life had just begun.

Waking up for me took guts, mass amounts of faith, and of course prayer. I only wanted attention from God. I wasn't going crazy; I just knew I had had enough of men for a while. When I put my focus elsewhere, my true passion began revealing itself to me. I realized the key was to allow myself to pay attention—pay attention to what I enjoyed and what I disliked. The attention paid off.

I married the man of my dreams, have a beautiful daughter who will know what a good dad is, created a business that is uniquely me and is a blessing to have, and am honored every day to work with amazing people.

You must have faith in you while learning you.

Having faith is never easy. It requires you to speak as if something is already done when you are looking at a circumstance that seems impossible. It also requires patience to know that at the perfect time what you desire will come to life.

Learning who you are and what you desire takes patience, courage, and the ability to be vulnerable while facing your past and your future. You can't be afraid to figure out what you want. And you certainly can't be afraid to tell others your story...How else will you make a difference in the lives of others?

Waking up took

a dose of reality

combined with an injection of courage.

It took

long nights of journaling,

being real,

and facing the multitude of fears

that I'd made my friends.

Waking up took

saying no to things

I had always said yes to,

saying good-bye to people

I had followed.

Now that I'm living,

I know who God called me to be,

when to say no and

when to forgive.

I know that being vulnerable

doesn't mean I'm weak,

and asking for help

doesn't mean I'm incapable.

Now that I'm really "here"

it's time to show up,

time to woman up,

and time to grow up.

Remembering when I woke up I know not a single day happened on accident and that everything has a purpose to inspire change.

Erin Giles is a business philanthropy expert and the founder of End Sex Trafficking Day. She teaches women how to rocket their revolution by building a big philanthropic gift they are passionate about into their business model as she did. You can find her online at ErinGiles.com.

THE FIREBALL KNOWN AS COURAGE
Sarah Burns

It was the summer of my junior year in high school. I had a boyfriend who I loved very much and who was on his way to college. I had the best group of girlfriends any girl could wish for. We lived in a home near the ocean, near my school, and near friends.

My days were filled with mornings spent at school and afternoons being a complete typical teenager. We'd hang out at the surf shop, go grab frozen yogurt, watch movies, do our nails, and hang at the beach.

My life was pretty vanilla, and it was great.

My father worked from a home office, and my mom took care of the family and home full time. My two older siblings lived out of state, one in Australia and one in Washington DC. It was nice being an only child after seventeen years of being "the baby" of the family. I loved this alone time with my parents. Although, of course I missed my brother and sister; they were like best friends to me, but with technology we stayed in touch.

"Knock, knock, knock."

One day as I was home alone, I heard a knock on the door. I peeked through the peephole and saw what looked to be a delivery man. I cracked the door open and said, "Hi."

The man was not a delivery person. Instead, he was serving my parents, and me, eviction papers.

I had to sign for them. Me...a seventeen-year-old. I was old enough to know what the words on the paper meant. I knew it meant that all that I knew would soon change.

That was the beginning of a new journey...a scary new journey.

The day we lost our house

That summer my father closed down his business and so began this crazy life of my parents traveling to go on job interviews. We had no money, we were losing our house, and here they were leaving me to go find jobs that could perhaps save us from being homeless.

No jobs were found. Instead we had one hell of a garage sale, sold nearly everything, and packed up the rest. Things were packed up as if they were traveling the ocean for their new destination because, as my mom put it, "We're not sure when we'll see our stuff again."

We were moving into my grandmother's home. She lived in Canada half of the year with her husband (a husband from her very late second marriage) and California the other half. She was currently in Canada and had opened her home to us but only "for a few weeks."

So we took only our clothes and a small box of my fun stuff—photos and a few other trinkets to remind me of my teenage life.

There I lived in a retirement fifty-five-plus neighborhood nowhere near the beach, nowhere near my friends, and nowhere near my school, in a room that was decorated for my long passed great grandmother. My parents slept on a pull-out couch in the den. This was our new home, for now.

Soon my grandmother came home and the house got really small, really fast. Without my parents saying anything, I knew that we couldn't stay there. I knew that what loomed was homelessness. We already felt that we were homeless. But now, the reality of literally not having a home to sleep in was becoming a reality.

This entire time, through all of the selling of our possessions and packing things away and living holed up in a home where we felt not at home at all, this entire time, my parents and I felt strong together. We got stronger together. We gave each other courage. After all, courage and hope were really all we had.

Asking for help...it takes courage

During the weekend of my senior homecoming dance, my boyfriend returned home from college. I stayed at his home with his mom, while my parents continued their journey of job interviews in a city eight hours away.

One morning over pancakes I talked with my boyfriend's mother about our situation. She had been there and done that. She was so sympathetic and understood and made me feel OK for sharing what we were going through. My family's situation wasn't typical for where we lived, a very affluent area of southern California.

She then made an offer that would forever change our lives.

"Why don't you and your parents come to live here?" she said. "It's not a big house, but there's room for all of you, and your dog can come too."

I was both excited and a bit hesitant at this offer. I thought for sure that my parents would never go for moving into the home of my boyfriend's mom. My parents were private people. They were people, who liked to do things on their own, and they weren't best friends with my boyfriend's mother; they only knew her as the overprotective mom that called our house a million times to find out if her son was there.

They were also full of pride. They had grown a family together, a life together. They had gotten married at the young ages of seventeen and twenty, and most everything they had done and achieved they did on their own.

The courage to let pride go and ask for help

I was stunned that my parents were open to the idea of living in my boyfriend's house. We had a dinner so everyone could talk and our dogs could meet. Dinner went well.

After dinner we went back to my grandmother's home and holed up in my parents' room. As we sat on their pull-out bed, we talked. I know that it took all the courage in the world for my mom, and especially my father, the patriarch of our family, to say "Yes, let's do it."

I know that it took courage for my parents to ask for help and to take it. There's really nothing more humiliating than having to move in with a relative stranger, your daughter's boyfriend's house. I knew this, I felt this, but I also felt proud.

I was proud of my parents for giving in and letting someone else take care of them. I was proud that my boyfriend's mom was so gracious and so nice and sympathetic and positive. I was proud that we had come through this together as a family, and we never let our love wane.

Months after our move, my parents found jobs, and soon we saved up enough money to move into a place of our own. It was small, but it was perfect for the three of us.

And life goes on

This story took place nearly twenty years ago, and when I truly allow myself to think about it, it brings tears to my eyes. The tears aren't from being sad, however. They aren't from all the emotions that run back into my soul as if it's happening all over again. The tears are from exuberance that "We made it."

The tears are from me now being a mother myself and understanding the courage it must have taken my parents to ask for help. The courage that it took to keep trying day after day to gain jobs. The courage that it took to not show fear to me, their baby, or sometimes to show that fear and let me hug them.

Since our experience with homelessness, I have gotten married to that boyfriend. His mom is now my mother-in-law. We have two beautiful children and live and love life in Hawaii. My parents just celebrated their forty-third wedding anniversary and are still two of my very best friends.

Life is good and I know that no matter what I get thrown my way, I'll dig up the courage to keep going.

The fireball known as courage

Every day we are all faced with challenges. Some are bigger than others. Some can feel like rock bottom. Some can make you want to run away or sleep forever. But courage will pick you back up. Courage will carry you through to find your way to get back on your feet.

Courage is within all of us, and we all have it in us to gather it up and throw it to the world, like a giant fireball, one that can lead the way to brighter beginnings.

We are never without hope if we have courage.

Sarah Burns is a mother of two and wife to her high school sweetheart. She lives on the beautiful island of Maui where she writes about their adventures on her blog, *The Ohana Mama*, and runs a social media implementation agency, Tadah. To learn more about Sarah, visit TheOhanaMama.com or TadahSocialMedia.com.

THE LIONESS WITHIN
Alexa Fischer

Dark streets are scary places. As a rule of thumb, I try to avoid them, but what bothers me the most about the creepy shadows of empty streets is my fear about what might occur there.

I spent three years in New Haven, Connecticut, in a graduate program at the Yale School of Drama. While some parts of the campus looked like they were right out of a Harry Potter set, the rest of the town could be pretty dicey. During orientation the school suggested the women (yes, the women) take a self-defense course. Not exactly the warm and fuzzy welcome I had in mind, but I did heed their advice. It was time I confronted this fear once and for all.

A few weeks after I took the course, I decided to walk home around 1:00 a.m. after rehearsal (admittedly, not what they suggested doing). Late-night rehearsals were so common that the school demanded we call campus security for escorts home, but it was late…I didn't want to wait…blah, blah, blah. I started down the street, knowing that I had a mere two blocks before I was safely stashed in my apartment. The street was dark. No one was around. I knew it was a bad idea, but there I was, praying that I would get lucky and nothing would happen.

Sure enough, I noticed a man coming toward me on the opposite side of the road. I said to myself, "Oh jeez…if he crosses the street, I'm in trouble."

As if he read my mind, the guy made a beeline for me. BAM. I remembered what I was taught. Be a lion, not a lamb.

Chest up, footsteps firm and measured, I headed right toward him. In a loud voice with my finger pointed directly at him, I moved into the center of the street and declared, "Hey. How ya doin' tonight? I see you're wearing a blue baseball hat, jeans, a red shirt…you look about six feet tall and you have a black backpack…" Throughout my rant, I kept my finger pointed with an outstretched arm between him and me, as I quickly moved past him toward my apartment. Looking somewhat confused, he backed off, sensing I was not to be messed with, either because I was crazy or because I would be able to recall exactly what he looked like in a lineup should anything happen. He was looking for a lamb, and I made him understand I was a lion. No one wants to mess with a lion, or in this case, a lioness.

I got home. My heart was racing. While I had been somewhat exhilarated that I implemented what I had been taught, I had learned my lesson. Do not walk home alone. Do not put yourself in vulnerable places, but more importantly, do not be a lamb. When you walk around this world with an imaginary target on your back, the world sends arrows.

As a lioness, you command respect. You are comfortable in your own skin, and you take pride as you navigate your way in the wild. You use your energy wisely, and you are keenly in tune with your environment. You are bold. You are breathtakingly powerful and magical…all at the same time.

Women are at a critical juncture now. We sense the lioness within, yet many of us are afraid to unleash its potential. Deep within we ask ourselves…What are we truly capable of achieving? Where will our dreams take us? What impact can we have in this world? And when we do tap into our power, what will that look like?

I am not imagining a world full of women dominating the men around them. To the contrary, I believe true power means working together in harmony and balance. As women, we are powerful in our grace. We are limitless with our compassion. We are divine with our bodies. There is no need to play like men when we can tap into our strengths as women. And the best part is that when we do, everyone wins.

There will always be dark places that scare us, but by tapping into our personal power, we ignite our inner light. This same light helps us overcome fear, confront challenges, and propel us toward our destiny. It's the light of a lioness.

Unleash the lioness within. The world is ready for you.

There's nothing like a one thousand-watt presence to make you realize you either have the "it" factor…or you don't. Fortunately, you don't have to be born with star qualities; you can actually buy them. Actress Alexa Fischer has turned normal civilians into major public speakers and wallflowers into power brokers. To learn more about Alexa and her work, visit AlexaFischer.com

THE DAY I STOPPED LYING TO MYSELF
Andrea Owen

If you're anything like me, when you hear the word "alcoholic" you get that vision of the dirty homeless man in the gutter, drinking from a paper bag, or maybe the leathery-skin woman at the bar, falling off the barstool, or any other pathetic image you can conjure up. Not often do you picture a successful, attractive, white life coach, living a great life in the suburbs complete with two kids and a husband.

And that story is a big part of what kept me drinking.

In terms of my drinking history, I was a "normal" girl throughout my twenties. I drank just like all my friends but could always put down the bottle without a fight. Sure, there were episodes where I made bad decisions (does anyone make good decisions drinking?) and had some embarrassing moments, but nothing so humiliating to write about. Throughout my twenties I struggled with an eating disorder, love addiction, and codependency—all things I got professional help for and recovered from. I thought I was "healed" and better. I had no idea what was in store for me.

Recently, what I've learned about alcoholism is that it's a progressive disease. Some research I've read has mentioned that with women the disease seems to progress more quickly than with men. I didn't just wake up one day and start drinking excessively. Quietly, my alcoholism snuck in like a lethal, poisonous gas that I couldn't see. I had really no problem quitting drinking when

I was pregnant, but after the birth of my second child in 2009 is when my drinking picked up serious speed and momentum.

I was bored as a stay-at-home mom. Laundry was simply more fun after two glasses of wine. Hell, anything was more fun after two glasses of wine. I found myself drinking nearly every day. And the days that I didn't were to prove to myself that I didn't need to. See? I could skip a day. I'm OK.

After about a year of this, the whispers in my head started.

"Normal people probably don't do this."

"Do I need to cut back?"

"This probably isn't good."

In December of 2010 I remember finishing an entire bottle of wine in one evening by myself. Soon after that, an entire bottle was pretty regular. I started hiding how much I was drinking from my husband, and pretty quickly the obsession started. This was a living hell. The more that I tried to not think about drinking and the feelings that surrounded it, the worse I felt. My first thoughts in the morning were guilt and shame about how much I drank the night before. Then the thoughts would move to planning on cutting back. Then thinking about what if I have a real problem. Then justifying my drinking. More guilt and shame. In an effort to numb the guilt and shame, I wanted to drink. The afternoon would come and I would watch the clock waiting for an "appropriate" time to pour my first glass. The times were getting earlier and earlier. If I remember correctly, my earliest drink was 2:30 p.m.

And the whispers got louder and clearer:

"Normal people don't do this."

"Why can't I stop thinking about this?"

"I think I have a problem."

I Googled "Am I an alcoholic?" I hoped Google and the Internets would magically pop up a "YES!" or "NO!" on the screen instead of a bunch of links. I kept reading "Only you know if you have a problem," and I wanted to scream. Mostly because I DID know I had a problem.

However...I was paralyzed with fear to quit drinking. I could not imagine my life without alcohol in it. I mean, I LOVE alcohol. I'm good at drinking. And, at the same time, there was a large part of me that was convinced there was NO WAY I could be an alcoholic. I mean, have you seen the show *Intervention*? Did you see the episode of *Oprah* where the mom was hiding bottles of chardonnay behind the kitchen trash and laundry room? That wasn't me! That's an alcoholic, right? And I JUDGED those women! But the whisper in my head politely tapped me on the shoulder and reminded me that those women were once where I was at that moment. They didn't just wake up one day and start hiding booze. But, I kept justifying my drinking. I was never drunk when I drank at home alone. I never drove, I never lost control with my kids, I never yelled. We had a house in the suburbs, two cars, two kids, and my marriage was actually pretty good.

And no one knew. No confrontations, no raised eyebrows. But, the hiding was becoming a full-time job. And one that I didn't want anymore. So, if no one knew, and I was doing a good job of controlling it (or so I convinced myself), then I didn't have to quit. Right? I mean, I didn't have a "rock bottom" that we always hear about. My life was great. All I did was drink too much. No DUIs. No arrests. No tragic story whatsoever.

Here was my turning point: I admitted that what was happening to me was happening fast. And it was out of my control. My drinking wasn't yet out of control, but this progression was. There's an ancient Chinese proverb that says, "If we don't change our direction, we are likely to end up where we are headed." And I knew where I was headed. My intuition, the whispers, were speaking more loudly at this point. I. Could. Not. Lie. Anymore. To. Myself. I felt like such a hypocrite writing and telling people how to live their best life. Their "kick-ass" life, for Christ's sake. And I was lying to myself every day. And numbing the pain with alcohol.

I knew I had two choices: Keep drinking and see what would happen. Or, quit drinking and see what happened. I was pretty sure I was an alcoholic, and true alcoholics don't get better if we keep drinking (no matter how desperately we try). We just get worse. I was more terrified to see what would happen if I kept drinking than to try sobriety. That was all I needed to realize to reach out and try sobriety.

And so I quit.

And it hasn't all been easy. Some days are, and some days aren't. I can't think about the rest of my life without alcohol. I just can't. Every day I make a decision and commitment to stay sober that day. Just that day. I'm human, I'm an alcoholic, and that's all I can do.

In all honesty, I'm not sure what's been harder—quitting drinking or telling the world that I'm an alcoholic. Both have taken the most courage I've ever had to muster up in all of my thirty-seven years. But, the cost of not doing it was my life.

Andrea Owen is a life coach, mom, writer, triathlete, and hell-raiser. She is passionate about empowering women to value themselves and fiercely love who they are. She helps women get what they want by managing their inner-critic, leveraging the Law of Attraction and stepping into their own badass version of themselves. Visit her at YourKickAssLife.com.

WHEN YOU'VE GOT NOTHING LEFT TO LOSE BUT WEIGHT
Rosie Battista

Some people don't know when they've hit rock bottom, but I did. I was slumped amid the dog hair and dust on the basement floor, sobbing uncontrollably about my miserable life.

I was forty-nine years old, and my life was crap. Crap boyfriend ditched me for a woman he swore he hated but who somehow was preferable to me (who he swore, for the last year, he loved); my finances were in the toilet after a bad investment, necessitating selling my family house in a dismal real estate market; I risked being thrown out on the street because crappy landlords wouldn't consider me with my two dogs; and my youngest just left home—was she really going to college or just anxious to get away from the misery that was me? And I knew I'd never find another boyfriend at this age, with this baditude and the extra thirty-eight pounds miserably packed on my body like the cherry on the top of a shit sundae.

My thoughts were as paralyzed as my potential. My stagnant mind could not spark even the tiniest suggestion for getting me out of this mess. I was hopeless.

Picture the runny nose, the red eyes leaking tears and mascara, and the crumpled heap of humanity I had become. And know this: there's something funny about rock bottom because when nothing matters, you can take that risk you'd always been too scared to try, because seriously, at this point, what difference would one more failure make.

I called on everyone for help: God, my angles, my guides in the form of my three deceased grandmothers, Sophie, Charlotte, and Violet. "Help me out here, ladies. Please plop a big huge sign in front of me telling me what to do now."

I guess so many rocks in one place can form a foundation of strength. I was able to muster up enough strength from my personal abyss to provide a strange source of courage.

At this low point in my life a bucket came to mind. Not the kick-the-bucket kind, thank God (and Sophie, Charlotte, and Violet too), but the bucket where you put your dreams and aspirations. If I could take something, anything, from my bucket list and get a win, a sense of accomplishment, a success, I knew I'd be on the other side of misery.

Looking back, I realize how fortunate I was to be completely drained of energy. I was so wiped out that during the time it took to solidify my goal, I couldn't muster the strength to make excuses for not giving my dream a shot. I tried out my resolve by admitting my goal out loud, first to an empty room and then to friends and family. And that goal was…

…To transform my body and enter a bodybuilding figure competition in celebration of turning fifty.

OK, which of you readers just spit out your latte reading the preposterous goal I chose? How quickly can you come up with five reasons a flabby, fifty, perimenopausal woman shouldn't pursue competitive bodybuilding?

You are not alone. "Friends" came out of the woodwork to suggest that setting myself up for yet another failure was a bad idea. No fifty-year-old should be prancing around in public in a bikini. Nature just didn't make us that way. It wasn't long before my own head joined the opposing team. My wounded psyche and the toxins in my body had grown accustomed to a sedentary life and were reluctant to give it up, so they lied to me, telling me I couldn't, exaggerating small physical complaints in an effort of fulfilling a dream.

I repeatedly asked my kids their thoughts. Son Number Two, frustrated with the question, shot back, "MOM, all you ever do is talk about it. Just do it already, and, yeah, I think you can...And, by the way, Mom, you can if YOU think you can."

Hey, that was a low blow. He used my words against me. I must have said that to him a million and one times in his formative years. Now, as an adult, it was his turn. It was not easy to hear. But I knew this was my chance to prove that it was good advice when I gave it to him.

"You can if you think you can" became my mantra and it pushed and sometimes dragged me toward my crazy-ass goal.

A skimpy sixteen weeks after that conversation, I unveiled myself on stage in a bling, string bikini, thirty-eight pounds lighter to compete in a figure competition. ZAP! I was electrically charged with renewed courage, confidence, self-esteem, and unstoppable resolve to accomplish anything and everything I wanted.

I want this renewed/revived life for you. I want it for every woman stuck in the mire of "Crap and Can't."

My one small win multiplied. I invested in training and studied with renowned experts in nutrition, physiology, and psychology. And I built my company, Sleeping Naked After 40, to empower women with good health for mind and body, to give them a hand up to a win and a recharged life like I'd experienced.

Don't start freaking out about the bikini. That was my goal. You get to come up with your own as long as it includes building the healthiest, sexiest version of yourself. As the pounds peel off, you will reveal the personal power you can call upon to accomplish what you have been squashing down or resisting for years. You will take charge of what you want in your life.

Your personal power propels you.

Your personal power makes your life amazing.

Your personal power reveals the beauty you've kept hidden for too long.

I get asked all the time how I did it and how I do what I do and stay motivated and on track. I used three tools during the competition, and they changed my challenge into a wonderful experience. I still employ them every day for everything I do. It started when I made the decision that mediocrity and "just OKness" are not good enough for my one very precious life.

So, are you ready to muster up the courage to drag yourself out of the crap?

Sleeping Naked After 40 is based on three core principles that will help you unleash your awesome personal power. Apply them to any area of your life that needs a boost. Together they will strengthen your "courage muscle" so that you can build your confidence.

1. Lose the Fake Stuff and Get Real – Get your body in the game. You only get one body, and it's an awesome one. Not only is it your right, but it is your obligation to take care of your body. The food you eat directly affects your mood, attitude, and health. It's important to participate fully in the process of nourishing yourself well. When you feed your body with processed, chemicalized, fake food (aka crap), it will show up on your body as unwanted weight and in your life as stagnation. If you nourish yourself with pure and naked food, the body of your dreams will show up.

2. Become Less Interested in Why You Can't – Get your head in the game. You can do, be, or have anything you want. If there is something that you want, go and get it. Screw excuses that tell you why you can't; instead, trust and believe that you can and take the steps necessary, one at a time. Make every meal an opportunity to improve your health. Make every workout an opportunity to feel better. Make every moment an opportunity to be your best.

3. Fall in Love with the Idea – Get your heart in the game. When you are in love, everything is so amazing. You have the energy and inspiration to do more than you ever thought possible. Every situation is viewed with fresh eyes in a different, lighter way. Fall in love with the idea of making the best, sexiest, most amazing person possible. Attack this journey with the exciting blush of new love and watch as your dreams get bigger and your body gets smaller and you get more comfortable sleeping naked after forty.

Rosie Battista teaches the world, one meal and one woman at a time, to become her most amazing, best, confident, sexiest self. She is a body stylist, confidence creator, noted speaker, and video star, as well as a food coach and a lazy cook (who concocts yum-azing recipes with ease and deliciousness). She has written a dozen books and cookbooks based on the principals of her Sleeping Naked After 40 program/experience. Visit her at SleepingNakedAfter40.com.

HOW LEARNING TO RIDE A BIKE GAVE ME THE COURAGE TO LIVE
Melissa Cassera

I'm not the least bit athletic.

At least that's the phrase I said thousands of times through my youth and even into my twenties.

You see, my parents (namely my mom) always shunned the soccer field for the stage. I spent my after-school hours and summer days acting my little heart out and loving every second of it. Around the age of ten, I began to notice that something was different. Every other kid in school would rally together, talking about their latest game or match while I shyly sat on the sidelines dreaming about a new role I could play.

My non-athleticism extended all the way to bike riding. That's right—I never learned how to ride a bike.

I vaguely remember having a bike with training wheels, but those wheels never came off. As the months and years went by, more of my friends and classmates would take their bikes and head out on adventures while I stayed inside. I would even have some kids knock on my door, asking if I could come along, and my cheeks burned with embarrassment when my mom told them, "Oh, she doesn't know how."

Sure, I could have learned, but I was so embarrassed to practice outside while the other experienced kids rode circles around me. It just felt shameful.

As I got older and my classmates started worrying more about boys and shopping than bike riding, I forgot about the skill I didn't have. I thought it would never really plague me again, so who cares if I never learned to ride?

The universe has a funny way of bringing things full circle.

In the winter of 2003, I met the man who I now call my husband. He was a great guy and an incredible athlete. Tennis pro, soccer player, diver—you name it. He could do it all. Dating someone like that also meant that instead of dinner and a movie, he wanted to do anything and everything athletic-style. One day we were at the beach and he mentioned wanting to ride a tandem bicycle. My eyes grew wide and I felt my cheeks get hot. I had to admit to him my shameful secret—I couldn't ride a bike.

He took the news in stride and said, "No worries. I'll teach you." The mere thought of this had me mortified. Not only was I in my twenties and didn't know how to ride a bike, but this man who I was supposed to be in the throes of passion with was now going to watch me stumble and fall off a bike. No way. I talked him out of it.

Over the years there were various opportunities to bike that cropped up. I always shot them down, making any excuse possible. I couldn't learn because I had a photo shoot and didn't want to risk scraping my knee. I couldn't learn because my balance was terrible. I couldn't learn because I had a headache. I was almost out of excuses.

It wasn't until I was thirty-one years old that I finally mustered the courage to learn how to ride a bike. In a very cold and rainy March, I enrolled in a fitness boot camp led by a former marine captain. The class was so intense that I threw up after the first one—in front of thirty people—a humbling experience.

After that day I became determined to conquer the class. I crawled through mud, sprinted in the pouring rain, and clenched my way up into my first real pull-up. I would leave class with scraped limbs, bruises, and so much mud on my clothes and shoes that I had to permanently keep my car seat lined with towels. It was awesome and empowering.

One day I told my husband it was time for me to conquer my fear of riding a bike. He coaxed me outside immediately, pulled his bike out of the garage, and we head out. As I tried (and failed) to keep my balance with my husband holding the back of the bike steady, a ten-year-old neighborhood kid came outside and shouted, "YOU don't know how to ride a bike?!" I was horrified.

I almost gave up right then and there, but my husband quickly interjected, "No, she doesn't. But she's learning. Do you want to help?"

"Sure," he said cheerily.

So there we were, me on the bike, desperately trying to keep balance, and my ten-year-old neighbor rallying me along. Soon after, my other neighbors started coming outside to watch the scene. One of my neighbors even revealed quietly that she never learned to ride a bike either.

Learning to ride at age thirty-one was humbling and at the same time incredibly powerful. I've always learned that the things that you cringe to talk about are often the things that impact the most people. I decided to share my experience with a small women's entrepreneur network I was a part of, and the response was astounding and not what I expected. Among the cheerleaders and "way-to-go's" there were hundreds of people that e-mailed me privately, revealing that they never learned to ride a bike, never learned to swim, and a host of other things they had been keeping secret. My revelation had inspired them to learn to ride a bike, take a swimming lesson, or just get out and try—no matter if they were thirty, forty, fifty, sixty, heck even ninety.

The great Nelson Mandela once said, "Courage is not the absence of fear, but the triumph over it." I was certainly scared that I would fall off that bike, that everyone would heckle me. But I kept going until I mastered it and can now proudly say I ride my bike everywhere in my new home of Northern California.

Melissa Cassera is a 'PR rock star' and CEO and president of PR consultancy Cassera Communications. When it comes to turning business owners into total celebrities, she's the real McCoy. Melissa doesn't just talk about fame and visibility—she lives by her own lessons, as a professional actress and TV spokesperson with more than ten films and one hundred TV credits to her name. For more behind-the-scenes scoop on Melissa, visit CasseraCommunications.com.

LEAN INTO THE UNKNOWN, LUSCIOUSLY
Allana Pratt

Even though I knew it would crush my dad, I just couldn't take over the pharmacy; it just wasn't me. I mean, I loved people and was grateful they adored me, but MY dream wasn't even to stay in my hometown, province, or even country.

I remember speech ten in my local Toastmaster's chapter, quoting a Styx song "Welcome to the Grand Illusion" that I couldn't do what I was "supposed" to do, that I was going to quit college, hop on Uncle Phil's semi, and head to Hollywood to "make it."

I stayed with connections from my California sister city from my pageant days and never looked back. I failed over and over, and I didn't have an American visa. I had the talent, the courage to leave home, to fly, to risk...yet visa technicalities stopped me? I didn't think so. I kept going, asked for help, and with forty dollars left to my name (and Dad's visa to come home if I failed), I ended up booking a gig in Japan where all the girls needed visas. Bingo. The flow continued with being an international model, spokesperson, and even English teacher!

I remember being so focused on my dream that "No" didn't stop me. I was scared at times, I wondered how it would all work out, yet I never questioned if I made a mistake. I was fueled by something bigger than me; I had given my dream over to the Divine. I had let go of control, while simultaneously being in divine action every day.

Once one decides on something, like a demand, and is willing to do whatever it takes, unwilling to take NO for an answer, yet simultaneously open to whatEVER it looks like...providence occurs. Demand first; then show up to receive what the universe has in store for you...Ask and it is given. How could it get better than modeling in Japan? Well, that attitude DID open a door to better backpacking adventures, being spokesperson for huge companies, and finding husband number one.

I remember several good times with this man, yet in the end, I would get in trouble for cutting a vegetable "wrong"—an external mirroring of my internal self-doubt. I remember knowing I had to leave, yet I STILL didn't have a visa to stay in the States. I could go back to Japan or home to Canada, so I took the plunge to move out, and on July Fourth weekend I said I wasn't going on the trip we'd planned and instead moved in with a girlfriend. THAT morning my green card came. Again...choose FIRST; then the universe can meet you.

This next period of life got cloudy in terms of courage with men, for my mom called to say she was tired of fighting the cancer. Months of alternative therapies, guiding her through affirmations on the phone, and even creating a special room of her own where we danced to Loreena Mckennitt to strung Christmas lights...she was done. I was giving my emotional, physical, financial, and spiritual reserves to my mom. I hopped on a plane to Canada to save her, yet I wasn't present enough to see I had meanwhile attracted a man who also drained those same reserves.

When I arrived in Canada, my aunt had downed most of those super-huge bottles of wine, there was morphine all over the kitchen, and Mom was in bed burning up. I slept at the foot of her bed all night, changing cold clothes that would burn up and

COURAGE

dry out, tossing every time she moaned. I called the ambulance in the morning knowing that I was taking her to the hospital to die.

They wouldn't give her more morphine so they could do some f-ing tests. I held her close, my whispers close to her cheek as she shrieked in pain: "Just inhale, Mom. Every exhale the pain drains away. Just inhale, Mom, and fill up with the light of Love." Finally they let her have morphine as my sister's flight arrived. We took shifts around the clock; every pain episode happened with me. Once she even sat straight up in bed, after not talking for three days, and asked me, "How do I die?" Shocked, I told her I think you decide when you're ready and the angels take you there. So she tried to get out of bed, catheter in, no more IV, just a morphine drip, and she was going to WALK AWAY to die. I tried to stop her, to hold her down, but this possessed voice took her over, and she told me to get out of her way, and then she bit my hand through the flesh, past tendons, and to the bone. We both screamed, a nurse came running, and I ended up in the ER.

Three mornings later when they woke me I had earplugs in... What? She's gone. Gone? I missed it! Yet I felt the pain to the core and experienced a soothing bath of love so pure and restorative, touching for a moment the timelessness she had transcended into.

The courage to disappoint Dad, to leave a failing relationship, to be present during a crisis, to keep my heart open when in pain, to receive blessings and continue on today into the unknown—this courage lives inside each of us. We are the only ones who hold us back from the prisons of our own making. I personally believe my methodology of self-care, feminine sensual practices, and oozing sexy self-love out of every pore of your skin is a delicious pathway to confidence, radiance, and magnetizing adoration and affection beyond your imagination. Today I have a successful business, a thriving son, luxurious male attention, and I know whatever happens, I will thrive. This allows me to lusciously lean into the unknown and create the life I choose, with a full heart of appreciation for the journey of Life.

Allana Pratt embodies 'Living Sexy,' loving exactly who you are, and being unapologetically radiant so your relationships thrive and your family flourishes. Author of *How To Be And Stay Sexy* for women, *The Missing Handbook to Motherhood* for moms, and *Get Her To Say Yes* for men, she's an intimacy expert on CBS, TLC, and FOX and a booked solid relationship coach. *People Magazine* reported Allana was the first person Leeza Gibbons called for coaching when she signed on with *Dancing with the Stars*. Visit her at AllanPratt.com.

TAKING THE LEAP
Amy Scott

On September 10, 2004, my friends dropped me off at San Francisco International Airport. As we stood at the curb to say our good-byes, my stuffed backpack and a big colorful bag of gifts for my host family at our feet, the tears started. I started shaking and my voice wavered as it finally sunk in what I was about to do. After two and a half years of planning, saving, dreaming, and scheming, I was finally getting on a plane to spend the next nine months or so traveling solo around the world.

I had never boarded a plane by myself except to visit friends or family or to attend a business convention, and I had never taken a trip longer than four weeks.

My friends had supported me through this entire adventure so far—spending untold hours listening to me hash out plane tickets and itineraries and packing lists, helping me cram my stuff into a storage unit, and driving me to the airport on that fateful day—and they'd probably never seen me scared, or even worried, about what I was getting myself into. I was so focused on my dream, so determined to make it happen, that there was barely time to be scared.

But then suddenly, there on the curb at SFO, I was scared shitless. What the hell was I getting myself into? What was I thinking? It may have been the first time I actually wondered what I would do if I didn't like traveling for so long, or traveling alone.

For a few brief moments, I longed to get back in the car, to be taken back to my cozy apartment (where my replacement had already moved in), and to forget this crazy idea had ever crossed my mind.

My breakdown surprised my friends, and it surprised me. Up until this moment, I'd never wavered, not even the year before when my boyfriend of seven years, with whom I'd been planning the trip, decided he didn't want to go and we broke up. The end of that relationship was difficult, and there were a lot of logistics to sort out, but it never crossed my mind to cancel the trip, and I never got freaked out about traveling alone. I simply tweaked the itinerary a little bit and continued planning.

But now that I was actually getting on the plane, it felt so real, so close, so...irrevocable.

My friends shared some kind and reassuring words and gave me a big hug. OK, I thought, calming myself down. What's the worst that could happen? You don't like it, and you just come home. No big deal. (OK, maybe the actual worst thing that could happen is dying in some freak mountain bus accident, but hey, at least I was living my dream; better than dying on the way to a job I hate!)

I took a deep breath, and I was on my way. First stop: Lima, Peru.

Almost exactly eight years later, I can hardly imagine what my life would be like if I hadn't gotten on that plane. Quite simply, quitting my job and spending nearly nine months traveling changed me, and it changed my life.

I met people traveling who showed me other ways to live: the Londoner who avoids the city's miserable winters by island-hopping in Thailand. The Minnesotan who's lived in Asia for nearly his whole adult life, rarely, if ever, going back to the United States. The innumerable European couples traveling for a year, or two. The Peruvian who lives in the jungle so he can share his country's magic with foreigners who visit his lodge.

By the time I returned to the States, I knew my life would be different from then on. Instead of getting tied down by another office job, I started working for myself so I could create the same freedom I'd seen others embrace.

Almost exactly two years later, I moved to Buenos Aires, Argentina. By then, I was more excited than scared as I boarded the plane. I knew that each step was taking me closer to my ideal life in one way or another.

In fact, I had no idea how right I was: I met my husband, Roberto, in a salsa club in Buenos Aires, and together we're now living and working anywhere in the world.

Why does quitting your job, or traveling alone, or starting a business, or moving to another country take courage? It's like any other decision where the outcome is unsure. It's a leap of faith to trust that things will work out, one way or another. You simply must believe that whatever happens will be worth the uncertainty. And the best part is, the outcome might be even better than you ever could have imagined.

They say travel can change your life, and it all starts with a simple step. Buy that plane ticket. Set a date. Sketch out your itinerary and make it happen. "Leap," as naturalist John Burroughs said, "and the net will appear."

Amy Scott writes about location-independent living at Nomadtopia.com and coaches others on how to create their ideal life, anywhere in the world. Through her other business, Nomad Editorial, she offers coaching and editing services to help writers finish their nonfiction books. To learn more about Amy, visit NomadEditorial.com.

FEAR LESS, MOXIE MORE
Danielle Dowling

I used to be afraid of getting what I wanted.

Truth? I didn't trust myself to take care of it.

I wasn't happy.

But I told myself I was.

A crafty expert, I believed the half-truths I told myself about how satisfied I was.

Satisfied with my career, romantic relationships, and their trajectory.

The lies were a sly weapon wielded for self-sabotage.

Self-sabotage had befriended me long ago, and she was mean and she was humiliating.

She had a way of making me feel five years old and powerless.

I was in my mid to late twenties and had, unconsciously, constructed what seemed to be a sustainable life blueprint.

The plan was to:

keep it small

keep it safe

keep it predictable.

In other words:

Soul-less.

Limited

Fearful.

You pick.

Occasionally wake-up calls come as gentle tappity-tap-tap.

Other times they hit you with the force of a bullet train, ushering in the complete dismantling of self.

The revolutions and upheavals hit me at a splintering one hundred miles an hour.

I was blindsided by a breakup that left me questioning my self-worth and decisiveness.

I had laid down roots in a job where dissatisfaction gnawed at my gut and left my heart a hollow shell.

I had fragile, underdeveloped ideas of who I was and what mattered to me.

I felt raw.

Bloody.

Cut to insomnia-filled nights and mascara-streaked pillows.

It felt really small.

And then finally, finally, too suffocating.

My patience with fear had run out.

I hauled my heavy heart and beat-up body into the fire of my truth.

Praying for healing and redemption.

Praying for more me.

I crawled back.

To life.

To love.

To creating work that matters in the world.

And along the way I learned (the hard way) three irrefutable truths:

1. Everyone, everyone is struggling with the same thing: fear of being her true self.

2. Meeting your highest creative capacity is inherently full of tension.

Ambition is always unrealistic. It's designed to be just a tad out of reach.

It requires s-t-r-e-t-c-h-i-n-g and that stretch demands moxie.

3. It takes nothing less than obstinate, unrelenting courage to excavate the truth of your identity and then live that truth even when it would be easier (way easier) to sell out.

Are you willing to love yourself through this "unsafe" process?

Are you willing to be on your own leading edge—exposed, vulnerable—and LEAN INTO IT rather than shy away and search for a familiar rabbit hole?

But here's the genius that underlies it all:

You are going to "work at" this life anyhow.

You will have to put elbow grease in either way.

You might as well spend that time removing the blocks to your unique truth instead of stitching together an awkward patchwork quilt of society's agenda for you.

Will this be easy?

Nope.

It will require a lot of courage.

Will it be worth it?

Yes.

So where do you get this moxie to fuel your courageous life?

We start with dismantling the fear.

We never want to let fear stay that way.

It must be developed into something that can help you reach that life you want.

Move it from a paralyzing, overwhelming emotion to an understood feeling—a state you can manipulate for your own benefit—a lens through which to build a plan.

I have an exercise I originally used on myself and learned from a book called *Feeling Good* that I now practice with my clients who are feeling paralyzed by angst.

I will repeat the same question two or three or even four times till we get to the root of the fear.

If someone is fearful of leaving a romantic relationship or venturing out into the wilds of entrepreneurship, I will say, "What are you scared of?"

And they may say: "I'm scared of dating again or losing money."

"What are you scared of?"

"I'm scared that no one will be interested in me or my product."

"What are you scared of?"

"I'm scared of being alone or I'm scared of failing."

"Why are you scared of failing?"

"Because I'm scared of being alone."

Ahhh. Well then. There you go. Let's talk about that.

Dissolving fear takes courage.

Choosing to be vulnerable in the world and feeling safe in that vulnerability takes courage.

Meeting your full potential and the ambition it requires takes courage.

Check in with your conscious dashboard.

Is the speedometer tipped in the direction of fear or moxie?

If it's fear, then this is a crisp call to action.

It is an invitation to excavate what drives you.

What inspires you?

Dig in. Your greatness is calling.

Danielle Dowling, MA, is a writer, relationship expert, and women's life coach. She is an intuitive strategist who works with women leaders who are ready to stop comprising on the things that matter most—soulful companionship, self-realization, and accessing their innate power. Learn more about Danielle at Danielle-Dowling.com.

TWENTY FIVE CENTS FOR FREEDOM
Denise Barry

I will never forget my first bully. I don't remember her name, only her eyes, and only because they had burned into mine with a hatred much too intense for someone who barely knew me.

"Hey girl," she barked in my ear.

I turned to find myself staring into those eyes. She was a tiny little thing, not much bigger than me. In fifth grade, I was as small as they came, and as unsure of myself as I was small.

"Where do you think you're goin'?" she demanded. Her breath smelled like hot dogs.

"To the cafeteria," I mumbled, trying miserably to maintain eye contact. I could guess what was on the lunch menu.

"You got any money?" she asked. I shook my head. "You ain't got no money? Girl, from now on, if you don't bring me a quarter every single day, I'm gonna beat the crap outta you."

In the face of so much hostility, I was speechless. She took my silence as a contractual agreement and stormed away. She didn't need a response. She knew I'd produce.

And I did, for a few days. Until my mother caught me stealing from her purse. Just like that, my safety supply was severed. The thought of telling my mother I was paying off a bully was worse than showing up without an installment. So, I went to school the next day, panicked and penniless.

Either this bully needed a better bookkeeping system, or she had so many paying customers she couldn't keep track of them because she never laid a finger on me!

Many years later, I came across another bully. This one made the first one seem like a pussycat. I mean, twenty-five cents to buy myself peace of mind? That seems like kibble to me now! This one wanted nothing less from me than my soul.

A few months ago, I was visiting the city of Sedona, Arizona, also known as "Red Rock Country." This is an area of the United States where both the view and the silence are equally spectacular.

Where else can you feast your eyes on sandstone rocks the size of mountains, that when illuminated by the sun, glow a brilliant terra-cotta? Or hear nothing (at all) but the flutter of a raven's wings as you stand on top of one of these formations, while the desert heat soothes your body and mind. It is easy to understand why Sedona is considered a mystical place.

As I sat in the middle of a conference room, in the midst of all this beauty, the last thing I expected was to find a bully—especially since I was surrounded by over one hundred people who were there for the same reason as me: to participate in a six-day retreat for personal growth.

Early in the retreat, I learned that all it took to advance from "stranger" to "friend" was the smallest hint of a smile. Which is why, just before lunch on that first day, when the facilitator asked us to pick a partner, I smiled at Delilah. She immediately moved her chair toward mine and settled in; we were officially friends now, as well as partners.

With her billowy clothes, soothing voice, and kind, intelligent eyes, I felt comfortable with her immediately. I felt free to be open and honest during our exercise, knowing I wouldn't be judged.

Even though I was enjoying the work we were doing, I was having trouble concentrating. I was distracted by the ring on Delilah's finger. I had never seen such a beautiful, unique stone before. It looked like the amethyst crystal had been plucked directly out of the earth, carelessly chiseled into a rough-edged circle, then popped into a silver band. The result was natural and spectacular.

I wanted that ring. But, not only was her ring beautiful, it was enormous, which meant I could never, ever, wear it.

I am on the small-to-very-small side; that hasn't changed since I was a kid. Therefore, I have always avoided big jewelry. I thought I looked ridiculous in it, like a little kid playing dress-up.

As I stared longingly at Delilah's ring, I heard, "Who says you can't wear a ring of that magnitude?"

My eyes widened in surprise. I knew that voice came from inside my head, but I didn't know who had put it there. I listened for it again...This was something worth hearing.

"Who says you can't wear big jewelry?" it repeated.

I burst out laughing and covered my mouth. I felt insane.

"I don't know who says!" I silently answered, shocked by this revelation.

Delilah looked at me, only slightly curious. Putting her head down, she busied herself in her workbook, allowing me to have this moment.

I realized then that "No, You Can't" came up regularly: "No, You Can't dance; you will be ridiculed!" "No, You Can't fly to Hawaii; you will surely crash and die!" "No, You Can't change jobs; you will fail miserably!" "No, You Can't wear oversized jewelry; you'll look like an idiot!"

I knew this was coming from inside of me, yet it didn't feel like me! The "me" I knew wanted to dance and travel and do work that she loved! Right now, I especially wanted to wear that ring! How dare this thing that sounded like me but wasn't tell me, "No, You Can't!" The BULLY!

When I finally shared this revelation with Delilah, she nodded her head knowingly. Unlike me, this wasn't her first retreat.

"That's a wonderful breakthrough, Denise," she sang. After a thoughtful pause she continued. "How would you like to go to lunch? Then afterward, we can go to the store where I bought my ring."

"Can we skip lunch?" I joked.

What fun I had trying on every ring in the store—the bigger, the better!

I'll teach that inner bully of mine who's in control! I promised. I bought a ring just like Delilah's—only bigger.

"Myring," as I naturally began calling it, became my closest friend that week. I never took it off except to wash my hands. Every time I touched it, I felt confident and safe. I rubbed it so much I'm surprised it didn't ignite.

Back home, I continued to wear "Myring" every day. It was a constant and welcome reminder of the incredible time I had spent in Sedona: the growth I had experienced, the friends I had made, and the beauty of the red rocks. It was the only thing that felt tangible, so far away from it all—which is why, when I lost it, I was devastated.

I tried to talk myself out of the pain I was feeling. Over and over I told myself I shouldn't be this upset over a piece of jewelry; I didn't need this to be happy; I am giving this ring way too much power! But it all sounded like blah, blah, blah to my troubled mind.

After a couple days of this, I realized I needed to come to terms with what I was feeling or the pain would never go away. So, I sat myself down and allowed the feelings to surface.

If you listen closely, feelings speak. This is what mine told me that day: "You are sad and grieving for your loss. It doesn't matter that it was 'only a ring.' It had meant a lot to you. It's OK to be sad...really, it is."

I had finally been granted permission, so I cried. I was shocked by how much sadness was inside of me. It felt good to release it and let it go.

In the process, I realized I had thought "Myring" was holding all of my memories, along with all of the progress I had made in Sedona. Losing it, to me, had meant losing that whole experience. It was a relief to realize this wasn't true.

I also realized that I had denied my feelings in order to protect myself from them. I was afraid to feel sad, so I downplayed the significance of losing the ring by telling myself I was overreacting.

Wait a minute...Isn't this what my inner bully had done? It didn't want me to feel embarrassed or scared or out of control, so it told me, "No, You Can't" do this and that. It was trying to protect me, albeit in a very futile way.

In the end, I was able to thank my ring for being in my life AND for ultimately leaving it. Although, admittedly, if it surfaced right here, right now, I wouldn't complain! But, I don't need it. I am the keeper of all my treasures.

As for my inner bully (and yours as well)...do this with me.

Take a quarter out of your pocket.

Give it a big, grateful smooch.

Toss it over your shoulder as you walk away.

Don't look back.

Denise Barry is a regular blogger for self-help guru, Karen Salmansohn and the author of the children's picture book, *What*

Does The Tooth Fairy Do With Our Teeth coming in the spring of 2013. Here you will find answers to the question kids have been asking for ages and learn just how clever (and naughty) the tooth fairy can be. To learn more about Denise and her work visit DeniseBarry.net.

COURAGE IS FOR THE CRAZY AT HEART
Hillary Rubin

Courage is a funny thing when you really think about it. We all have heard amazing stories of courage that uplift us—and then we wonder if we could ever be that person. Do we have it in us?

I believe that courage is in all of us, even if we think we don't have it or we've lost it, or we have yet to experience it.

For years people said I was courageous, and I could not see what they were talking about. I just knew that making changes lit me up and kept me feeling ALIVE. That's just how I was wired as a child. Out of survival I had to do things that looked courageous to others, while on the inside it was basically life or death. It took me a long time to see my courage and honor the role it has played in my life.

Courage shows up in lots of different ways. For one thing, it's standing up for what you believe and not backing down. Sometimes courage is asking for the un-askable. Sometimes it's having the "balls" to go for it even when it may not seem like it's going to work—and not giving up just because other people think it's nuts. And sometimes it's following through on things even when it's not fun, because you are serving your heart's desire.

A good test of courage is when your plan passes the "crazy test." That's when you share it with someone and they say, "Are you crazy?! You think that would work?" When that happens for me, I know I've hit a nerve, and what I'm doing is probably going to be life-changing.

One of the most memorable times in my life, and one that definitely passed the crazy test, was when I left New York City for Los Angeles.

At the time I had just landed a new job working as a PR director for a well-known fashion company. I was good at PR and liked the company, but I knew I wanted more for myself than just working in fashion: I wanted to teach yoga.

Yes, yoga. It had become a huge part of my life while I healed myself of my severe medical diagnosis, multiple sclerosis, and it helped me survive the craziness of Manhattan for several years. Deep down inside I really wanted to help others the way my teachers had helped me.

That wouldn't have been such a big deal—there were yoga teacher trainings in NYC—but my soul was telling me I really wanted to do it in Los Angeles. So here's where the courageous part comes in: I decided to convince my brand new company that I should keep my PR job AND go to Los Angeles to study to be a yoga teacher.

That idea definitely passed the "crazy test" for everyone I shared it with.

What was in front of me was a HUGE leap, and I did not know if it would work. That did not stop me because I knew in my heart I had to do it. I HAD to get them to agree to keep me on board. And I had to get accepted into the program for this plan to work.

After a month of waiting, I was accepted, and the steps I needed to take unfolded very quickly.

First, I had a meeting with my boss and said, "Hey, I have a great opportunity to go to Los Angeles and do a yoga teacher training.

I believe I can do my job even better while I study." And it was true. I really believed I would be able to do a better job in LA than in the NYC office.

Then I told him, "All I need is an assistant and a computer, and I promise to get you into *Vogue, Harper's Bazaar,* and *W Magazine.*"

And THEN said I needed them to keep my pay the same. Gulp! This was the courage of asking for the un-askable.

I was not sure what they would think about this. They were a pretty conservative company. But after forty-eight hours of waiting, they came back with a YES.

OK, now I had to make it work! Insert lots of deep breaths and thanks to yoga for keeping me sane.

Woosh! I found an assistant, rented my apartment, found a place in LA, and set myself up to be mobile. Oh, and I had just gotten my license to drive, so I not only had to figure out what to do for a car, but I had to get over the scary thought of driving on the highway in LA.

Before I knew it, it was bye-bye, NYC and hello, LA. I found myself sitting at the first night of the yoga teacher training, not sure I was going to be a yoga teacher. It was pretty overwhelming.

Everything happened so fast, and now here I was: I worked in the mornings doing PR and placed the product in the magazines I promised, and in the afternoons I studied yoga. I got lots of parking tickets and did meetings while driving on Sunset Boulevard. I was living my dream.

Pretty soon I knew I wanted to move to LA for real, so I went back to NYC, packed up my things, and came back to start my new life in LA.

Though it was exactly what I wanted, there were plenty of challenging moments in this new life—like being screamed at by a fashion editor while driving to my yoga teacher training. I wasn't sure how long this would work for us both; however, I worked for that company for about two more years before I went off to teach yoga full time. The real courage here was that I really thought of what was best for my company, not just for myself. I put them first, fulfilled my commitments, and delivered more than they expected most of the time. And ultimately, I got where my soul was longing to go.

Since then, I have taken many more leaps of courage, including going from full-time yoga teacher to spiritual lifestyle design coach. What I have learned is that there is never an end to living life with courage. It is a practice, and the more you do it, the more comfortable you get with living with uncertainty and trusting your soul to get you where you need to go.

Now let's look at where you are. What have you wanted to do that you are putting off? To make it happen, first you must to believe it can work. Then you have to see how it will bring more value to others. Lastly, you must give 100 percent to what you are doing and trust in yourself. The steps are there inside you, so list them out, ask for help, and surround yourself with at least one person who is on your team cheering you on.

Courage is not about following someone else's plan. It's about going for what you truly believe in your heart is possible. What is it for you?

Hillary Rubin is a spiritual life and career coach and founder of Your Souls University. She helps women integrate who they are with who they want to be. She has been featured on Fit TV, in *The Los Angeles Times*, *The Independent*, and *Yoga Journal*, and she was named one of the 25 Women Entrepreneurs to Love in 2012 by SheOwnsit.com. Visit Hillary at HillaryRubin.com.

COURAGE CRED
Jenn Burton

My very first memory was at four years old...and let me tell you it was a beauty. I was helping my mother scrub blood stains off the wall. Apparently my father took it upon himself to beat my mother's boyfriend's head in. Charming memory indeed.

In fact, my entire childhood was heavily sprinkled with these types of charming memories, especially after my parents reunited while I was in third grade. Between the fistfights, slapping, broken ribs, head gashes, daily screaming, alcoholism, cheating, and even gunplay, you could easily say that my family was one hot, dysfunctional mess. I was an extremely scared child most of the time. I spent a good amount of time praying, asking to live with someone else, and even fantasizing about turning eighteen so I could leave for college to get away from these memories-turned-nightmares.

Over the years, I was admitted to groups for children of alcoholics and given access to school counselors on a regular basis, but no one could give me what I desperately wanted. No one offered to open their home to me, to give me a permanent break from the madness I suffered through every day. Well, there was one person. My friend's father graciously said that I could stay with him, though he warned me that I'd have to be OK with waking up in bed with him—his offer accompanied by him rubbing my nipple through my bathing suit top. Needless to say, I declined.

In a word, I was trapped because let's face it: mentally abusing a child isn't a high priority for our system in the States and most of the physical violence in our household was parent-on-parent. I spent years telling my story to anyone who would listen, still hoping that someone would swoop in and rescue me. I wore my story like a badge of honor, letting it define me in my success, in my failure, in my friendships, and in my romantic relationships. Little did I understand that this definition of myself was actually keeping me from the things I wanted most in life, especially with men.

Ever since I can remember, I've been boy crazy:

Danny in kindergarten

Jimmy in third grade

Scott in seventh (when I developed my affection for big noses).

There have been few moments in my life when I wasn't "in love" with someone. Problem was being this boy crazy didn't do much to help me actually get the guy. My childhood story that I professed to anyone who would listen wasn't exactly my sexiest attribute either. I actually grew up pretty scared of men in general, which of course was relatively easy to do with an alcoholic, verbally abusive dad who used to scare the crap out me and belittle me on a regular, sometimes daily, basis. (Fortunately, he recovered and is not the same man anymore.)

For years I was immensely intimidated by men. I definitely believed that I would never have a happy, healthy relationship. I thought I was too fat, not attractive enough, fundamentally broken, but most of all, I had very little romantic courage.

I have been That Woman—the one that men consistently treated poorly, the one that men overlooked. I have been That Woman who stayed in bed for a month, crying over a guy who left me for another woman. I felt ignored and unlikeable most of the time, not dissimilar to my childhood. Now, don't get me wrong—I did meet a few great guys. But I had the unfortunate knack for turning a relationship dysfunctional in under six months. I could manage to get rid of a guy in no time at all. Basically, I sucked at dating and attracting men, and essentially, it was my story that was killing my romantic life.

For years I believed the mere act of living my story made me courageous. As I continued to share my victim status with he who would listen, I unknowingly built a toxic wall around me, making healthy romantic relationships next to impossible. I was constantly looking for outside validation and connection through my victim status. Now I did get lots of "poor you's", hugs, and such, but none of it got me any closer to an amazing love life... something I wanted desperately.

In 2006 in the midst of a divorce and brand new dating adventures, I discovered something game-changing. I decided that in the pursuit of more pleasure that I was going to focus on what was awesome about my life instead of victimhood. This meant no longer would I attempt to bond with men about my childhood wounds. Men would now learn how much fun I was to be around instead of how much shit I had previously gone through. The results were unbelievable.

For the first time, I truly understood and experienced what it felt like to be adored and cherished by men. I let my strengths, intelligence, wit, and, shall we say, naughty sense of humor define me. I no longer allowed the focus to be on what I thought was broken in me. Men responded in ways that I never could have imagined and beyond my wildest dreams. My new approach led me to my healthiest, happiest, and most amazing relationship to date.

Several years before I made this change, I had decided that my raison d'être, my personal mission in this world, was to help women feel safer...but I had no clue how to do it. It's such an easy thing to want, as a victim, but it is only accomplishable when you give up that victim status. By giving up my identity as a victim, a martyr, and a survivor, I had been able to give myself amazing dating adventures and had been able to shake off my fear of men—and thus, my career as a dating coach was born. I now help women build their romantic courage with men, and voila! I found how I could fulfill a unique version of my mission.

The biggest lesson that I've learned has been that courage has little to do with what we've specifically been through. People are not courageous simply because of what they have survived. The truth is that almost all of us have experienced some extremely difficult situations. Being courageous is about who you become from these situations. Do you use these situations to grow mentally and physically stronger? Do you use them to become more creative or more disenchanted? Do you use them to push more people away or draw them closer?

Do you use your story to create change in the world?

The best part is that I feel much freer. My story now is an asset for me because I use it to relate to people instead of building barriers between us. But I had to learn the not-so-fun way that being a victim, martyr, or survivor doesn't give me "courage cred." You have to be courageous enough to use your story to start your own revolution—personal or global—you decide.

Jenn Burton is founder of Have Him Your Way. After years of dysfunctional relationships and crappy dating experiences, she decided to take matters in her own hands. Jenn developed a method to help women create the most amazing dating adventures and learn how to go from feeling ignored to absolutely adored. To learn more about Jenn, visit HaveHimYourWay.com.

TURNING TOWARD LOVE
Alana Sheeren

Five months and seven days after the wedding of my dreams, my marriage fell apart. My new husband left his e-mail up on the computer, and curious, I looked. What I found made my head spin and my body crumble. I spent that first night with my two best friends, drinking wine, crying, and throwing up. I wondered who knew. I felt like a fool. My anger throbbed as my heart lay shattered on the floor.

It took a week for the story to unfold and for my life as I knew it to unravel. I went home and asked him to move out. I called my therapist. I wept and raged. I told him I wasn't keeping it a secret. We talked with our friends and family, divulging whatever details were necessary. They listened, told us they loved us, and offered support. I lost my appetite and my ability to sleep.

I'd had boyfriends cheat on me before. Somehow as a kid I absorbed the message that men weren't to be trusted, and that's what life gave me more often than not. But this was my husband. The man I'd met after the last boyfriend dumped me for his cocaine habit and his newest temporary love. The man who had looked me in the eyes in front of one hundred fifty people and made me laugh and cry with his vows. Despite the pain and anger, I was surprised that I never questioned my love for him. My therapist told me to leave, but other people in our lives were suddenly saying, "Us too…this happened to us and we made it through." I wanted to believe it was possible.

My husband was falling apart too, living on a friend's couch, desperate for a second chance. I knew I had a choice: walk away and risk repeating the lesson with the next relationship I entered into, or take a deep breath, get a new therapist, and slowly relearn trust.

Intuitively I'd known something was wrong. I'd sensed a disconnect between us, despite the laughter and love. We were living on the surface, each of us with a deep sense of shame that was a perfect match for the other. But I only saw it in hindsight. His work kept him on the road. On the days I'd get up at 5:00 a.m. to teach Pilates in Beverly Hills, he'd stay up late with his computer games. We were busy, there were excuses, and I figured we just had a few kinks to work out.

We separated for three months. We started therapy. There were very clear rules as I began to explore what would make me feel safe again in our relationship. It was brutally hard. But I loved him, and he was willing to do the work, on himself and on us, that this Herculean overhaul required.

I'd been taught that when there is infidelity, the relationship ends or one person suffers in silence while the other does what they want. History and literature are full of philandering husbands and unhappy wives. I didn't know there was another way, until that other way changed the course of my life.

Sitting with my husband, the space between us thick with history and emotion, I began to find a voice I didn't know I had. I began to ask for what I needed and say no to what I didn't want. I began to believe I was worthy of the kind of love I craved. In finding the courage to risk being hurt again, in opening my heart instead of allowing the pain to shut it down, I began to walk the path of trust. Not only did I have to learn to trust my husband, I needed to be able to trust myself.

It turned out that the process of mending our marriage was preparation for what was to come. Eight years have passed since I found the e-mail that rocked my world. In that time we've experienced two miscarriages, the birth of our daughter, and the stillbirth of our son. Infidelity aside, the marriage we had early on wouldn't have survived parenthood, never mind the grief that followed our son's death. In those months—and years—of rebuilding, I learned the skill that would carry me forward: to live and speak my truth with love.

There are days when fear shows up, when memories and old pain return. There are tears to be shed, questions to be asked, and hard conversations to be had. But with practice I've grown less afraid. With time I've gotten clearer on the roles I play and the ways I hold my husband at arm's length. With repeated effort we've softened into each other and forgiven again and again. I believe staying together is a daily choice. Sometimes we make it by default as we fall into the patterns and rhythms of work and parenting. Then there are the moments, so small as to seem insignificant, that add up to a happy or unhappy life. It is those moments when the choice is hardest to see and we can begin to turn away from each other in almost unnoticeable increments. The awareness that came from our experiences of loss is a safety net that catches us before we fall too far apart.

When we open our hearts to love, we risk the pain of loss. Life asks much of us, and it's easy to harden, to isolate, to ignore the bigness of our feelings. It takes courage to be vulnerable and say yes to love after we've been hurt, to say yes to another child after one dies, to say yes to life when it has felt cruel and unkind. There is magic in yes. There is possibility, hope, and strength. My life is more beautiful than my wildest dreams, though it's nothing like I'd imagined. The times of grief and despair opened my eyes to the light of my own soul, shining through the cracks in my heart. I cultivate that light and I honor the courage it took to bring me here. Unable to see into the future, I pray for more joy than pain, for more ease than struggle, but I trust that whatever life brings, I will set my sights on joy and I will thrive.

Alana Sheeren is an emotional alchemist, deep conversation catalyst, Reiki Master, Kundalini yogi and proud mama of two children, a five-year-old daughter and a stillborn son. Her unique blend of compassion, insight and expertise creates a warm, judgment-free space for deep exploration and self-realization. To pick up her e-book *Picking Up the Pieces: thoughts on grief and growth* or to learn more about Alana, visit AlanaSheeren.com.

PANACEA LOVE
Jennifer Louden

I.

There is a story my father told my entire life. It is 1964. I am two and he is forty-three. We live on Park Lane in Bloomington, Indiana, and every morning when my mother releases me from my crib, I bump down the stairs in my night diaper. I crawl across the kitchen tile and down two more stairs to the half bath off the family room, where my father is preparing to shave. Dad reaches down and seats me on the closed toilet seat, where, according to legend, I raptly watch him moisten his morning stubble, measure out the Old Spice shaving cream, and carve precise paths through the aromatic snow to reveal Daddy cheeks. Smooth. Ready for my kiss.

Dad always finishes this story with, "Your mother must have put you up to it." He shakes his head in wonderment. "You came every morning."

II.

My dad and mom often stop by with a container of chicken soup or a small gift for my ten-year-old daughter, so I was not surprised when midmorning one day last month, the front door opened and I heard my parents' voices. I got up from the computer and headed to the front door. Mom had been crying. Dad was pale. "I have pancreatic cancer," Dad blurted out from the entryway, before I'd even reached the living room. "We just came from the doctor's."

I almost say, "You're kidding," but I only allow myself a fifth of a second of denial before slap! Gut-clenched, iron-lunged, acid esophagus: so this is how my dad's life will end.

III.

The pancreas: mysterious hermit of the abdomen. The unwritten credo of medical students is "Eat when you can, sleep when you can, and don't mess with the pancreas." An alchemist when happy, it transmutes tiny particles of food into an enzymatic energy drink that plaits bone and braids muscle, nurtures dendrites and regenerates skin. A stingy tyrant when crossed, it lies hidden while making any manner of mischief: no more insulin from its islets of Langerhans (imagine Norse gods brandishing swords against angry skies while cursing, "No more sweetness for you!"); pancreatitis (acute, chronic, infectious, recurrent, and interstitial relapsing); cysts and pseudo cysts; atrophy; calculus; fibrosis; cirrhosis; and, like every other part of the body, cancerous. In the United States, pancreatic cancer is the ninth most commonly diagnosed cancer and the third cause of cancer death in men. The median survival period from the time of diagnosis until death for untreated advanced cancer of the pancreas is about three and a half months; with good treatment this increases to about six months. Later, I wonder how, somehow, I knew, in the instant Dad said pancreatic cancer, that it meant all this—hidden, dangerous, sweet.

IV.

Kant believed the soul permeated every part of the human body. Carl du Prel, a German philosopher who lived in the mid-1800s, argued that our emotional center originates in the solar plexus, located just above the navel, near the pancreas. One new age guru maintains a diseased pancreas is the result of rejecting the sweetness of life.

V.

Two weeks before the news about Dad's pancreas, I am flying home from a job in New York, feeling horrendous. I had a glass of wine the night before, waiting for my college friend to call, but this morning it feels like I drank two bottles—of rotgut. I write it off to a lingering cold and jet lag. Days pass. I don't recover. I get worse. Then a bit better. Worse again. Weeks pass. I decide I have a low-grade bug. Go to my naturopath. Take more herbs. Feel worse. Waves of nausea and fatigue that resemble the sudden, chilling onslaught of the flu. Scurry to the bathroom. Seems to strike between ten and two.

VI.

What I have learned from my father: admit when you are wrong; do the numbers and don't hide from the truth; when you have nothing left to go on, go on your nerve; don't fence me in; humility; cordiality; a habit of driving myself toward a future where things will be better; and too often, a visceral sense of being one step removed from the breathtaking moments of life. Just yesterday, walking in the Grand Forest near my home, puppy darting ahead and then back to my side, a floppy silver streak, I came around a turn and the autumnal sunlight lit up a stand of cedars and a single big leaf maple, all velutinous with fairy light. The air was saturated with cedar, fir, neon-new moss. I stood still, feeling a swell of well-being, connectedness, gratitude—or did I watch myself feel? The sweetness is there, but sometimes I can only gain tiny sips.

My father always murmurs the same thing when life shines brightest: "This is wonderful. This is so wonderful. Isn't this wonderful?"

VII.

I finally go to the doctor, expecting a quick prescription for antibiotics. She orders a full blood panel. When she calls with the results, she tells me my pancreatic enzymes are elevated, very unusual. She asks if I know where the pancreas is. I picture the various diagrams of the pancreas I have seen in the last two weeks: at the oncologist, at the surgeon, at the oncologist's again, not to mention the thirty or so websites I have visited obsessively, clicking for hope.

Each doctor asked my father, "Do you know where the pancreas is?"

VIII.

I tell my daughter that Grandpa is very sick. I tell her while we are in the car doing errands. She cries easily, immediately. "I mean, I love him, he's the best grandpa, but, Mommy, he always says to you, 'Don't make her hug me.' I want to hug him!" She asks why Grandpa doesn't believe we love him for himself, without Mom as mediator. Staring at the highway, I open and close my mouth. How to explain to a child the jumbled stories we create to survive?

That weekend, Lilly takes Dad outside to the patio. Dad sits in a plastic patio chair. Lilly dances around him and tells him how much she loves him. That nobody makes her love him—or anybody else for that matter. She punctuates her declaration with a cartwheel.

IX.

An ultrasound shows my pancreas is smooth and tumorless. No one knows why I am feeling poorly or my lipases are elevated. When anybody hints at a connection to my father, I protest, "But I started feeling ill two weeks before we learned about Dad."

X.

A coaching client remarks, "You are on the edge of a mystery." I feel lost and guided, terrified and brave. The sweetness my dad has denied himself calls to me. It calls to my dad too. Will we be tender enough to answer? I am, once again, bumping down the stairs in my night diaper, and this time, perhaps, my Dad will know I come for him.

Jen Louden is a personal growth pioneer who helped launch the self-care movement with her first book *The Woman's Comfort Book*. She's the author of five additional books on well-being, including *The Woman's Retreat Book* and *The Life Organizer* that have inspired close to a million women in nine languages. She's at work on a novel and leads retreats around the country. Visit her at JenniferLouden.com.

THE ROCK
Leah Shapiro

It's pitch black, I'm cold, and my mind is in hyper-overdrive.

"Where am I going? What's going to happen next? Man, I hope I don't trip!"

I'm being led down a dark path through an unknown forest on a Quest for self-knowledge. I have no idea where I'm going or what I'll encounter. My feelings are all jumbled together: curiosity, nervousness, and excitement all at the same time.

This Quest was part of a really cool woman's mystery school and leadership program I was part of back in 2003. On this Quest, there are many interesting stops along the way designed to challenge me and make me think about my fears, desires, and beliefs.

At one stop, I come across a woman dressed in black, and she asks me how heavily my past experiences weighed on me. We talk about the boyfriend who dumped me when my mother was dying, my struggle to trust and find happiness, my crappy corporate job that didn't care about my needs, and my fears of making a mistake and failing. I also say that I'm nervous because I don't know HOW things are going to turn out.

The woman in black hands me a big rock and says that I am to carry it the rest of the way along my journey. This rock represents all the emotional baggage I carry with me as I move through my life.

Let me tell you, carrying that rock sucked! It was awkward and took so much energy. It weighed me down. At each new stop along the trail, it became more and more irritating. The longer I carried it, the heavier it became and the more I focused on it. I was not able to enjoy the cool stuff I was coming across along the way because I was so focused on carrying the rock and how much it sucked. The rock became the focus of everything.

Finally, I got fed up and decide to throw the rock off into the woods. Boy, what a relief! I felt free. The Quest was fun again. I wondered why I did not ditch the rock sooner.

Interestingly enough, I was the only one who chose to ditch their rock. Everyone else kept lugging the thing along until they came to a stop where someone else relieved them of it. It never occurred to them that they might have a choice in the matter.

Flash-forward ten years and I find myself on another kind of Quest. This one is the Entrepreneurs' Journey. I often feel like I'm stumbling down an unknown path in the darkness. Half the time I have no idea what's going to happen or how things will turn out. Half the time it is a well-rewarded journey. What I'm offering is a hit, and I feel deeply satisfied. The other half of the time I trip and fall and have to pick myself up and try a different path.

After a particularly painful failure that rocked my confidence, I found myself once again carrying a rock down an unknown path. I was afraid of failing again. The last one was weighing heavily on me, and I was second-guessing myself and questioning everything I was doing. I had invested a lot of time and money in what I thought would be a successful mastermind program, only to have no one sign up. I didn't want to put myself out there again and risk another flop.

The weight of this rock was taking up much of my energy, and as a result, I was playing very small and holding back my creative juices. I was comparing everything I was considering doing to my past failures. I was focusing on all the ways things wouldn't work because they hadn't worked in the past.

The rock began to take over and become the center of my focus. I felt irritated and vulnerable. I wasn't having fun, and I considered closing down my coaching business and going out and getting another job.

Then I remembered that I could ditch the rock!

I gathered up my courage and tossed that sucker out into the virtual woods. Boy, did I feel free!

Focusing on the rock limited my ability to see the cool, amazing opportunities that were happening around me. I totally missed out on all the joy, fun, and possibilities because I was too busy thinking about all the stuff I didn't want to experience again.

I decided to completely change things up and do things in a whole new way. I took a big risk and started working with a partner. I challenged myself to only focus on what I wanted to create and all the ways it could work. I made having fun a top priority in my business. A few months later, I launched my most successful program ever, and my future looks bright.

Are you carrying around a rock of your own?

Make the choice to ditch it! This rock holds you back and keeps you playing small in your life. It inhibits your ability to look to the future and focus on how you want it to be. The rock keeps us in the past. That is no way to live!

Ditch the rock! There is always a choice.

Choose to let it go and focus on what feels good to you right now.

Choose to enjoy the adventure.

Ditch the Rock!

Leah Shapiro is a life activator and kick-ass catalyst. Her super power is helping you identify and break free of the stories that hold you back and keep you playing small. She is an expert at helping you own your super powers and bring more YOU-NESS out in the world so you can finally live the life you are here to live. For more information about Leah, visit LeahShapiro.com.

MY TRUTH, THE REAL TRUTH
Lisa Consiglio Ryan

There's a lot of talk about being authentic…being your true self. As humans, we thrive on making connections, gaining trust, and being real.

But what is being real actually?

You might think that I'm a little crazy because I'm not certain about this authentic stuff. It's not like I downright lie or steal. In fact, it's the total opposite. Growing up, I was a good girl, making sure to follow the rules. Even now when I feel my "real" self coming out, that good girl shows up just to remind me of my past.

Ever since I can remember, I lived in fear. Fear of my parents arguing and thinking I caused their unhappiness. Fear of being left out on the playground and not popular in school. Fear of being alone so that I clung to any boyfriend for as long as I could, even if they treated me like crap. I just couldn't risk being all by myself in this world.

Since this fear washed over me so deeply, I learned to hide my truth—push it way, way down inside. In fact, I learned to be accommodating. I accommodated everyone. Whether someone played guitar or lacrosse, I either learned how to do it or researched how so that I could fit in. I had no interest in learning guitar (I play the piano), and lacrosse, well, I did join a team in college, but that didn't go too far. I learned to accommodate my friends and family, not to get them mad at me, and to say what made them feel better. I made sure not to shine too brightly so that the people around me wouldn't feel intimidated.

I went to every party, baptism (maybe the Catholic thing had something to do with my "good girl" act), and any event possible, even if it meant that I would sacrifice something I really wanted to do. I did whatever someone wanted so that I could hide my real truth. That way I didn't have to risk showing my true colors because that was too scary. I was afraid to just be me because I actually probably lost "me" a long time ago.

I'm not exactly sure when I lost my true self, but I can put big money on the fact that being told I was fat had a lot to do with it.

I remember the exact day. It was in the early summer just before my dance recital. I was eight years old and wearing my yellow cowgirl dance outfit. Pictures were being taken, and then someone I loved dearly told me I was getting fat and to be careful or soon I would be as big as a house. I was crushed.

Then I stopped eating. I stopped being me.

I can remember writing down each item of food in a journal. I only allowed five things a day, such as one piece of toast, one stick of bubblegum, one slice of pizza, etc…Of course I was growing child, and I was constantly starving; therefore, a trip to McDonald's would happen at the end of the day. I would feel defeated, resentful, and above all, disconnected from myself.

My years with an eating disorder are difficult to talk about, but I've learned that it is just a part of me…it's in my cells, and my body remembers. I respect this and am able to let go and speak of my experience. This has taken a long time, however, but each time I bring up the truth, my body gives me a gentle squeeze and trust is deepened.

As I healed, it was terrifying to let bits and pieces of the real me be seen by others. Since I have accommodated everyone in my life for so long, it was extremely frightening to let go of that control. Just like with food, I can control my reactions and even words just to please others. Even though I felt my truth stirring restlessly in my whole being, I still felt I was betraying that fat "good girl," and I really couldn't tell where my truth began and ended because I learned to blend into others.

My authentic self couldn't hide any longer, however.

I knew deep down that until I spoke my full truth, I would still live in fear, loneliness, and dishonesty.

As I work my way with speaking my full truth, I still find myself swallowing it. What if someone doesn't like what I say? What if no one agrees with me? Even if I express my authentic self, a hesitation pops in at times. The old feelings try to take first place, but I'm determined to have my truth win.

My truth. It begins with me. I can be grumpy. I can be silly. I can be anything—just me. And that is OK.

My truth. Giving others a chance first instead of beating them to the punch and figuring out what they want me to say. I used to pride myself on that, knowing how to please everyone and keep them happy—any quirky, random thought or genuine need. Let myself be me. Really feel it.

My truth. Learning to give people the opportunity to love me first and to react to me. For so long I have wanted to experience really being seen, to be cherished for who I am. I'm learning to share true feelings coming from love, and it's so freeing.

How do I truly feel? The courage to say it. Uncensored.

My truth. The real truth. As I grow and begin to trust that the universe wants me to be the real me, I recognize that my talents and creations and my voice are needed. Building up my spiritual and emotional muscle helps me be comfortable with my truth each day. It will come…I'm in an absolutely divine place.

I trust that my journey was built just for me. I know better, I know the answers, I can trust myself. I can trust my own judgment without looking out there but within me.

My truth. The real truth. Life is rooting for me, for my truth. Living life uncensored is liberating and gets easier each day. No more swallowing the truth. Never again.

Lisa Consiglio Ryan is the founder of Whole Health Designs, a juicy clean living advocate, and a mama of two. She loves her Bikram yoga practice and running; she is on a mission to spread the word that "Food is love," and she provides detox programs and private coaching for women who desire to embrace clean living. She has written for TinyBuddha, Crazy Sexy Life, and Mind Body Green. To learn more about Lisa, visit WholeHealthDesigns.com.

PLEASURE SAVES THE DAY
LiYana Silver

I just took a break from writing to nurse my seven-month-old son. His exuberant, dewy existence has broken me open into a higher octave of love, which is a good thing, since I am a student—and steward—of extraordinary love stories.

Seven years ago, freshly free of my Fatal Attraction tendencies that had plagued my early relationships, a big, hairy question began to loom over my horizon. This question, ripe to completely derail my love affair with my now husband, Nathan, was, "Hey, are we going to have a kid?"

He: "No." Me: "Yes. I really think so. Yes."

I have the fortunate habit of finding wizard-mentors and oracle-teachers in unlikely places. Enter Morehouse, an unlikely bastion of sanity and intentional community in Northern California. In the 1960s, these folks formed an experimental living collective based around answering the audacious question "How can we have the most fun and pleasure, while only doing what we want to do?" The experiment never ended and yielded some of the most impressive courses I've yet to encounter on communication, sensuality, and partnership.

Nathan and I sat our tushies down in their Basic Sensuality course—still one of my favorites—waiting for a lightning bolt of clarity around the kid question. I was a teary, snotty mess, and he was cold and distant—a general replay of how we both dealt with most difficult issues. No lightning. No clarity. So we booked a private session with the teachers, putting our fate in their hands.

It was fifty minutes into our hour-long private session that they said, "Look, we don't know if you should have a kid or not. It's a lot of work. But what we do know is that you are having a really crappy time figuring it out. What if you had a really fun and pleasurable time figuring it out?"

Have FUN working on a problem? Have PLEASURE from chewing on a conundrum? My inner sufferer was mortally offended by the sheer audacity! Regardless, in that spectacular moment of cognitive dissonance, a crack appeared in the kid conundrum. Here's how.

Turns out the main reason Nathan was a no to having a child was due to what he thought he would lose. Over our three years, he had plenty of opportunity to see the way I dealt with stressful times and tough issues: sliding into murky pits of overwhelm, despair, and self-criticism. Out winked the lights of my happiness. Gone was his joyful, vibrant, juicy partner. Add a baby to the mix and the only sure results he could foresee were exponential misery and loss of his lover. I had to admit he was probably right. I seemed committed to having the crappiest time possible in tough times, so as times got tougher, they were likely to get crappier.

But how in the world might I party my ass off when I found myself between a rock and a hard place? What if instead of despair I brought pleasure? The questions set me to realize I was chronically overwhelmed, relentlessly out of touch with my bodily wisdom, and constantly disappointed with the world and the people in it. On closer examination, I saw myself to be a woman who was unable to be generally happy. I decided a breakup was the only answer. With my sourpuss outlook and beliefs, I mean.

I started to ask myself a question. It's the single-most important question any woman can ask herself as part of a practice of taking ownership of her happiness. It's made up of the nine most important words you may ever read. "How can I make this more pleasurable for myself?"

I applied it to already crap situations, like when packed between sweaty armpits in crowded subway train cars in August in New York City. (Answer: Imagine everyone painted in full blue body paint, a la the Blue Man Group. Hold belly while laughing.) I applied it to already pleasurable situations, like mid-orgasm. (Answer: Imagine sensations spreading out to toetips and fingertips and entwining in my lover's heart, a la full-body cosmic bliss).

I traded up bowing to the gods of productivity and instead worshipped at the altar of fun and pleasure. I realized I was going to die with things on my to-do list, so maybe it was OK to feel good even though I left my desk with boxes unchecked. I prioritized going to dance class, painting, eating kale, and hanging out with girlfriends. I spelunked into my own being to inquire what really fed me, lit me up, felt good, and called me out of my cave of hopelessness. And then I did those things as a meditative, devotional daily practice.

Nathan started to notice. My juice and joy were less dependent on circumstances going well. I was happier more of the time, if not most of the time. Around me, people had fun and liked themselves more. I'd pause in the middle of having a hard time and call "grumpy-pants" on myself. When a snarled issue came up, my light didn't dim. My sensuality ran deeper, which made me a much more enticing lover. I was at the epicenter of the party of life.

Nathan started to notice that I was in the active inquiry and exploration of how to make each moment more pleasurable than the last. No longer having to guard against losing the good parts of me, his "no" around having a child teetered into the gray area of "OK, maybe."

By embracing pleasure and fun did I become a hedonist, on the hunt for more and better bodily sensations? In a way, yes. I'm a proponent of life feeling as good as it possibly can to our sweet animal body and our beloved servant mind. But the word "pleasure" began to take on an even fuller meaning, beyond fully savoring life through the five senses.

The definition of pleasure as I see it is a feeling or state of enjoyment, satisfaction, and gratification. Gratification comes from the same Latin root as does the word "gratitude." The root "gratus" means "pleasing and thankful." There is, therefore, an etymological and visceral loop between pleasure and gratitude. The Twelve-Step Process folks have a saying: "A grateful heart doesn't drink." I understand that to mean that you can't be in a state of gratitude (the real thing: on-your-knees, whole-heart-panting) and feel shitty at the same time. The two can't coexist. You can't feel self-loathing, despair, and overwhelm—and hope to drink, snort, shop, vomit, or exercise those intense emotions away—while you're thankful.

I didn't stuff down my shadows and plaster a saccharine smile on top. I applied the "pleasure question" to every area of my life, asking how excavating my dark parts could be more pleasurable too. Pleasure became a state-changer, a means for easier communication—and waaaay better sex—with Nathan and a context for a more abundant life. Instead of needing everything in the world around me to go my way in order to feel good, I realized I carried "good" around inside me. I felt hooked up to the creative life-force power source of the universe itself, and I could flip the switch to "on" any time I wished. I called off the fraught search for my true self and instead found she was right here with me, right where I left her, all along.

Pleasure has shown itself to be a potent concept. By asking myself—and then answering—how I could make this more pleasurable and fun for myself, my whole outlook on life, womanhood, and partnership has changed irrevocably. Nathan asked similarly, how could having a child be more pleasurable and fun than not?

And thus pleasure manifested itself quite concretely. This baby—his cheek against my collarbone, his body soft and floppy with sleep, his chubby fingers wrapped around my thumb—pleasure did this. Pleasure made this. Pleasure saved the day.

LiYana Silver wasn't born a relationship revolutionary; her mastery was forged in the crucible of multiple and massive screw-ups. A recovering self-loathing anorexic dancer, she's learned to take the term "starving artist" less literally and get mighty comfortable with the skin she's in. As a lifelong student of Love, she's managed to shake her Fatal Attraction tendencies and co-create a work of living, loving art with her husband of over ten years. To learn more about LiYana, visit her at Love3Point0.com.

YOU ARE ALL YOU EVER NEED TO BE
Marlee Ward

"Our deepest fear is not that we are inadequate. Our deepest fear is that we are powerful beyond measure. It is our light, not our darkness, that most frightens us. We ask ourselves, who am I to be brilliant, gorgeous, talented, and fabulous? Actually, who are you not to be?" – Marianne Williamson

I'm a brave girl. I don't mean to sound cocky. I've just always been a tough cookie.

When I was thirteen, I helped my mom pack my father's belongings in garbage bags (and put them on the street) after a "friend" approached us in the mall and confirmed my mother's suspicion that my dad was having an affair (for the second time).

Later that year, when I came home to a barren house (because my father took the furniture without notice), I wrapped my arms around my mom and said, "I like it just you and me," because I wanted her to know that I was strong.

After high school, I attended college in a city where my race mattered more than my substance. I wasn't black enough to be black. I wasn't white enough to be white. And, the Hispanic crowd made it pretty clear I wasn't one of them. Despite their efforts, I refused to let others define me.

And then, I fell in love. It was magnetic, electric, and breathtaking. But the pain it brought me was relentless. After years of riding the rollercoaster of "love me-love me not," I flew five thousand miles to make a final stand for what I thought was the love of a lifetime. I did not leave "standing," but I promised to love bigger and better next time.

Years later, as a newly minted lawyer with student debt the size of a mortgage, I stood face-to-face with the fact that I hated my career choice. Practicing law was killing me from the inside out, and I felt tempted to settle for less than what I could offer the world. But, I refused to settle.

And just this year, as a new mother and wife, I learned that my migraine headaches weren't due to my voracious reading and work on the computer but that a pea-sized tumor growing inside my pituitary gland was the culprit. Now, I take medication that makes it difficult to stand (or do much of anything at times). But, the inconvenience is nothing compared to the myriad difficulties so many others face. That tiny tumor won't stop me. I won't let it.

I know these aren't particularly tragic experiences. But they are reasons why I consider myself a brave girl. I know how to get going when the going gets tough.

So it shocked me when, for the first time in my life, I feared something so much it paralyzed me mentally, emotionally, and physically.

This fear made my heart race. It made my breath shorten. It made my voice quake.

This fear was a fear of myself.

After so many years of being "tough," I discovered that fully stepping into who I've been created to be terrified me to death. Ironically, doing so has given me the most life.

Allow me to explain.

When I left my career as an attorney for life as an entrepreneur, I had no idea what to expect. I only knew that I needed to make money—fast.

So, I leveraged my marketing and business skills and built a business that made money from day one.

At first, the thrill of "pulling it off" carried me for a while. But it didn't take long for my dream of becoming a "badass business woman" to become a nightmare of my making.

Somewhere in the process of building my business, I got so caught up in creating a business that worked, I never asked myself what I really wanted.

So there I was, at the height of a recession, running a profitable business that was making me miserable.

And then, the still small voice that called me into entrepreneurship the first time reappeared. And just like the time before it whispered, "You were made for more than this."

Because once again, it wasn't that my work wasn't challenging, profitable, or worthwhile…It just wasn't what I was meant to do.

That is when I realized something that sent total shock through my system.

I wasn't living my truth.

I wasn't saying or doing the things that only I have been placed on this earth to say and do.

I didn't want to be judged. I didn't want to be rejected. I didn't want to be confronted.

I didn't want to be me—fully and completely. It was just too scary.

But, I knew I couldn't live as only a portion of who I am. My inner woman wouldn't let me.

With fear and trembling, I started over and built a business that allowed me to be ALL of who I am. The moment I committed to doing that, I set myself free.

Free from judgment, because some people don't get it (and thankfully, they don't have to).

Free from rejection, because you can't and shouldn't try to please everyone.

Free from confrontation, because when you love yourself fully, you give love more than anything else.

Free to be me—fully and completely.

It was the scariest thing I ever did. Thank God, He gave me the strength to do it.

When I look back at the woman who feared her own truth, I'm startled by the small game I played. I'm surprised how much I limited my potential. I'm amazed at the possibilities I ignored.

I could have missed my purpose, and I'm so relieved I didn't.

So, just in case you didn't know, you are amazing. You are wonderfully and marvelously made. You are a child of God. There will never be another you.

You are a gift. You contain greatness. You have presents the world desperately needs.

Have the courage to give them out generously.

Marlee Ward helps entrepreneurs build spiritually, emotionally, and financially rewarding businesses through her marketing and faith-based mindset coaching programs. She resides in sunny central Florida with her husband and son. Learn more at MarleeWard.com.

MAKING FEAR YOUR BITCH
Michelle Leath

"Life begins at the end of your comfort zone." – Neale Donald Walsch

I used to believe that courage was about being fearless. But now I know otherwise.

I sometimes feel as though I've spent the last few years at the University of Courage, gettin' schooled on the true meaning of the word! It started when my dad passed away, my marriage crumbled, and I came to a career crossroads all within a few months' time. I had reached that critical and somewhat cliché point in life when I realized that I needed to make some big changes. The universe obviously had a plan to teach me about courage, and thus began a series of opportunities for me to explore and experience it in a variety of forms.

Early in the process of my divorce, I had adopted a personal mantra of "making fear my bitch," and I certainly put that to the test. But two particular moments in time stand out vividly in my mind—the moments in which I came face-to-face with the meaning of courage.

August 2010 After sixteen years of marriage, my ex-husband and I told our two children that we were splitting up. A few days later, I was alone with the kids on a planned vacation to Seattle, the pain and fear around breaking up my family heavy on my mind.

One afternoon I took the kids to a water park. Now, if you knew me you'd know that the germy, soggy amusement park is not really my thing. But I wanted to create a new bond with my kids as a single mom; their dad had always been the one who played. So rather than my usual, "I'll just hang out in the sun and keep an eye on the stuff" approach, I decided to suit up and get my feet (and my hair) wet. I decided that instead of being a "no" mom, I was going to be a "yes" mom. I was going to engage and participate. I was determined to show the kids that I could lead and support them on my own. (With everything so fresh, I naively believed I had to have it figured out and resolved all at once!) Now that I look back, I think I was also looking for reassurance that they didn't hate me for shattering their family stability.

As we explored the park, we came upon the Sky Coaster, a towering and somewhat foreboding bungee jump apparatus, to which I was double-teamed with an excited, "Mom, can we do that???" My answer, of course (per the deal), was YES. About twenty minutes later—harnessed in tandem between both of my children, hoisted 125 feet in the air, and facedown with the ripcord in my hand—I was seriously rethinking that decision!

But here's the thing. I knew in the moment that I said "yes" exactly why I was doing this. As I ran back to the locker to get the money to pay for the ride, I realized that I wasn't jumping for fun or entertainment. I was jumping for our new life.

I was already in an emotional free fall, leaping into the unknown, breaking the status quo, plunging into divorce, single motherhood, and all the social and financial ramifications that go along with it. The Sky Coaster was the perfect metaphor for what I was experiencing in my life. If I had the courage to change my life, free-falling 125 feet out of the sky was a no-brainer. Or maybe it was the other way around.

I looked at both kids with terrified eyes, the three of us sharing a classic "holy shit" moment. I asked myself what kind of mother would tie herself to her kids and have them dropped from the sky with no net or protection? I guess the same kind of mother who would leave the safety of her marriage to stand for her own happiness, who'd let her husband go on to find the happiness he deserved, and who'd take a leap of faith for the chance to teach her children about courage and someday show them an example of a healthy, loving relationship.

I pulled, we plunged. Just before we reached the earth, the bungee recoiled according to plan and we were propelled back into the sky in a swinging motion, soaring high above the park, supported once again, and woo-hooing together as we flew into the new chapter of our lives.

December 2010 A Friday night in Washington DC. I was waiting backstage with nine other contestants in the Ready for the Stage competition, an *American Idol* type contest for aspiring public speakers in the coaching/helping/entrepreneurial world. I wasn't exactly sure how I'd gotten here, other than having submitted a video application after receiving an e-mail about the competition a few weeks prior. The rules: make a five-minute video stating what the big message of your business is and why you believe you are ready for the stage. And I'd been chosen.

The funny thing was I didn't even technically have a business yet. In fact I had just started coaching school. But I knew that I wanted to be on stage (I'm a known karaoke microphone hog), and I knew that I wanted to help people heal their troubled relationships with food. That had been my own journey. Actually, for twenty years, it had been my deepest, darkest secret. And so that's what I made my video about.

And now here I stood, about to go before a live audience of three hundred and a global webcast, and prepared to give a ten-minute speech on my experience with bulimia. I'd never spoken publicly about this before. Ever. Even most of my closest friends and family were unaware of my struggle.

But over the prior several months, there had been a growing pull on me. As I found my way through recovery, I was feeling called to help other women who were feeling powerless, trapped, and afraid. I had discovered a hidden doorway to healing, and I was compelled to share what I had learned.

In order to do that, I needed to step through my own shame. And I had to let myself be seen. I had to stand up and say this is me, the real me. Naked, exposed, raw. And I'm OK anyway.

So I'd submitted the video, fallen out of my chair when my name was announced as a semifinalist, boarded a plane, and spent several days preparing my speech and my public declaration of imperfection. The kicker was this: of the ten semifinalists only four finalists would be picked to deliver their speeches, and those contestants would be announced live on the air. None of us knew if we'd actually be speaking or not. And those who did speak would be publicly critiqued by the judges, and the audience would choose the winner.

I'll never forget the elevator ride down to the ballroom that night. Floor by floor it was as if layer upon layer of my self-protection was being stripped away. What if they called my name? What if everyone I knew was watching? What if everyone looked at me like a freak? A psycho? Couldn't I just have written a nice uplifting speech about finding your life purpose or something? Why did I have to talk about this? I wanted to run, withdraw, go to the bar for tequila shots…anything but give this damn speech!

And yet I knew that if I had done anything differently I wouldn't be here, and I knew that if my name was called I would go on.

As I gathered with the other contestants in a prayer circle, moments before showtime, my trembling had become so intense that my jaw was literally locked up. I could not open my mouth. How would I even form words?

Out we went, in front of the live and webcast audience, everyone anxiously anticipating the announcement of the finalists. One by one, four names were called, and none of them were mine. I was flooded with relief but also a feeling of victory. Being willing to give that speech was the biggest win I'd ever achieved.

I used to think that courage meant having no fear. Now I know that it really means being terrified beyond belief and acting anyway.

So what's the change you are yearning to make? What's the story you are longing to tell? What's the gift you are dying to share? You know you have one.

What's stopping you? If you're waiting for the fear to go away and the courage to "arrive" you'll be waiting a long time. Courage is a choice. It's simply the moment when you make a decision to act on something bigger than your terror. And it's a process. It's when you say, again and again, "Yes, fear, I see you there, but today I am making you my bitch."

Michelle Leath is a coach, mentor, speaker, and the founder of Unlock Your Possibility. Michelle works with women, who are fed up with dieting and deprivation, and she teaches them how to find freedom from unwanted weight or eating habits and how to create a relationship with food and with life that truly nourishes them. Michelle is a certified food psychology coach and a Co-Active life coach and has been helping women connect to their potential in various ways for over twenty years. To learn more, visit UnlockYourPossibility.com.

LEARNING TO SHOW UP AS ME
Nicole Mangina

Rolling Stone magazine had an article a few years ago about the latest overnight singing sensation, and he talked about it taking ten long years to become an overnight success. That quote has stuck with me and offered encouragement when the going got tough and I doubted my ability to succeed. Not that everything takes ten years, but it serves as a reminder that success is a process and we all have our struggles along the way. It's easy to look at someone who has "made it" and assume that it has always been easy for them. Know that we all have our stories.

Admittedly, I had an outwardly easy childhood. My parents loved me, and we had everything we needed in life. Internally, things were a different story. I was very shy and insecure, never feeling like I fit in. Interacting with others and building friendships was hard for me, and so I was often the quiet one on my own.

After college I started my career in real estate, which requires confidence and communication skills in order to succeed—two things I did not have at the time. I remember being so overwhelmed. My education background is in math and science, and I kept thinking, "I am smart, why can't I figure this out?" One night I was so scared about a client meeting scheduled for the next day that I cried all night afraid I couldn't do it and had to ice my face in the morning because it was so puffy.

The one thing I have always had, though, is determination and a willingness to learn. None of the skills necessary to succeed in real estate came naturally to me. I attended classes, hired a coach, and paid attention to those around me. I also implemented what I learned, and before long I started having success.

The three biggest things that worked for me were the following:

1. Showing up as me,
2. Focusing on small consistent actions, and
3. Letting go of the need to be perfect.

In the beginning, since I lacked self-confidence, I took all of the classes on how to profile your client's personality so that I would know what to say to them. There were endless scripts to memorize. None of it worked. I was so awkward and could not genuinely connect with anyone. As a result I was struggling in my business. Finally my coach gave me permission to show up as me. Forget the scripts and the personality types. She told me to just show up as me as if I was chatting with a good friend. As soon as I did that, my business turned around. I was open, talkative, and focused on connecting with my clients rather than fitting into some ill-fitting mold. It was about serving my clients to help them, not closing the sale. Give yourself permission to be you. You bring your own "flavor" to all that you do, and that is what your clients will love about you.

Since everything about real estate was so foreign to me, it was easy to get overwhelmed. I have always been an overachiever, wanting to do it all right now, and so figuring out what to do next in order to grow my business was frustrating. It's natural to assume that the bigger the action, the bigger the result, but I found the opposite to be the case. Big actions often scare and intimidate us into inaction, and they are not sustainable. It's too much, too fast, too soon. A lot of success is about sneaking up on it. For me it was about making changes that have impact, but are not too far out of my comfort zone. Many classes talk about the importance of calling your clients to stay in touch with them. Ideally they want you to call ten clients or more each day. When you are not making any phone calls, ten is enough to make someone hyperventilate. Rather than beating myself up for not doing the ten, I finally decided that I would start with one phone call. The results were amazing. There were still days that I did not want to pick up the phone and call a client, but it was easier to do knowing that I only had to do one. In less than five minutes a day, I could accomplish my goal. It worked. Consistently doing something as small as making one call a day had a compound effect and helped to double my business that year.

Letting go of the need to be perfect was a big one for me too. I wasted so much time not taking action because I was afraid that something was not perfect. No sooner would I get a marketing piece put together than I would see what someone else had done and shelve mine, assuming theirs was better. What I finally realized is that my clients usually didn't know if it was perfect or not. Even if there was something not quite right, it was more about connecting with my clients than anything else. Perfection is a moving target. Something that feels perfect today might not be tomorrow based on new information. When someone tells me that they have a hard time getting things done in their life because they want everything to be perfect, what I hear is that they are scared—scared of failure. Failure comes with success. You cannot have one without the other. It's about forward motion. Imperfect action beats perfect planning any day.

Each day is a new adventure. I still get sidetracked and nervous at times, but now I have a foundation to bring myself back to and refocus. When I start to get scared and overwhelmed, it's usually because I am overthinking things, trying to do too much at one time or doing something that is not true to who I am. As soon as I realize this, I can take a step back and ask myself what is the best next step for *me*, and the answer is usually pretty clear.

Nicole Mangina is a real estate agent and trainer in the Seattle area. Nicole's passion is helping agents simplify their business, boost their income, and love their life. Her specialty is in the real world application of ideas to truly reap the benefits in business. To find out more about Nicole, go to TheSuccessPerspective.com.

COURAGE: F-IT, WE'LL NEVER KNOW UNLESS WE TRY

Sheila Viers

I remember the day so clearly. I was sitting in my office—the office I had just moved into only four months prior—in my comfy high-back chair, staring out the giant window.

I look over at my clock, waiting for the time to count down. It was 3:54 and I had a meeting scheduled at four to talk with the vice president of my department to let her know that I was unhappy in my position.

I had been feeling this way for a while and had been pushing the feelings away, telling myself I was crazy to even be slightly discontented. I had just been promoted into a brand new department within our company in a role that had a lot of room for growth. The only problem was I wondered, "Is this the right role and the right growth for me?"

I had a strong feeling from the depths of my core that the answer was no. And I was scared.

What does this mean for me? My career? My future? I had worked so hard to get here, and now I'm here…and I'm miserable! I'm bored. I'm restless. I want more, but I'm not exactly sure what more means to me. I feel like I've been climbing this ladder only to realize my ladder is up against the wrong building.

3:59…It's time. I went to her office, sweaty palms and all, and explained how I felt. I had heard a rumor that a round of layoffs was coming, and I asked to be included. Cut me and save someone else. What was I doing? Who does this? What was my plan?

The truth was, I didn't really have one. I knew that my passion lay elsewhere, and I knew this was going to mean a serious adjustment for my husband, Ryan, and me financially, but luckily he was supportive and we both knew that we'd figure it out. My VP agreed and things were set in motion. I was gone in less than two weeks.

Fast-forward 5 years, a cross-country move, and a new business later, and things are better than good. They are great. Don't get me wrong, there were many challenges along the way, and even still, we face our share of challenges daily, but Ryan and I are finally following our dreams.

Funnily enough, six months after I was laid off, Ryan did the same thing. He negotiated himself out of his position as well. We sold our house (at a huge loss), moved in with family, and soon after made the cross-country move from Michigan to southern California with six boxes shipped ahead of time and whatever fit in our car.

Typical with us, we had a vague plan. Make the drive, stay with friends for a few days, find a place to settle, then get Ryan a job until our new business could really take off.

After I left the corporate world, I ended up starting a blog, detailing our road to health and fitness. Ryan had lost eighty pounds and I had lost thirty-five pounds, and as we went through this journey, we learned a lot that we felt we could share with others like us.

Yet that wasn't enough for us. We wanted to do more for our growing community of people serious about fitness, so after much deliberation and research, we decided to branch out into design and manufacturing…We wanted to produce the most kickass line of fitness and yoga bags known to the world of fitness.

Oh yes, one more thing that we had never done before, but we figured we could figure it out as we went. Two years later, we had our first bag, fittingly called the Core, up for sale on the website. A year later, we had expanded the line, with two more bags, each with its own unique purpose, and had already been featured in two top fitness publications, *Oxygen Magazine* and the German edition of *Shape*.

Another interesting twist to the story is that upon our arrival in California, by a seemingly random sequence of occurrences, Ryan was able to land a job, which has given us the opportunity to continue to grow our fitness bag and lifestyle brand, Live Well 360, organically without investment funding.

Looking back, this all sounds so surreal. How do things like this all come together? It all sounds so easy and effortless. Well, it wasn't. I will be straight with you: it was hard. It took all the faith I had and then some that somehow, someway things would work out.

There were many stressful nights and fearful fights. It's tested our relationship and our sanity, but you know what? It was worth it. We're building a kickass business—together. We live on the beach in sunny Santa Monica, where people flock by the thousands to vacation, and we get to live here.

And none of this would have ever happened had we not had the courage to stand up and say, "Hey, this American dream that I've been chasing, with the thirty-year corporate position and the house with the white picket fence…this is just not for me."

We had the courage to say, "I want more and I trust myself enough to figure out what more means for me"—courage enough to get off the path of seeming stability and take a chance…a chance on ourselves.

We had a willingness to try something new and make mistakes. To be honest, failure has never really been an option in our minds, but we sure had our share of "F-it, we'll never know unless we try" moments.

So I share this with you, not because I am saying that you too should say, "F-it, let's do it," but rather to have the courage to wake up to the voice inside that is guiding you to what you truly want for your life—courage to listen to your internal guidance above all else. You have all of the answers you will ever need; the key is to have the courage to listen and then trust.

Sheila Viers is the cofounder of the premium fitness and yoga bag brand Live Well 360 and the author of the book *ROCK Your Dream Body*. Instead of staying on the traditional "corporate" path out of college, in 2008 Sheila took a leap of faith, leaving her comfy yet unfulfilling job with a Fortune 500 company, to pursue her passion of entrepreneurship and to share her message of living well in every way. Sheila has been featured in top health and fitness publications including Yahoo! Shine, Glo MSN, *FITNESS Magazine*, LiveStrong, FitSugar, and TinyBuddha. To learn more about Sheila, visit LiveWell360.com or SheilaViers.com.

FROM DESTRUCTIVE TO DAZZLING
Goddess Star Monroe

How do you turn your life around when everything is falling apart around the seams? How do you step up and step out when your self-belief and your self-worth is in shatters? How do you make positive choices when your life has been built on one mistake after another? How do you fall in love with yourself when you have spent the past thirty-seven years hating yourself?

Hello, gorgeous one. My name is Goddess Star Monroe, and I am honored to share my story with you—my story that took me from absolutely destructive to beautifully dazzling. You see, I nearly ruined my life with my destructive behaviors, but over the past five years, I have rebuilt my life on my terms: I have created a life, a body, and a mind that I am totally in love with.

So make yourself a cup of tea, snuggle up on the couch, get comfy, and let me tell you more.

My earliest memory of self-hate was when I opened the *Vogue* Beauty Bible and it said that to be a true woman you had to have three perfect ovals between your legs when standing with your legs together and you had to be able to rest a ruler across your hips bones when lying down. Well, that was it for me—this was the ideal I strived for in my early teenage years. Enter in my first eating disorder—anorexia and a ton of self-hate (bulimia came later in my twenties).

Not only did I battle with my body image, I was bullied nonstop at school. My parents did nothing really to help, so I cocooned myself into my own fantasy world and stopped speaking to anyone. I become shy, defensive, and so very unhappy. I really didn't know what to do to make it better. (Does any teenager really know how to make a situation like this better?)

As I moved through my teenage years, the anorexia slipped away, and I slowly emerged out of myself. Outwardly I became more confident, but inside I was still a vulnerable mess of insecurities and doubts.

When I hit seventeen, I discovered boys and alcohol, and boy did I discover them! I spent my weekends and most of the weeknights drunk and sleeping with random men. I was a lost soul, and I was searching, searching for love, and I equated sex with love. Needless to say, this left me empty, alone, and with my self-esteem in tatters. But instead of facing up to my deep feelings, I carried on masking the pain by drinking more and partying hard.

As I moved into my twenties, I met my future husband. I still am not sure if you really know what love is at twenty, but we "fell in love" and traveled the world.

Looking back, my life was a whirlwind, and I never really had the chance to stop and really look at what I wanted. To be honest, the thought of looking at what I wanted never really crossed my mind.

So in my mid-twenties I walked up the aisle in Las Vegas and married this man. I vividly remember saying to myself as I said my vows that I really didn't love this man but thought, "Hey, it will all be OK."

We were married for four years and had a child together, but eventually the marriage broke down and we split up when I was thirty.

So there I was at thirty suddenly free and very wild. On one hand I was happy, but on the other hand I was so lost. So what did I do?

That's right, I discovered alcohol again, and this time I added a class A drug—cocaine.

Enter my super destructive years. From the ages of thirty to thirty-seven, I absolutely destroyed my life. I partied hard all the time, and I became addicted to cocaine and became an alcoholic. I was drinking two bottles of wine a day and got into the habit of taking two sleeping tablets a night.

I was overspending on all my credit cards, and my intimate relationships were appalling. I moved from one abusive boyfriend to another. I got beaten up, talked to like I was worthless, and walked over time and time again.

My life hit rock bottom when I found myself on a hotel floor, curled up in a fetal position. Let me say at this point I was using one gram of cocaine a day and drinking two bottles of wine, and I was in yet another abusive relationship and was addicted to sleeping tablets.

When I was lying on the floor, I looked at myself from above and just saw what destruction I was causing, not only to myself but to my son too. At that moment I decided that enough was enough, and I knew that I had to make some changes. I just knew that I couldn't go on anymore. The pain was too fierce and the reality of me doing this for another year, if not more, scared me senseless.

So within the next two weeks, I stopped drinking and stopped the cocaine, and I did this myself without the help of any addiction therapy or group.

Now, gorgeous one, I'm not sure where you are in your life, but let me tell you: anything is possible when you put your mind to it and decide that you want to change. People often ask me how I did it, and my reply is always "I just made a decision to do it." I was strong, I dug deep into my reserves of womanly strength, and I formulated a beautiful plan of action that kept me going when times were tough.

I still remember the date. It was July 1, 2008. I marked it on my calendar and said that this was the start of my new life. I started to journal daily. After years of locking away my feelings, all my thoughts, fears, and emotions came spilling out. I was committed to writing daily, and I believe that this practice really helped me to not only face up to my fears, but to start to get to know who I really was and what I really wanted in life.

I also set myself three daily rituals that I could do time and time again. These were to get out of bed at eight every day, to make a green juice, and to walk my dog. I also started to say to myself, almost mantra-like, that I was a lovely woman, I deserved love, and that I am loved. After years and years of self-hate and self-destruction, this was like a balm to me. And over a period of three to six months, I started to believe these words for the first time in my life.

I also decluttered my life. You know nature abhors a vacuum, right? I totally decluttered my house (and made a fortune on eBay!), I decluttered my friends—I only wanted to be surrounded by amazing people—I dumped the abusive boyfriend I had, and I started to properly cleanse and nourish my body.

Now, I'm not saying this path from destructive to dazzling was easy, but the above practices (which you can do) really supported me and gave me the energy and motivation to continue. One other practice that totally transformed my life was monthly goal-setting. I used to get a friend around, and we would have fun creating glittery, gorgeous goal boards each month. Having a goal—a purpose—really, really helped.

So, let's fast-forward to today, and do you know what?

I have completely created a life that I love. I honor that I cannot have too much stress in my life. I create, work, and live much better when I am calm. I have an adorable mini-empire where I mentor women and teach them how to tap into their womanly superpowers. I spend soooo much time with my son, and we have a supersonic bond that is just exquisite. I am surrounded by yummy friends, and I have absolutely fallen in love with who I am as a woman.

I could have easily let everything in my past destroy me, but I decided to use my past mistakes to my advantage. They are, indeed, what has made me a strong, beautiful, and wise woman.

So, gorgeous one, I want to let you know that whatever you have done in your past, let it go and forgive yourself. Understand that it happened for a reason. You are an extraordinary person with unique gifts that the world needs to see, feel, and hear. I am on your side. I'm cheering for you. And remember, anything is possible. xo

Goddess Star Monroe is a mistress of womanly superpowers and RED HOT confidence expert, combining confidence with common sense and a delicious dose of glamour. She has over twenty-one years of experience crafting deeply feminine coaching programs that combine powerful and wise philosophies, sensual dance, and ardent self-love amplification. She is a former competitive figure athlete and professional showgirl, a published author, and an inspirational speaker with added va-va-voom. To learn more about Star, visit GoddessStarMonroe.com.

THE MOST COURAGEOUS THING YOU'LL EVER DO... JUST BE YOU
Stephenie Zamora

"It takes courage to grow up and become who you really are." – E. E. Cummings

We're all born unique and beautiful individuals. We have our own talents, opinions, and views of the world. It's absolutely remarkable how amazing and different we all are, yet many of us work so hard to conceal our beautiful nature—simply because we feel different.

As a young girl, I was very introverted, wildly imaginative, deeply troubled, and highly creative. I would ponder possibilities, dream and scheme, write for hours, and make art just for the sake of making something. It felt like any time I was alone in my room, magic would happen.

When it came to being anywhere else with pretty much anyone, I felt like I didn't belong. I felt different, so I did my best to fly under the radar. I had my few friends and did the occasional mall hangouts and sleepovers, but mostly I kept to myself. That is, I kept my TRUE self, to myself.

Honestly, as far back as I can remember, I felt out of place. It was very apparent that I saw the world in a much different way. I didn't care about the things everyone cared about, and I didn't want to do what they wanted to do. I didn't understand them, but worse, I didn't understand myself. Because of this, I worked very hard to conceal my truth. I developed a talent for always keeping the spotlight on everyone else, along with an artful avoidance of sharing anything I thought, felt, or desired.

All of my talents, opinions, strengths, and beliefs were only exposed in the safety of my room. Before long, though, it was time to move out and head to college. I moved in with my high school sweetheart, and suddenly I no longer had the safety of my own space to let my truth free. I was now living and sharing a six hundred square foot apartment with a man I loved, but who didn't really know me inside and out. Being the master I was at keeping my truth tucked safely inside, it was impossible for anyone to really know and see me.

Between college, my part-time jobs, and working to create a life living with someone else, I completely lost sight of what made me ME—my beliefs, my depth, my soul, and my creative expression. I stopped writing, only created when homework for my design degree required it of me, and I stopped journaling. I fell into a whole new world...one that found me striving to be the best and most accomplished. This drive gave me a false sense of purpose.

By the time I was twenty-one, I'd graduated from college at the top of my class, I had an amazing job at a local graphic design firm, and I had a brand new townhouse, a boyfriend of almost seven years, and a shiny little car in my own name. I had built myself the perfect little life.

The trouble is, when you build a life around a false purpose (one that is usually created by trying to fit into what you think you should be), you wind up completely losing sight of yourself. In my case, I ended up deeply depressed, lost, confused, stressed out, and overwhelmed by the obligations that came with the life I created. I had to keep the job I no longer felt was right for me to keep the house I'd purchased with someone I now knew wasn't "the one." I felt trapped, yet clueless as to what I'd even want to with myself instead.

Then one day, with nothing left to do and no more tears to give, I started to write. It was an anonymous blog, but it served as a space for me to explore what I was REALLY feeling. I wrote about feeling lost and unhappy. I wrote through the many chaotic changes I'd thrown myself into in an attempt to "get happy." I wrote through my breakup and diving into a new relationship.

I wrote about what I thought I wanted...how I didn't really know, but that I knew there was more to life than all the "accomplishments" I'd racked up. I began to dream of the life I'd left behind and wanted to recreate—one where I was expressive, creating, spiritual, and deep.

Before long, I started drawing. Again, so used to hiding myself from the world, I did it without letting anyone know. I doodled and colored simply because I needed to. It's what my soul was crying out for. I started reading creative books, exploring personal development, and learning about spirituality. I bought a real journal and started pouring my heart and soul onto the pages.

It was terrifying every single time I started to share a little bit more of myself with the world, but what I found was almost unbelievable to me...acceptance—love, appreciation, praise. As I opened up about who I was and what I really wanted, my relationship deepened. As I shared more of my art with the world, I found more courage and inspiration to try new things and be more open. As I wrote, I received such love and support for my words and my truth.

The most terrifying moment of my life was creating a blog under my own name. At this point, I was getting pretty good at sharing my truth—MY view of the world—my beliefs, my hopes and dreams, my goals and my experiences. I had found my voice and was sharing my mind—something I'd always worked so hard to hide because I felt like no one would understand me. For months, I published with high levels of anxiety, despite never having actually shared the blog with anyone I knew.

And then one day I worked up the courage to share my words in a very public space. I expected people to make fun of me or knock my opinions and feelings. Instead, I received some of the most loving and supportive comments from friends and family.

The most amazing moments of my life to this date are when people I know and don't know e-mail me to say thank you for sharing MY mind. My view of the world. My beliefs.

My words and work are my truth. They are the bits of me that I thought didn't belong, when really they are what make me unique.

The things that make you different are your truth. They're what make you so unbelievably amazing and special. They're not meant to be hidden! Quite the opposite...they're meant to be shouted from the rooftops and to shine blazingly bright. Because when you step into your truth and you live life as you are, you attract the most amazing, loving, and supportive people. You find your passion and your calling. You do good work in the world. You change lives.

Being who you are can feel scary; I know this better than anyone. But I also know that when you stop hiding and let people see the real you, despite the fear and anxiety it may cause, you will experience love, joy, passion, and fulfillment like you never have before.

I am so grateful for the amazing people, experiences, and opportunities in my life that have come directly from sharing my truth. Don't waste another moment hiding yourself from the world. Shine bright; it's the most courageous thing you'll ever do, but I promise, it is also the most life-changing thing as well.

Stephenie Zamora is the founder of a full-service, life-purpose development, design, and branding boutique. Here she merges the worlds of personal development and branding to help young women build passion-based businesses. Her articles have been featured in The Huffington Post, Yahoo Shine, Positively Positive, and Brian Tracy International. To learn more about Stephenie, visit StephenieZamora.com.

REMIND ME
Sue Ann Gleason

I enter the room and I'm greeted by a blast of heat from the registers that line the wall beside my father's bed. The smell of disinfectant assaults my nose. The sun is bright outside, but the blinds are drawn. I glance at the poinsettia and wonder how it thrives in this dark, oppressive place. It's been two months since I've seen him. He's noticeably thinner. No, that's an understatement. He is emaciated.

He tries to get out of his chair to greet me, but his spindly legs won't hold him. I bend down to give him a hug. "That's OK, Dad," I say. He feels so fragile I can barely stand the embrace.

"Have you eaten today?" I ask.

"Yes, I had breakfast."

"What did you have for breakfast, Dad?"

"Scrambled eggs," he replies.

I note the bottle of Ensure on his end table. There are "doctor's orders" to administer a liquid supplement when he misses a meal. "At least he'll get his vitamins," they say. I imagine taking those little bottles of "Ensure" and hurling them out the window.

"I'm having a little trouble with my leg," he says, interrupting the explosions in my head.

This is new. My dad no longer expresses emotion, desire, wants, or needs. He doesn't complain of pain.

I ask him, "Where does it hurt, Dad?"

He points to his thigh. Well, his femur. There is no longer enough flesh on that bone to call it a thigh. He tries to stand.

"Maybe I should rest," he says, falling back into the chair.

"Yes, you rest a bit longer, Dad," I say. "I'll be right back."

I leave him for a moment and walk down the hall to find the staff member on duty. It's Kay. I feel a slight pang of trepidation. Kay and I had "words" on my last trip. I fear she will resent my questions. Even more than that, I worry that she will not take care of my father in my absence.

"Hi, Kay," I say, approaching. "My dad is complaining of some pain in his left leg. Do you know anything about that?"

"I can't check his leg," she replies briskly. "I can only offer him Tylenol."

"Let's do that," I respond, not knowing what else to say, though the voice inside my head wants to scream out loud, "Please… help me help him."

Kay follows me back to the lonely little room. The threadbare carpets in these halls look nothing like the parquet floor in the front lobby. My father is sitting in his chair with his hat on, ready to go anywhere I wish to take him, but without the strength in his legs to get up.

I ask Kay, "Has he eaten today?"

She replies, "He had some breakfast, but he didn't come down for lunch."

I glance at the clock. It's one thirty.

I ask Kay, "Can we get him some lunch?"

"The only thing we can get him at this point is a ham sandwich," she replies.

"Great! Let's get him a ham sandwich."

She says, "No, he needs to want the ham sandwich." There are RULES in this assisted living facility. They cannot "force" a resident to eat.

I do everything in my power not to leap out of my skin. "Great! Let's ask him if he'd like a ham sandwich."

She turns her back to me and says to my father, "Sam, would you like a ham sandwich?"

He says, "Sure, I'll eat a ham sandwich." I breathe a sigh of relief.

"Let's go down to the dining room and grab that sandwich, Dad," I say hopefully.

I reach for his walker and gingerly lift him out of the chair. His pants slip down and rest on his hipbones.

"Do you have a belt, Dad? Is there a belt we can use to hold those pants up?"

He opens his drawer, one hand on the walker to steady himself. He tries valiantly to get the belt through the loops. I try valiantly to keep from crying as I help him guide it around his too-big pants.

We walk down to the dining room. Kay drops a ham sandwich on the table. My father picks it up. I note the band spinning around a knobby finger on his left hand. I try not to think about the day he called me to say, "Your mother is kicking me out."

"The sandwich is very cold," he says, a look of confusion crossing his face.

"We keep them in the refrigerator," Kay replies hastily.

"Can you toast it?" he asks, hope in his voice.

She grabs the sandwich and takes it to the microwave. My heart leaps. He actually expressed a need. This is big. My father rarely asks for anything anymore.

Kay returns with the sandwich. She takes the opportunity to show him the dinner menu. "What would you like for dinner, Sam," she asks. "Meatloaf or chicken?"

His eyes look to mine, as if to say, "What do I want? Remind me, Sue Ann, what do I like to eat?"

My heart cracks open. Everything, Dad. You used to eat everything.

Epilogue

The dictionary defines courage as the "ability to confront fear, pain, danger, uncertainty, or intimidation." For me, courage meant listening to my intuition and being fiercely committed to finding the best possible situation for my dad, even in the face of adversity.

After seven weeks in Colorado, I moved through mountains of bureaucratic red tape and finally got my father placed in a much better elder care facility.

This wasn't about fighting the system. There was no giant act of bravery here. Instead, the fortitude to find my father a new home lay in a series of small daily choices to stay the course and stand firmly in my power as his daughter. Courage was acting with intention, humor, and heart.

Two months later, my ninety-year-old father was released from hospice care. He had gained nine pounds and was, once again, eating chocolate for breakfast. But this time, in a room with a view.

Sue Ann Gleason is a food lover, food writer, and food-based healer. Founder of the Well-Nourished Woman, she inspires women to trust their intuition, unravel their food stories, and take back their plates, one luscious bite at a time. Her entertaining, cutting-edge articles on nourishment, the psychology of eating, and the blissful benefits of chocolate have appeared in various publications, most recently *Oprah Magazine*, as well as her own eco-friendly blog *Chocolate for Breakfast* (ChocolateforBreakfast.com). To learn more about Sue Ann, visit ConsciousBitesNutrition.com.

YOU WERE BORN TO SHINE
Tracey Selingo

There is a seed of courage nestled in your soul between the seeds of love and hope. The three grow in unison from the minute your soul enters your body.

Their roots tangle together, forcing their way below the depths of your surface, creating a profound dependency on each other to survive.

The only time you become certain of their growth is the minute you think it's not within you.

This is the power of absence, of discovering truth in trust, light in darkness, strength in weakness.

Courage shines its light effortlessly in fight or flight, in your not knowing what you're made of. It rises to your surface in your rescue of self.

It does this effortlessly in your abandonment of ego. That's the nut: the minute you're willing to put aside any notion of pomp and circumstance you give courage the ability to thrive with love and hope.

Love and hope feed courage. Courage feeds love and hope. It's impossible to have one without the other. And so the minute you realize that fact, then you realize how much you have within you.

Most people can measure their love and hope levels, but courage eludes them. And that's only because you don't know how much courage you have until you need to use it. Using it is like calling a power from within. It requires a willingness to empower it, and in doing so you empower yourself.

Consider the amount of love you're willing to give to anyone—a family member, a lover, a child, a friend, a neighbor—then why not imagine your courage level equal or greater to that? If you can imagine hope in the same way... what's there?

That's all it takes (written with a wink and a smile). It's really not imagining as much as it's conjuring—conjuring the fire to erupt within your heart.

This starts by rubbing love and hope together. And that takes trust. Trust in the ability to move from spark to fire. Trust in the sustainability of yourself. Trust that there is a divine source that can ignite your desire to thrive.

Courage isn't about survival, but survival is about courage. When you are surviving, you're tapping into the potential of your courage. Survival is evidence that is there with or without your aid. It's what happens when the divine takes over when you're not strong enough to thrive.

Courage is stepping into your survival mode, acknowledging and allowing strength to well up or spring forth. It's handing yourself over to the power of belief that you can shine. That you will shine. That you were born to shine.

And you were. Source your love. Embrace your hope. Power through.

Tracey Selingo is a promise-spinner, truth-seeker, and creative solopreneur with a fierce love for empowering communication, mainly yours. She helps people discover their soulprint full of promise. To learn more about Tracey, visit TraceySelingo.com.

EVERYTHING YOU WANT IS ON THE OTHER SIDE OF FEAR
Liz Dennery Sanders

Most of us are spending way too much time in our comfort zone. We cling to the familiar, the commonplace, what we already know.

Anything of value, anything worth doing that's going to make a real impact, often brings up fear. If you want to make a dent in the universe, you need to get out of your comfort zone.

If you're not feeling fear in some area of your life, you're probably not challenging yourself, let alone going to change the world.

After a decade of running my own PR and marketing firm, I founded SheBrand because I want to help other women find their voice, step into their power, and be successful. Philanthropically, I've been working with underserved women and girls for more than twelve years and have loved seeing them have lightbulb moments.

When I realized that I could use my expertise and experience to actually change lives for the better, I went back to school for my coaching certification to hone my skills and add more tools to my toolbox.

Yet almost four years later, I found I could only work with so many women at once. Given the nature of our work together, I discovered that I could best serve about seven or eight women in any given month.

How could I fulfill my vision of helping thousands of women if I could only work directly with a small number?

I saw others scaling their businesses by developing group programs, putting together workshops, and taking on speaking engagements. It was certainly the next stage of growth and made perfect sense to me.

But I was petrified. Some days, I still am.

I've never been completely comfortable in the spotlight. PR and marketing was always a cinch for me because it's about promoting someone or something else. I got to use my well-honed people skills and communications strengths and stay right where I was most comfortable: behind the scenes.

It was easy for me to stay there—but it wasn't of service to me, or to the women I wanted to serve.

The SheBrand community has been asking me to offer a group program for a couple of years now. But I have shied away from it—found excuses not to move forward—for fear of putting my voice out there in a bigger way. Fear of it not being well-received, or, God forbid, not perfect.

The irony is not lost on me that one of the things I help my clients do best—connect to their voice and step into their power as entrepreneurs—is something that I myself struggle with.

One of my business coaches and collaborators calls it kryptonite. It's the thing that happens to be one of your superpowers in working with others, but it's also a great personal challenge.

There's an old saying: "We teach what we ourselves most need to learn." I would add that we often hide from those things that are our greatest opportunities for growth.

How often have you found yourself making excuses to not do something, even though, if you were to really tap into your intuition, you knew it was the exact thing you should be doing to take you to the next level?

There's a reason that certain things or certain situations make us uncomfortable. We often retreat from the things that scare us the most.

And why do they scare us?

Marianne Williamson once wrote, "Our deepest fear is not that we are inadequate. Our deepest fear is that we are powerful beyond measure. It is our light, not our darkness, that most frightens us."

We all carry a certain amount of insecurity and self-doubt, and those fearful thoughts tend to rear their ugly heads when we're about to embark on anything new.

Anyone who tells you that they've never had a thought like, "Who am I to be doing this," or "I'm just not good enough," is lying through their pearly-white veneers.

You'll never completely get over fear. A shift in perception would be to consider it your friend. The way I look at it now is if I'm feeling anxious and fearful, it's often a positive signal that I need to get to the other side of something.

It's all about using a muscle that you haven't used before. Once you start, it strengthens and the fear subsides.

As you build your confidence at trying new things, it actually becomes easier to do them. It doesn't mean that the fear completely goes away; it just means that you become more adept at managing it.

The real secret is not to eliminate fear, but to make peace with it. In other words, you have to learn how to amicably cohabitate with the enemy.

These feelings are nothing more than a signal that you're about to learn, grow, and step out of your comfort zone. It also means you're about to make a creative contribution to the world. And what a loss it would be for us if you decide to recoil, fearful of what we might see if you give us what you've got.

Fear comes as a teacher bearing gifts. If you are open to the lessons and can get past your own resistance, you could make a dent in the universe and get exactly what you want, while making a difference in the lives of others along the way.

I'm happy to report that my first group program, The Awesome Brand, served thirty women entrepreneurs with much success over a six-week period earlier this year.

Did I feel fear putting it together and presenting the material? Hell, yeah.

Did I push through to the other side? You bet.

Now that I've exercised that muscle, I'm ready to step out of my comfort zone once again.

I hope you'll join me.

Liz Sanders is a brand and creative strategist, personal development coach, and the founder of She Brand, a global online business dedicated to helping women entrepreneurs build their confidence, their brands, and their bank accounts. As the past chair of the Los Angeles Board of Directors for Step Up Women's Network and a founding member of the organization's Luminary Circle, Liz pens the monthly column "Step Up To Success" for Step Up's national newsletter. She is also a regular contributor to MariaShriver.com. To learn more about Liz, visit SheBrand.com.

QUALIFICATION: PAIN
Vanessa Katsoolis

I sometimes go back to that little house in Palm Beach in my mind. I can see the waxy shine on the leaves of the peace lily that sits on the small wooden table in the living room and can smell the oil finish on the new chopping board, and I can hear the gate tap, tap, tap against the latch in the wind.

It is a Monday and my son is sitting at his drums and trying to reach the pedal of the bass drum with his little toes, and the blond curls that hug his ears are blowing back because the door is open and the breeze is inviting itself in.

I am standing back from the kitchen sink because my seven-month pregnant belly is getting in my way, and while I slowly wash the dishes, I plan the suicide in my mind.

By Friday night I will be no more, and the relief of that thought is so overwhelming that I smile and sigh and feel such a peace.

I had suggested that my husband take our son camping for the weekend, and he took to the idea without hesitance, not picking up on my uncharacteristic excitement, not raising his eyebrows at my overzealousness, not discerning that something was very, very wrong.

I tell him he will have fun and that Asa will enjoy the trip, and I decide I will commit the suicide late on Friday night, as that way they will be far, far away, and even if it were to rain and they returned early on the Saturday, it would be too late and I would be very, very gone.

The baby in my stomach moves around, and I don't feel any regret or love or sadness or shame. The fact I am pregnant with my second son does not deter me from the plan any more than the fact I had just bought new shampoo. It was a shame, perhaps a waste, but nothing more.

My world had disappeared long before this day, and I had been breathing in and out and eating and sleeping, but I wasn't really there. The lights were on but no one was home.

I needed something from the store, so I put my son in his pram and we make our way up the street. The sun is very hot, and I remember thinking that sunscreen isn't important for me anymore because sunburn doesn't matter when you have a few days left to live.

The last thing I remember is squinting my eyes at the brightness of the sun reflecting off the shiny grill of a large approaching truck, and then there is blackness.

There is a flash of me in a medical kind of room on a chair. I have a tissue in my hand, and I can feel a tear dripping off my chin, and then it is black again.

Suddenly I am back in my house sitting on the lounge chair with my hands folded in my lap, and I am watching the door, waiting for them to come. The knock finally comes, and my husband looks at me, sees I am not getting up to answer, and wrinkles his forehead at me, confused.

At the door are two men with clipboards and name tags. Somberness stands beside them ready to invade the house with its heaviness.

The next hour is occupied by the mental health interventionists recounting the story of my breakdown to my husband while he sits, staring at me in disbelief. He shakes his head as they speak of the suicide, the mental illness, and how it's been years now and I never told a soul.

I must have given them this information, but I don't remember when. Maybe when I was in that office holding that tissue…wherever that was.

The next few months are broken pieces of memory.

There are appointments with a man who wears a white coat and gives me the pills, which make me tired and cause my jaw to clench up in the mornings and chatter uncontrollably at night. Arrangements for me to fly home to New Zealand to be with my mother are made immediately.

So, at seven months pregnant, halfway up Palm Beach Avenue, on the Gold Coast of Australia at about 11:00 a.m. on a Wednesday morning, after many years of battling a deep and unrelenting depression, I had a nervous breakdown.

The factors that contributed to developing such a life-threatening mental illness were a series of utterly unbearable circumstances and events and crimes, which I never spoke of. I carried the memories of them on my shoulders, but the burden took its toll and it was my mind that paid the price for it.

I didn't want to speak of any of it because I didn't want anyone to ever think I wasn't coping, that I wasn't happy. I wanted people to think that I had it together, that I wasn't a failure.

I hated the circumstances that made me sick. I hated the memories of nights sitting in my car at the top of hills trying to muster the nerve to drive off the cliff because I couldn't bear life anymore.

I wondered if things would ever get better, if there could possibly be a purpose in my suffering. But what good could possibly come from living through circumstances so painful that you no longer have any hope that anything will ever be any better and that the pain will never subside and you don't want to live anymore. What good could possibly come from that?

Years later I am in the living room of the psych ward where I am doing my clinical placement for my nursing degree. I notice a new face come in through the doors. The woman seems small, and not because she is short or slim, but because she is shrinking into herself. Her arms are trembling, and she looks lost and afraid. There is a cannula in her arm, which means she has been treated medically in another ward and is now being transferred to us.

I bet she took an overdose.

After she scribbles her name on the bottom of the forms, she is left alone and she drifts into the living room and takes a seat beside me. After a few minutes, I turn to her. "Hello, my name is Vanessa. I am one of the nurses."

She looks at me and bursts into tears. "I don't know why I'm here. I took so many pills, and I don't know why. What's wrong with me?"

She is shaking her head, and I put my hand on her arm and I tell her, "It's OK. I know, I know."

And in that moment I realize that I do know. I recognize that frightened look on her face because I have seen the same one looking back at me in my own mirror. I understand the confusion of having someone tell you that you tried to take your own life and sitting there thinking, "This isn't me…is it? This isn't the real me…" And what that woman needed right in that moment was not someone who had been studying at university and would practice using the fancy new mental health terminology she had been memorizing for months; she needed someone to grab her by the arm and say, "I know."

There are thousands of degrees to choose from at hundreds of universities—degrees that will teach you how to write or how to build a business or degrees that will teach you how to protect someone's legal rights and degrees like mine where you learn how to make people well.

But, reader, listen to me…There is no qualification quite like pain.

Experiencing deep and wrenching pain qualifies you in a way that no book or course or degree could ever hope to do because the memory of your pain and the way you may have beat at the walls with your fists at night with tears burning the makeup off your cheeks and demanding that God tell you what the meaning of this cruel and horrible circumstance in your life was, gives you a unique insight and compassion that enables you to take hold of someone who is falling apart beside you and say, "I've been there."

Today I am no longer angry about the circumstances that led me to the breakdown that nearly cost me my life. I know now that every last shred of compassion and love that I have the ability to feel is because I have known brokenness.

I am glad it happened, and if I could live my life again, I would not change one thing, not even the worst of my suffering because it has become the best part of me. It is the only reason I know compassion and probably love.

As a people we don't typically speak of our pain. If we have suffered, or are suffering, we habitually keep it behind closed doors.

Even you as you read this may have friends that you have known for a good part of your life that have no idea you are sleeping in a separate bed to your wife, that the house is getting sold by the bank because you lost your job, that you had a miscarriage, or that you were abused as a child…but if you keep it to yourself and pile it upon your shoulders never to speak of it again, then it all happened for nothing. There is no fruit, and that is when it really does become tragic.

When we are facing something unbearable, we want to speak to someone who has been there, who has been bruised the same way and has survived so that we can have hope, and yet no one talks about it, and so the suffering believe they are suffering alone.

I feel deeply sorry that it took me having to sit in the middle of a psych ward to realize that my pain and heartbreak is what makes me able to feel compassion and understanding for others who are weak and that it is a wonderful privilege.

I feel sorry for every person up until this point I may have been able to help had I just spoken about my own experience with depression, suicide, tears, disappointment, and pain but didn't because I wanted everyone to think I was coping just fine.

I wrote this because while it is lovely for people to praise you for your strength, I would much prefer someone draw comfort or hope from my survival.

Everyone has a story, but the pain you are going through or the pain you have gone through in the past may very well be your highest qualification and a qualification the world desperately needs because you have no idea what it means to be in the depths of despair and have someone grab you by the arm and tell you "It's OK…I know."

With her blog *One Thousand Single Days,* Australian-based blogger Vanessa Katsoolis has turned into a rising star on the blogosphere. Writing personal stories about her upbringing in a bohemian Kiwi-Greek family and about her self-created challenge—staying single and celibate for one thousand days until March 14, 2015—Vanessa has found unexpected success in writing, with the blog being read over one hundred thousand times in 140 countries just four months since her first post hit the Internet. Vanessa's commitment to complete transparency in writing and her willingness to tackle sensitive and taboo subjects head-on invites readers into her heart as she explores her recovery from depression, her survival of abuse, and her discovery of identity and self-esteem. To learn more, visit OneThousandSingleDays.com.

LIVE IN COURAGE AND THRIVE
Debra Oakland

Being a courage advocate is most meaningful to me on this particular journey. Life throws us curveballs appearing as challenges. I have had quite a few thrown at me in my life. We can choose to let them strengthen us or break our spirit. I choose to grow and become strengthened by them, which has led me to talking about courage with others.

After going through so much loss and grief in a six-year period of time, I started thinking about how I could live more courageously. Throughout these many challenges I will talk about, my husband Cody and I supported each other, growing stronger and more resilient together. I feel so much compassion for people going through loss and grief, so I decided to become a courage advocate. I also realized that many people around me didn't understand my perspective on death or the way I dealt with so much loss in my life. I found myself having to be strong for many other people who were falling apart. Maybe that was one of the ways I got through some of the deep grief. After each person passed, beginning with my brother Tim to AIDS, then losing my unborn daughter in the eighth month of pregnancy, my brother Ted to AIDS, my twenty-one-year-old son Wade in a car accident, and my father Jim to cancer, all in a six-year period, the question I consistently asked myself was "What would they want most for me?"

I knew with all my heart and soul they would want me to be happy because they loved me. I believe that love only wants the highest and greatest good for us, and we should want that for ourselves as well. LOVE RULES...LOVE TRUMPS ALL! I decided that since I couldn't bring their physicality back, I could choose to honor each by carrying them in my heart as the precious gift they were. I also decided to be grateful for the time I had with them and to remember the joy we shared when they were here. Now, when I am thinking about any one of them, it always brings a smile to my face. They each continue to bring joy into my life in so many ways, and I have to say I became a better person for knowing them and a stronger, more courageous person in their absence.

Tell the people you love that you love them because you never know the moment they will be gone. Stop worrying about the little things that are so inconsequential and direct your attention to what truly matters. Love yourself for who you are and give yourself permission to FORGIVE those who have hurt or harmed you in any way. Forgiveness sets you free! It really does. I am living proof, as is my mother and all who embrace forgiveness in their life.

I believe that courage is constancy under the most trying of circumstances and action at the moment when it is needed most. Work with the principles of life that are your true nature. Play the game of life with determination to live in joy. Courageously maneuver yourself into a positive state of mind. As you become a courageous, thriving individual playing the game of life, become a messenger, a living example to others. You will be able to provide your family and friends with insight as to how you thrive. This encouragement will spread from you and others out into the world. This provides invaluable wisdom into how to play the game of life, where everyone wins. Inspire greatness in yourself, share it, and people will pass it on.

The original definition of the word "courage" came into the English language from Old French *corage*, derived from the Latin word *cor*, meaning heart: to tell the story of who you are with your whole heart. My deepest wish is for us all to live courageously from the heart. I can't think of a better place to live from. We're incredibly powerful beings, and yet, as Sting sings, "how fragile we are." There's a bridge between being broken and living in power. We get to choose which side of the bridge to be on and who we'll assist to the other side. It takes courage to believe in ourselves, to be our true authentic selves, never apologizing for who we are. If we can create a spiritual space inside ourselves, a place where we can overcome life's biggest challenges, we'll truly begin to thrive in courage. By navigating the bumps in the road wisely, joy becomes a very good travel partner.

Here is my personal definition of courage: I see courage as the will to act from the strength and power within the heart. Courage is a quality you gain through overcoming life's biggest challenges and something you become through experience. Living a courageous life happens when we allow the true essence of who we are to rise up and shine for all the world to see, regardless of other people's opinions. Courageous individuals who are true to themselves feel a powerful resolve that's unshakable, a true conviction of purpose, a willingness to carry on in the face of any challenge.

Courage is required, down to the very fiber of our existence. Use your will, desire, and persistence to develop the qualities you need to materialize your dreams, whether they are mental, physical, or spiritual.

Debra is a courage advocate, writer, and joy-full experiencer. Debra became a courage advocate through the loss of many immediate family members over a six-year period. Feeling so much compassion for people going through loss and grief, Debra decided to create a website called Living in Courage Online - "A Spiritual Oasis for Overcoming Life's Biggest Challenges." To learn more about Debra, visit LivingInCourageOnline.com.

STRENGTH

"In the end, some of your greatest pains become your greatest strengths."

– Drew Barrymore

SHAME HELPED ME FIND STRENGTH
Charly Emery

It is often during our darkest times that we discover the creative power and strength we have within. Like a lifeline in the sea of our emotions, we must grasp it with all we've got. For no matter how rough the waters become, we will indeed reach the shore. We will have also gathered the strength needed to rise to greater heights along the way. This I learned firsthand, and if there's one thing I want you to know, it's that no matter what you've endured in life, you can recycle it into strength and insight that will propel you forward in ways you may have never dreamed possible.

The scuffed beige floors looked virtually colorless as I sat between the aisles crumbled by shame against a mirrored column in the store. I can still see the clothing hanging on the racks just above my head and the dust bunnies dancing around me as the tears streamed down my face. Two incidences of rape had taken ownership of my life, my dreams, and my body. I'd been hiding in a well-designed reality that was not mine for more than five years at this point. Now, in a surprising twist, the shame of disregarding myself was about to become my savior and connect me with the strength I didn't know I had.

Infinitely curious and passionately provoked by thought, I traversed my college campus with determination and excitement about what I'd learn to contribute to the world. I never saw the assault during my sophomore year coming. After that first rape, I took my education and college experience away from me. It would be less than a year later, during a night of underage drinking with friends, that I'd be raped again. After this second attack, I took the rest of my dreams and desires for my future away from me. I didn't believe I deserved them anymore. Then, in an effort to conceal what I'd been through, I created a false persona to convince everyone I was still designing my future. Who knew I'd begin to believe the illusion as well. Now huddled in a heap on the floor, my attempt to flee from someone the old me had known, acquainted me more intimately than ever with the shame thriving inside me.

We often assign negative connotations to emotions when in truth emotions are simply beacons that we can use to strengthen our awareness of ourselves. It's the conclusions and beliefs we create from those emotions that pose the actual threat. That day, shame was my savior. In feeling its intensity, I was acquainted with the desire to free myself of that heart-wrenching pain. I'd packed more than forty-five pounds onto my petite five-foot-two frame. Now my safe shell of a hiding place had become a prison I was desperate to escape from. Hence, I joined a weight loss center and began to exercise my way to strength.

I've learned that transforming your life happens in stages with certain steps providing platforms on which you can gain the additional strength you'll need for the next part of your journey that you may not expect. This is precisely what happened on my path through weight loss. With every pound and every inch, my feelings about myself began to change, not because of how I looked, but because of the effort I was investing in me to achieve the results. By the time I celebrated my twenty-fifth birthday, I had reached my fitness goals. I had recycled my feelings of shame into desire and then recycled my desire to escape that shame into a new level of strength and self-confidence. It was a triumphant time, though I had no idea what I had actually been preparing myself for.

In the midst of our struggles, we often isolate ourselves, believing we don't belong, when in truth, our experiences, fears, and imperfections unite us. I've learned that you can connect with others to grasp a sense of strength or find your strength and then use it to reach out to others. Whichever way you go about it, sharing that strength is the most powerful way to deepen and further develop it. I hid under oversized T-shirts and avoided eye contact until I realized that including others in my quest empowered me to achieve my results even faster. Doing so helped me take ownership of my weight challenge. It turned my focus toward what I was accomplishing and away from what I had or hadn't done in the past. This is powerful for healing and transforming any aspect of your life. This lesson came just in time for the next stage I didn't see coming.

The post-traumatic episodes started four months after my twenty-fifty birthday. From waking up with mysterious symptoms that left me virtually paralyzed with pain to debilitating migraines that increased in frequency, I was terrified. The strength I'd gained from losing my extra weight and building my confidence had prepared me to face my past. These symptoms were signs that my memories were about to reemerge. When they did, the truth felt like a double-edged sword. On one side I was finally free to be my real self, and on the other I had built an entire life that included a marriage I could no longer sustain. Clutching to the strength I'd developed, I began asking myself who I wanted to be and in essence already was…

Two more of the greatest tools for building strength are honesty and self-forgiveness. When I looked at my actions closely with honesty, I realized that I'd mistakenly believed I could no longer be the person I wanted to be or enjoy the life I wanted to have after being raped. This awareness increased my strength because I knew that if I changed my beliefs I could create new results just as powerfully. What beliefs did you change about you after enduring a challenge?

We're also often quick to judge ourselves for things we did yesterday using wisdom we have today that we didn't have at the time. Do you need to forgive yourself and accept that you did the best you could at that time? I learned that if I was going to heal and build a fulfilling life, I had to give myself permission. That meant

I had to forgive myself for what I'd done to me, in addition to how I'd included others in my attempts to survive after trauma, so I could finally stop the process of re-victimizing myself. This journey was not as easy as losing weight, yet using my shame, sadness, desire, honesty, and forgiveness gave me the strength to transform my life, heal my wounds, and touch people's lives in ways I couldn't have imagined. You can use your emotions to access your strength in the same way.

You don't need to possess strength to build it or find strength to use it. By giving yourself permission to be your best self and find out who that is, strength will reveal itself to you and stay with you throughout your journey. By owning what you've been through and using it to give you a voice instead of silencing you, your inner strength will reveal itself to you. I believe that emotional baggage is the accumulation of lessons not yet learned just waiting to be transformed into arrows of insight that you can use to reach your goals. As long as you don't give up, your darkest times will connect you with strength and power you may never have known you had. Grasp it with all you've got and know that no matter what you've been through, the best of life and love await you.

Charly Emery is a personal strategist, author, and TV personality who specializes in recycling your experiences into tools and insights that propel you forward faster. She's a trauma survivor who used her own instincts to transform virtually every aspect of her life before becoming the expert resource for others that she couldn't find. Author of *Thank Goodness You Dumped His Ass—Use Those Mr. Wrongs to Lead You Straight to Mr. Right*, Charly brought her cutting-edge coaching to TV on *Opening Act* and is currently developing a show of her own. Connect with Charly at CharlySense.com.

BEAUTIFULLY BROKEN: FINDING STRENGTH THROUGH LOSS
Amy E. Smith

It was May 2007, but I remember it as if it were yesterday. My lovely and frail father was hooked up to a multitude of cords and contraptions in this cold and icy intensive care unit. He was still and quiet…the life slowly slipping from his body. The doctors had informed us that there was no longer a choice to be made. They had done everything in their power. It was now simply a matter of time. We had one hour—one hour to see if he would miraculously respond to the desperate medication administered or one hour to say our good-byes, the latter being the more probable of outcomes.

I sat there by his bedside, consumed by my own humanity, feeling the weight of sorrow and grief, the anxiousness of loss at my heart's doorstep. My mother was on the opposite side of him, reading scripture as her way of processing the end. A few days earlier they had celebrated their thirty-year wedding anniversary. So many of life's chapters they had lived out together, side by side. Partners. And now he was nearly gone. My brothers were sitting in silence, heads in hands, handling the weight of this day in the only way they knew how…as twentysomething boys tend to do. Just silent.

The clock was ticking. The second hand felt like a heartbeat, slowly decreasing in speed while simultaneously growing louder in volume.

We were told that he would most likely flatline before us…his body no longer able to push through the trauma of such assistance in survival. Surely it wouldn't be much longer. I was heavy. Heavy with anxiety. And fear. Sadness and grief. I vacillated between wanting it all to end and wanting to hang on forever.

He had lived such an incredibly rich life. He had influenced many in his life's work. He was a genius father, husband, and teacher. He was at peace with the beautiful legacy he could potentially leave behind.

In preparation for his fourteen-hour surgery, I had asked him, "Are you scared?" Surely he must have had trepidations as he prepared for a rigorous spinal surgery designed to prevent his near folding in half—a surgery that would interrupt his destined path of slowly suffocating over the next five years. I'll never forget his humble response. He looked at me calmly, his eyes smiling as they always did, and he replied, "I suppose if my purpose was to simply live this life here on earth, then I guess I would be scared. But I know that it's not."

What strength my father had. What a profound ability to see past his limited human shell—a shell plagued with polio in the 1950s… one that prevented him to swim and run like others who were able-bodied. Instead of allowing that body to limit him, it became a vehicle of truth. He crafted the sharp tongue of his youth (his defensive against aggressive peers) into an articulate, passionate portal to express his true calling and gift…his beliefs and convictions of his spirituality—a message that permeated thousands.

Of course, this was hardly my focus as my eyes darted between the constantly decreasing beeping of the hospital machines and the pesky clock on the wall. My focus was, in fact, scattered. I was feeling like I was distant from my own body, my mind repeating over and over, "This isn't happening, this isn't happening."

Then, as if time stood still, the beeping ceased and became one continuous beep. The life force at the end of the cords and contraptions had left this plane of existence. There was no need for the artificial life any longer. He had gone. The life that had just been there was now absent. And it had happened right in front of me. It felt like an eternity. And like a blink of an eye.

The sobering reality began to sink in as I cried and wailed for the loss of my father. I could feel the grief shake me to my core, and my entire being felt alive with the intensity of human emotion. I was shaking and sobbing. I felt volatile and fragile. Surely, this was all just a nightmare and I would awaken at any moment.

In the weeks that followed, my spirituality was ablaze…an internal dialogue like no other. An interesting dichotomy ensued: having extreme anger at the universe and simultaneously wanting to learn my lesson. Although in the depths of despair, I knew I had a very distinct choice: I could either be defined by my circumstance, or I could be defined by how I dealt with it. Victim or survivor. Which was it going to be?

I found it so curious to speak to others about this incident, and they would often comment that they wouldn't ever be able to handle something like this. My retort was always the same: "Prior to this experience, I would have told you the same thing—that I would never be able to deal with losing a parent." The lesson I've learned, however, is that we summon our strength when needed, like a little arsenal we never knew we had.

I realized that I had more strength than I ever knew I possessed. In fact, I was redefining the role of strength in my life. It was a monumental piece of my spiritual journey. As the weeks turned to months, I dove deeper into my questioning around this life-changing experience. What was the meaning? What purpose did it serve? What was I meant to learn? My internal voice answered softly, "Gratitude." I had lived the better part of my life with little to no hardship up until that point, and this experience cloaked me with gratitude. Grateful that I had been there with him. Grateful that he was at peace leaving. Grateful that I had said all I needed to say. And grateful for no regrets.

And as those months have since turned to years, I am still grateful. Grateful to have experienced such an incredible and vibrant father. Beyond honored to watch a soul leave a body. Blessed to feel such extremes of human emotions. And beyond it all, grateful to experience my own capacity of strength. Sometimes it's not about coming out unscathed…It's simply about making it out at all. Celebrating the strength of your survival. Regardless the tribulation, it is always our choice—our choice to create a future riddled with victimhood and sorrow or to create something brilliant. A life defined by strength of character. I, my friends, choose the latter.

In honor of all those who have lost and in doing so have found their strength.

Owner and founder of Joy Junkie Enterprises, Amy Smith is a certified and credentialed individual and couples life coach, speaker, and writer. As a life enthusiast and love advocate, she has been able to move people beyond limiting beliefs and negative self-talk to a place of personal empowerment and self-love. She fervently calls the masses to "Get Your Shit Together" through self-discovery, bravery, and personal empowerment. Hang with Amy at TheJoyJunkie.com.

BEING BENDI
Kristin McGee (the Bendigirl)

I study with an amazing teacher, Nevine Michaan. She has a magical way with words; and she has helped me grow as a yoga teacher, student, and person in so many ways. The one thing she tries to instill in all of her students is how to find our own center then build a circumference around it so we become buoyant and flexible.

Everyone is going to fall in life, and the goal is to learn how to bounce back instead of break. If we can get comfortable with that knowledge, the world is ours to explore and thrive in! We can't prevent the fall, nor do we want to; the magic in life is going out on a limb and bouncing back if that limb breaks.

Yoga is a way for us to become "bendi," not just in our bodies, but also in our minds. If we're rigid in our thoughts, we are rigid in our bodies and vice versa. Yoga lets us explore our edge and find a way to test the boundaries on our sticky mat. Once we push ourselves further in our practice, we find ways to journey into the unknown in our lives.

I truly think that this mindset that we can cultivate over and over again through yoga asana, pranayama, and meditation, can help us in ways beyond imaginable. I am not a doctor or psychologist; but I do think if we can continue to come back to our center, come back to our home and our midline, we can find ways to eliminate the underlying fear inside. It is that fear inside of us all that can lead to problems such as anxiety, depression, eating issues, drug abuse, and relationship troubles.

I've always been an overly sensitive girl, and I found ways to protect myself through my perfectionism and holding myself up to such crazy standards. I would get very anxious about failing that so many times I'd limit myself from truly letting go and enjoying the moment. It's so easy for us to hide behind these mechanisms and think we are protecting ourselves in some way.

When I go to Nevine's or do her practice at home, I find my fear start to melt away. I find that I don't have to hide or try to protect myself from failure and that perfectionism is truly limiting and rigid. The beauty lies in imperfection and finding a deep connection within, an inner smile.

I was nicknamed the Bendigirl years ago by my producer on set when I was shooting my first MTV Yoga DVD. He meant it as a joke since I could bend in so many ways that were incomprehensible to him. The name stuck with me; and it's grown to mean so much more over the years.

My goal is to continue to find my inner "Bendigirl." I want to be flexible on the inside and outside so I can continue to bounce back in life. I want to broaden my circumference and open myself up to amazing circumstances in life. I want to be comfortable falling and find the thrill in bouncing back. I want to share these principles as much as I can when I teach and continue to cultivate them in myself.

* * *

I want to share a simple exercise I learned from Nevine; it has helped me in so many ways.

Sit comfortably in Sukhasana or Virasana and rest your hands on your knees with the palms open to the ceiling, hands in chin mudra. Close your eyes and envision the earth as one giant socket and your sits bones as one giant plug.

Let your mind rest on your breath and imagine an arrow from your heart center shooting down through your perineum to south below you and tap into that support. Make effort by engaging your pelvic floor and feel the energy rising up your spine.

Go back to your heart center and shoot an arrow up above you to north and open up to the grace of the universe that rains down upon you. You don't need to make any effort, just be open and receptive to receive the gifts that are yours.

Next, shoot an arrow from your heart center to east in front of you and see your visions and goals ahead of you in the future. Always make sure to shoot an arrow behind you to the western hemisphere and anchor yourself in your past and your memories and everything that has brought you to this place.

Now find yourself right in the middle of your own universe and expand your breath (the universal ujayii breath) so you can broaden your circumference and open up to all the awesome circumstances in your life. Be bendi, be brave, be bold, and don't be afraid to fall! The universe is here to support you, and if you free yourself up from rigidity or constraints, you'll bounce right back and never be broken.

Kristin McGee is a celebrity yoga and Pilates instructor and personal trainer. She is the star of over one hundred fitness DVDs, a Fila personal performance ambassador, host on HSN, and *Health Magazine*'s contributing yoga and fitness editor. For more information visit KristinMcGee.com

TO BE FULLY SELF-EXPRESSED
Allison Braun

Once upon a time there was a young girl named Allison. She lived in a great neighborhood in the prairies and had two loving parents. Allison was very comfortable in her body and felt strong and curious—curious about sex and sexuality. She didn't learn about any of this from anyone else but seemed to have this innate knowing inside of her.

As Allison got older, she was told by the world and her church that her behavior and curiosities were inappropriate. She didn't like that feeling. She wanted to be approved of by others and to fit in. She thought to herself, "If I express myself, I won't fit in and I will be judged, which hurts, so maybe if I don't expressed myself and just hide out in the background no one will need to judge me."

As she got older, she started to see all these groups of friends laughing and having fun, and that made her feel lonelier than ever before. "Why don't I fit in?" she wondered to herself.

Seeing as she didn't fit in with girls, she started seeking approval from guys instead. Getting the attention she craved from a guy made her feel wanted and appreciated, and it subdued her loneliness. However, she was so addicted to this feeling of belonging that she would sometimes even date guys that she wasn't attracted to.

Soon enough she started longing for more, asking herself, "What is my purpose?" Allison didn't realize at the time how hiding her true self for so long, just to be liked by others, blocked her ability to truly know and appreciate who she really was.

Allison felt extremely anxious about her life, which left her feeling tired, stressed, and generally unhealthy. Something had to change.

One day after wanting to be accepted so badly and being diagnosed with skin cancer, Allison hit her breaking point. She knew she had to change, and so her path of personal growth began. After doing some research, Allison felt drawn to go to school to learn about natural health and energy medicine, but still something was missing…She needed to learn more.

Then a guy started to like her and she thought and felt, "I should be single right now; I don't want to date this guy." He was very convincing, manipulative even. Because Allison had still not gotten to a place of total self-trust, she trusted this guy more than her own intuition.

Her intuition was right, for after dating for a couple months, the drama escalated between them. Allison knew she HAD to end the relationship, but when she did something terrible happened. This guy was so unstable that he completely lost his temper and started punching holes in the walls of her house and locked her inside to witness his breakdown. If it hadn't already been clear enough, she now knew the consequences of not trusting her intuition. This intense experience caused Allison to make a decision; she was going to trust herself once and for all no matter what. She was so scared: "What if I'm myself and people still don't like me for who I really am? What if I'm not good enough? What if I am judged again? What if I never find my purpose? What if I never find a man I truly connect with?" The "what ifs" were running rampant through her mind.

Even though all the questions were causing Allison some stress, they were also propelling her toward her next step in this journey. That's when she came across a women's education-focused product store called Positive Passions. She immediately knew when she applied to work there that this would be the safest place for her to fully express herself, sexuality and all.

Working in this space taught her that connecting to sexuality, even at a young age, was a gift, one that shone when she allowed herself to be fully expressed. The more she embraced this gift, the more she was shown how she could use it to help others; even complete strangers would talk with her about their sex lives and relationships for hours.

Eventually Allison realized that in all those years of trying to figure out her purpose it was right under her nose. Although at first many people she knew didn't understand what she was doing, she felt really liberated and strong on her path. She knew deep down others would benefit from her openness and the safety she provided around this taboo topic of sex.

Allison's true purpose was to be herself, fully self-expressed—sexuality and all—and to empower other women to do the same. When Allison decided to truly be herself, thousands of other women around the world started to benefit. Thousands more women will benefit when each new woman trusts her intuition and lives fully self-expressed and shines who she truly is.

Now when others judge her she has the strength, trust, and knowing to keep going forward—to keep sharing her truth, no matter what others think or say. On top of that, she has now attracted both a loving and supportive husband and friends who celebrate who she is on all levels.

Allison knows that following her path may not always be easy, but with inner strength and knowing along with support from key friends and mentors, there is a greater purpose to it all; that being fully expressed in who you are (sexuality and all) allows you to serve a higher purpose.

Allison Braun, aka The Bedroom Joyologist, helps women (often with a conservative background) let go of guilt and sexual suppression so they can experience the deep connection they desire with a partner—in and out of the bedroom. Having suppressed her sexuality for years, Allison is able to utilize her past experiences, intuition, as well as her extensive background in holistic health and coaching to have you feeling more connection, passion, and playfulness than ever before. To learn more about Allison, visit AllisonBraun.ca.

CHALLENGE ACCEPTED
Amanda Howell

I've been raped. I've been molested. I've been in an abusive marriage. I was assaulted not once, but twice while I was serving my country. But this isn't a story about them. This isn't a story about what happened. This is a story about how I moved on from mere survival into a total life transformation.

Do you know the worst part of being abused? Not knowing you're being abused. It sounds crazy, unless you've been there. They get into your head. They know what you need to hear. But worst of all, they can sense when you're fed up and ready to leave.

Six years ago, I didn't know I was being abused. All I knew was that I was lucky. I was lucky to be with someone who was willing to overlook all my flaws. After all, I couldn't cook or clean. I was stupid and unfunny. And I was the reason that no one came around. But he told me he could overlook all that.

Five years ago, I was out of the bad marriage. But over the next year, I was in bad relationship after bad relationship. One shoved me into a wall. One got angry and stormed off, leaving me in the path of an oncoming tornado.

Four years ago, I was assaulted by a superior in my job. I reported it through the proper channels and I was blown off. Then they started creating paperwork to kick me out. While this was going on, I was seeing a shrink for anxiety. I was tired of being anxious all the time. I asked my shrink when I'd be better. They said that all the experiences had added up and that it would be a long road to recovery. But they said even when I was better I would never be the same. I would NEVER be completely OK.

I said this story isn't about them. So why have I told you all this? Because that's the day my life was changed forever. They were right when they said I would never be the same. But that's the only part they got right.

When they said that, righteous anger welled up in me. How dare they give my attackers that much power over the rest of my life? How dare they say that I would always be afraid? I left that day and purposed that I would prove them wrong.

At first I went backward. I cried. I cut. I slept. I avoided. I didn't care if I was ever in another relationship ever again. And whenever I did briefly dive into a relationship, I would quickly bail out of it to prevent being hurt.

Then one day I was perusing stories of other women's attacks. And time after time, I saw women in the comments telling them that they needed to get used to how they felt. They'd always be afraid. They'd never trust again. Over and over they gave all the credit to the attackers. That strengthened my resolve…This attitude had to stop!

So I got healthy. I got counseling. I got back in church. One of the most important things I did was build myself a support network—people who believed in me and believed that I could do anything I set out to do. Some of my loneliest days were my most vulnerable. And the more I was attacked, the more I felt like I was unworthy of being loved or supported. I had to end that lie. I had to retrain my brain…What happened was not my fault. I didn't do or say anything to make it happen. I wasn't "asking" for it.

Once I knew that I wasn't at fault and that I did not deserve what had happened, the next step was to build myself up. I am worthy of love. I am worthy of respect. I deserve to have good things happen. I deserve to be happy. I deserve to live my life without fear. Caution, always. But I should not live in fear of what "they" might say or what "they" might do.

At first I resolved to never speak of these things again. But silence gets us nowhere. Silence won't end the stigma that's associated with rape, assault, and molestation. Our society extends the victim's suffering, by continuing to give their attackers the power. Stop it! This is my driving force now: spreading the word that you are strong enough to make it through. Do not let what others have done define you. To continue to live in fear of them is to forever give them power over you. You're better than that. You're worth more than that. You're stronger than that.

Amanda Sue Howell is mother of three beautiful children, veteran of the USAF, a military spouse, virtual assistant, and business coach. In her spare time, she enjoys photography, singing, and going crazy on Pinterest. She's also the author of *10 Things That Kill Creativity*. To learn more about Amanda, visit AmandaSueHowell.com.

YOU WERE BORN WITH IT
Baeth Davis

Before I discovered my life purpose from my palm prints as a "business owner and spiritual teacher with a special message of love for the masses," I was an office worker in the marketing department of a small design firm. While the job paid decently and the work was varied, I was going home many a night and crying myself to sleep. There had to be more to life than just going through the motions day after day to pay the bills.

I was also suffering from an unexplained chronic cough, depression, and fatigue, as well as an emotionally abusive romantic entanglement. To say I was in charge of my life at that time would be a gross overstatement.

My sadness escalated to the point of suicidal thoughts. Late one night, I called a close friend and told her that I didn't want to be on earth anymore. There was a long pause, and then she said, "Baeth, that is the most selfish thing I've heard you say. Don't you know how loved you are?"

"Well, what should I do?" I said.

"Pray," she said with force. "I'm going back to sleep now. If you're going to do anything drastic call me back; otherwise, let me sleep."

I did as she commanded. I kneeled by my bed, folded my hands, and whispered, "God, universe, whatever is out there, this is my prayer: if you will show me my life's purpose, I will forever be your humble servant. I go where you ask me to go, and I will do what you ask me to do."

A few weeks later, thanks to the recommendation of another friend who knew of my weakened state, I received a hand analysis session. The "hand analyst," upon looking at my palms, said to me, "Baeth, you are not living the life you were meant to live—you are not living your life's purpose."

I got a bit woozy hearing the phrase "life's purpose" since I had uttered it just weeks before during my prayer.

She went on to tell me about my life's purpose as a business woman using spiritual tools and spiritual exploration to create more love and money and success in people's lives. She also told me I had gift markings in my hands that indicated I had abilities as a writer, speaker, leader, intuitive, and more.

It was the best thing I had heard about myself in a while—no, it was the best thing I had ever heard ever. My life did have a purpose after all! My prayer was answered. And I intended to follow through on the deal I made with God.

I decided, then and there, that there was no turning back. I prayed for my life's purpose—and it was handed to me directly through my very own hands. Of course, nature would give each of us a blueprint, a map, a GPS to our own lives in our physical hands! How simple, how obvious, how perfect!

I later found out that your fingerprints form in utero between the fourteenth and sixteenth week of development and do not change during your lifetime. They carry a code for your life's purpose and its fulfillment.

After discovering my life's purpose, my depression completely disappeared. I was so fascinated by the impact a simple deciphering of my palms had for me that I had to make hand analysis my life's work and share it with others. That was fourteen years ago.

I have since read nearly eight thousand pairs of hands and have thousands of clients around the globe.

I have personally witnessed thousands of clients quickly lose as much as eighty pounds of excess weight, release unhealthy relationships, find their soul mates, create their dream careers or businesses, or pursue their artistic visions after discovering their life's purpose and gifts. They also figure out how to get paid for their passions! No more working at unfulfilling, dead-end j-o-b-s!

YOU too have a life purpose. When you know this life purpose and set about fulfilling it, you connect directly to your highest self and put yourself on the master path to your life. What could be better? I can think of NOTHING more important than knowing and living your purpose. You were born with it. It's what you were put on this earth to do.

I want to share a little secret with you. Do you ever notice a person and say, "Wow, that person has amazing energy?" The reason for their sparkling, magnetic presence is that they know who they are and where they are going. You can't fake that. If you don't know what you are doing tomorrow, your presence is much weaker than someone who has a vision that extends beyond their own physical lifetime. When you know your life purpose, you vibrate that frequency. If you know your purpose and determine the legacy you want to leave, you become a leader and healer to others.

As for my own legacy, it is my personal wish that in my lifetime, every child is born and raised in an environment where their life's purpose is acknowledged, honored, and nurtured. In our YourPurpose.com community, we currently donate five percent of our product sale revenue to VillageEmpowerment.org, a nonprofit that builds schools in Malawi and the Philippines.

Here in the US, my goal is to help enact legislation that makes life purpose discovery and fulfillment a priority in the public school system. We are currently building technology that will allow for rapid hand analysis reports to be utilized by students and teachers alike.

My wish for you is that you know, deep in your soul, that you are necessary to the evolution of the universe and what the world craves is you in your full glory, expressing and creating from your life's purpose.

You were born with it! Go BE IT!

Baeth Davis, known as the "Love and Money On Purpose Mentor," is founder of YourPurpose.com, a company devoted to helping entrepreneurs and spiritual seekers of truth to discover and unleash their life purposes so they can get paid for their passions. As featured in *Women's World, Cosmopolitan,* and *Los Angeles Times* and heard on Radio Europe, NPR, and the BBC-5, as well as seen regularly on the Internet and network television, Baeth is an advisor to people in the healing professions, coaching, business, the arts, and many other industries, using her extensive intuitive abilities and a unique personality profiling system called scientific hand analysis. Visit her at BaethDavis.com.

STRENGTH OVER FEAR
Danielle Diamond

As a yoga teacher, people assume that I hear the word strength and immediately think of holding myself up in a one-armed handstand. While that's definitely exhilarating, the strength I've built that I'm most proud of is that which has gotten me over my biggest fear.

Some people fear spiders or driving through tunnels, but those aren't fears that keep us up at night; they don't keep people from functioning day to day or paralyze them in relationships with others.

I've always had a fear of people leaving me, not leaving me by going to work or on vacation, but leaving me and never coming back. I've had this fear ever since I was three. Yes, that may seem a bit young to start fearing death, but most three-year-olds have never caught their mother trying to commit suicide.

It wasn't easy growing up in the constant state of awareness one has when living with a bipolar mother. I figured out early on that she wasn't going to be the person I could count on when times were tough—God, she couldn't even handle days that seemed like a breeze.

Eventually I realized it would be easier to deal with my mother the way she dealt with her bad days—not at all. I didn't stay in bed all day, but chose to put up a wall. That way, I figured I wouldn't be hurt by her lack of involvement in my childhood—or the next suicide attempt that didn't just leave her feeling foolish.

In fairness to her, it wasn't for lack of trying. She took Prozac before it was even legal in this country, had shock treatments, and even went away to a fancy hospital in Boston. Unfortunately, after witnessing all this, I didn't want to have a relationship with her. Who knew how long she was going to be around, and I didn't want to enjoy that level of connectedness with her only to have it disappear.

At age twenty-one, I finally realized I wasn't only punishing myself, but ultimately I was hurting her for reasons over which she had no control. I thought maybe it was time I let down my guard and love her like I always wanted to—to have a "normal" mother/daughter bond.

That year I took her out for dinner, and she let me know how extremely proud she was of me—dealing with the mess that was my childhood, putting myself through NYU, and now starting a job at the place I always dreamed of. The way she described it was her being happy that I was finally "all set." Those words were a hint of things to come, but I was too high on the joy I was feeling from our newfound friendship to give the comment a second thought.

We had what I look back upon as the best two hours of our lives spent together. The next day I stopped by to say hi, and ultimately good-bye—not just for that day, but forever. I didn't know it at the time, for if I did, I would never have let go of the hug I had her in.

After her death, I built the equivalent of Fort Knox around my heart, reasoning I'd rather be alone than feel the pain from a loss like that again. Flying solo seemed to be my destiny, until I met my husband- who happened to be fourteen years older than me.

I fell in love with him the first time I saw him speak. We got really close, really fast—and then I wanted to run. I kept reasoning in my head that when I was forty, he'd be fifty-four, and when I was fifty-four, he'd be—gasp—almost seventy. I told him I couldn't handle getting close to someone and losing them again; but then he proposed.

It was the turning point. I had to decide if I was going to be paralyzed by this fear and let it keep me from living, or if I was going to kick it to the curb. It wasn't easy. The strength I cultivated to decide to live in the present and enjoy each day with those around me was harder to develop than any arm balance I've ever contorted myself into.

We got married that fall, and now we have two incredible sons. Sometimes I watch them on the playground and worry they're going to crack their heads open or think about my husband constantly flying across the country for work and think, "What would happen if…"

And then I stop. I think how blessed I am to have this family, for whatever amount of time we are together. I try to enjoy each moment, and each time I say good-bye, I hug them like it could be the last.

Danielle Diamond, ERYT- 500hr+, teaches a kick-butt class focusing on alignment, strength, and breath that opens your body through an insightful, creative sequence where you'll laugh as much as you'll sweat. Danielle has sold thousands of copies of her Xen Strength DVD, has appeared on *The Today Show* and *Dr. Oz*, and is also the wellness contributor for Bobbi Brown's blog. She looks forward to the launch of the book she is writing with Dr. Barry Sears, which combines the Zone Diet with yoga and meditation. Visit her at XenStrength.com.

THE SOUL OF SAFETY
Dara McKinley

Though I live in Seattle, I have the biggest love affair with Colorado. I spent my twenties there, and I often say that moving from the Bronx, NY, to Boulder, CO, was one of the best decisions I ever made. This summer my man's family organized a reunion in Crested Butte, CO. However, a dark cloud loomed over this reunion; six months previous, we lost our thirteen-year-old nephew Taft, my sister-in-law's son, in an avalanche. So, in the sunny and idyllic Colorado mountain ski town of Crested Butte, we all met up…with cracked hearts.

Despite this immense tragedy, this family is a bunch of troopers who lives for fun activities, and so we all carried on. One day we went to the top of the Crested Butte ski mountain that has a ton of summer activities for young kids, like miniature golf and toddler bungee bouncing. You can also take the ski lift up to the very top, and we decided to do that first. Though I don't hate ski lifts, I don't love them either, as they don't seem very secure with only a simple bar holding passengers in place. Nevertheless, I lined up with my husband, my three-year-old son, and my six-year-old daughter to board.

Swoooooooooosh! The lift picked us up, and once my arms were super snug around my little guy, I looked up and took in the peaceful silence, the fresh air, and the beautiful mountains. I turned to my husband and beamed. Then my mind assessed that I was in the air with my entire family on this metal chair with nothing but a single bar keeping us safe, and the next thought I had was, "Am I going to be OK?" To which I had no answer. Then, like a wave crashing over my body, fear filled my being. I turned to my husband and told him I wasn't feeling so great and that I needed a mantra. He suggested, "I am safe and I always will be." Though one might think that was the perfect thing he could have said (and it was,) it was like he was speaking Chinese. His words made no dent in the fear I was encased in.

I don't know how I made it through the nine-minute ride to the top, but eventually we landed, and I was beyond relieved to have my feet touch the ground…sort of. Although I was finally on the ground, I felt so separated from the earth, like there was a piece of cold metal between us. So shaky and stunned by what had just happened to me, I hung with the group for a while, and then I followed my intuition and went into the woods for twenty minutes and…cried.

Why was I crying? Was it just my excellent maternal instincts that kicked in because the truth is that ski lifts are really not that safe (especially for young children)? Yes. Was it that riding a ski lift was one of the last things Taft did before he died and I was channeling a bunch of grief? Yes. Was it that I generally don't feel safe and this quasi-dangerous nine minutes was just too much for me? Yes.

While we normally associate safety with protecting ourselves from physical harm, did you know that safety has a soul? The soul of safety is belonging and is very much an emotional experience. Belonging to the earth and belonging to a tribe of people are two significant ways that an internal feeling of security is cultivated.

Felt in the legs and feet, energy speak calls the felt sense of safety a root chakra and says it is influenced by our first family experiences. In the human pursuit for safety and security, we buy homes, build a military, purchase insurance policies, earn money, get dogs, construct fences, and install home alarm systems. Yet all this focus on protecting ourselves from outside invasions overlooks the other, and perhaps more important, side of feeling safe: did we derive a sense of safety from our first relationships AKA our family of origin? You can have all the external protection in the world, but feeling fundamentally safe inside is the breeding ground for a trust-filled life.

If there was constant conflict, alcoholism, divorce, financial stress, single parenting, constant criticism, or significant trauma/loss early on, you may have had good reason to feel unsafe, and this rocky foundation may be shaping your adult experiences.

I've had many an energy healer tell me that while my crown chakra (one's connection to spirit) is miles and miles long, my root chakra, (one's sense of belonging) is inches deep. I cannot deny that this is what it feels like in my body. Although my parents did many things right, for me it was constant conflict and a dragged-out divorce that went snip-snip to my root chakra. Through all the years that this went down, one important question was never asked or answered: am I going to be OK?

When you are a little kid, it is not only your physical safety but your relationships that create a safe internal world. It is through relationships that we establish our sense of belonging. As a feminine essence junkie, the power of affirming relationships is the first thing I teach. Feminine power not only exists in relationships, it is the force that creates healthy ones. Whether you are aware of it or not, your relationships, the ones that truly see you and believe in you, are the foundation for your emotional well-being. Consistent, affirming, and emotionally honest relationships are the soul of safety, and it is the feminine essence, which resides in both men and women, that weaves this experience.

So how do you get belonging's muscles nice and strong? Super easy. Frequently tell the people that are important to you:

What you appreciate about them.

What is special about them.

That their feelings matter.

That their dreams are beautiful.

That you think about them.

That you believe in them.

That they're going to be OK.

Of course there are many other things that could be said, especially around being supported. We are unique and it's important to know what you specifically need to hear in order to feel belonging in your body. These mentioned are just some of my favs that make the wheel of belonging, and thus the soul of safety, go round.

Dara McKinley is a complete junkie for the actualizing power of the feminine essence. Creator of The Goddess Process, Dara stirs a cauldron filled with the divine power of belonging, desire, and self-love. She desires a world where all men and women have the capacity to live from the depths of their souls. Visit her at DaraMcKinley.com.

REDEFINING SUCCESS FOR STRONG, POWERFUL WOMEN
Denise Duffield-Thomas

"You can bend the rules plenty once you get to the top,

but not while you're trying to get there.

And if you're someone like me,

you can't get there without bending the rules."

Tess McGill, *Working Girl*

When I was a little girl, my vision of a strong, powerful woman involved shoulder pads, a sharp suit, and an insanely busy job. Nobody I knew worked in an office, so I felt like I had to forge my own path. From university onward, I was independent to the point of obsession. Four part-time jobs plus full-time class plus club president equaled stress-related glandular fever.

I don't need fun. I'm strong and can take care of myself.

From the time I could talk, I remember hearing the women in my family talk about the men and their frustration and disappointment with their marriages. They would look down at me, the eldest grandchild, and say,

"Denise, don't you ever trust a man."

I think they were joking, but I took it as gospel truth and was determined never to be "trapped" like they were.

"I won't!"

I vowed at eight years old to be stronger than they were—a vow that took me about twenty years to break. So I left the men before they left me. If I hadn't met a sweet guy while working in London, I would have probably been a crazy cat lady.

I WILL be strong and independent. I will not rely on a man.

My first "professional" job was a disaster, despite the long-coveted proper suit and sensible heels. My first real boss, a very important senior partner, middle-aged, semi-alcoholic, and borderline sociopath, brought up all sorts of unresolved daddy issues and sent me into daily panic attacks and mysteriously itchy arms.

The two assistants on my windowless floor bore scars of the pressure of corporate success. One lady's hands shook regularly before meeting with the boss. The other had recovered from cancer, no doubt stress-related, but was back to work as soon as she was mobile. The air was always tense and unhappy, especially when he came back from a long, boozy lunch.

He was powerful and I felt powerless to change my job, so I changed my route to the restroom so I wouldn't have to go past his office. I dropped my pen on the floor when he passed so I could hide under my desk.

I am strong, I can stick it out. Think of my resume.

I have a thousand examples of sheer bloody mindedness, of mistaking isolation and stubbornness for independence. Workaholism gave me grim pleasure (and is there an addiction more socially acceptable as workaholism?).

Being a "strong, powerful woman" kinda sucked. My version of success sent me to the hospital with stress-related pneumonia, dried up my sex drive, and made me self-hate to the point of suicidal thoughts. What was missing? How long could I keep this up?

STRENGTH

I had it all wrong. Strength and power wasn't defined by a busy schedule. It was having the courage to forgive myself and others for not being perfect. It was redefining my boundaries enough that I wasn't afraid to disappoint others or piss them off by saying no, declining invitations, or pushing back on arbitrary deadlines.

It was treating myself like I mattered, doing work I enjoyed (maybe even loved) not just because I was competent at taking direction and bending time and space to make things happen. The strength had to come from within. The power was already there; it was just funneled into no-win games with people I was afraid of.

Rules of traditional success have changed, and the old way is crumbling. There are no rules. Being strong and powerful is entirely yours to define, and every aspect is 100 percent negotiable.

But, gorgeous, at every stage of your quest for your own version of success, even if you manage to fight and wrestle your own internal resistance, you'll come across the well-meaning, the jealous, or the downright evil who will push your buttons and dredge the fear from the past.

You'll be criticized, you'll get endless "feedback," thinly disguised disapproval, and yes, even haters. But find your tribe of supportive and loving women and you'll grow even quicker, fuelled by examples of strong, powerful chicks getting it together and loving their lives.

But whatever you do, don't keep it to yourself. Redefining strength and power for yourself gives permission for other women to do the same.

And when we do that…we change the world.

Denise Duffield-Thomas is a success coach and the author of *Lucky Bitch*. She inspires women all around the world to create exceptional lives. Get her popular free manifesting guide, *The Lucky Bitch Secrets of Outrageous Success* at DeniseDuffieldThomas.com.

FIND YOURSELF
Jenelle Montilone

"Find yourself" is inscribed on the pendant of my necklace. As I roll it between my fingers at the train station, I convince myself that I'm not running away. I'm embarking on an adventure to discover who I am. For my whole life, I had been in denial of what I could become. I questioned my worth. I had been plagued with fears, insecurities, guilt, and the anxiety of others' expectations, no doubt remaining scars of a childhood peppered with every type of abuse, abandonment, and zero stability.

Homeless, reckless, brave, alcoholic, victim, helpless, scared—yes, I've been these.

Did I find myself, or any of the answers, on that train ride? No, I didn't. I got all the way to New Mexico before I realized that, instead of a journey, what I longed for was staying. A journey, the process of going, needs direction. To find myself, I simply needed to stay.

Stay open to life and the amazing possibilities tomorrow brings.

Stay courageous enough to say hell yes to opportunities that scare me.

Stay strong when I feel like I cannot take anymore.

Stay true to myself no matter what.

It's the staying that leads us to the finding, the knowing of who we truly are, what we are called to do, and to discovering our own unique genius. We don't have to find ourselves on the road of life somewhere; we just have to come home to who we already are.

Creative activist and entrepreneur, Jenelle Montilone is changing the way we consume and create through TrashN2Tees and The Create Change Movement. She believes that each of us has the ability to inspire and change the world around us. Visit her at TrashN2Tees.com.

THE ACCIDENTAL PARENT
Jessica Kupferman

In 1996, I got miraculously pregnant with my daughter. I was a senior in college; I had been on the pill. I already had four years of school under my belt, even though I had a few more credits to go before graduation. But since I was twenty-one, since I was "highly educated," and since I really loved their dad, I decided the right thing to do was to get married and have the baby.

I was wrong about the get married part. Turns out that knowing and dating someone for six months before deciding to have a baby with them isn't the smartest decision one can make. Once we decided to get married, we moved in together, and I found out that we were totally incompatible in the same living quarters. We weren't just incompatible; we were total opposites. We watched different TV shows. We ate different food. We didn't want to do the same things on weekends. We couldn't agree on anything. It was like living with an alien from another planet.

Why did this elude me prior to getting engaged? Well, as a senior in college, I ended up doing a lot of partying. I drank a lot and smoked a little weed here and there (OK, and everywhere), and turns out everything you think you know about a person is sort of null and void once you're forced to be sober around them ALL the time. He wasn't as funny as I thought he was, and he definitely wasn't as responsible as I hoped he'd be. That wouldn't come until years after we were divorced.

I knew on our wedding night we were not meant to stay together. And I cried.

A few months went by, I gave birth to my beautiful daughter, and I tried to gain some sort of employment. Day after day I looked for jobs, and all I seemed qualified for was waitressing and clerical work. I fed the baby, took her for walks, looked for jobs, and cleaned the basement we lived in. Oh, I didn't mention that we lived in his mother's basement? YEAH.

Life was not awesome. There was a bathroom, a shower stall, and the L-shaped room was sectioned off with a crib at one end and a couch at the other. The ceiling was low and there were no windows. It was like being trapped in my life.

One day I was complaining about my misery to one of my bridesmaids, my bestest friend Kay. I assumed she would just listen and be sympathetic, but instead she said, "You should finish school. You're never going to get out of that marriage unless you finish."

Wait, what? "How the hell am I supposed to do that?" I asked. After all, since my last few months there were spent not really studying, I didn't exactly have the best GPA or even a leg to stand on as far as them letting me back in.

Kay said, "It's July. Go to the school tomorrow. Don't wait. See if you can get financial aid. Get in for next semester. See if they'll let you back in. You have to finish, because if you don't, this will be your life for the rest of your life. Promise me you will go TOMORROW."

I owe everything wonderful about my current life to Kay. She friggin' terrified me. I believed her that I'd never have the strength or salary power without finishing college. I'd always just be some young mom who almost had potential. For my own self-esteem, for my own empowerment, Kay was right. I had to do it. I looked at my baby daughter, so sweet, smart, and full of joy, and I knew I couldn't let her be the reason I didn't finish college. I wanted her to have an example of a woman who could do anything, regardless of the situation she found herself in. So the next morning I made an appointment to see the head of the department.

When the day came for me to go in, I decided that bringing the baby would be a good way to go. I didn't have any day care anyway, and I thought maybe it would prove that I was more motivated than ever to finish my education and be a positive influence on society. Determined, I sat down at his desk with Emily on my lap and pleaded my case. No, I hadn't done well while I was there, and yes, I had taken my college education for granted. But now that I had my daughter, I had to finish. I didn't want her to have a mother who quit college. I didn't want anything to ever be an excuse for HER not to finish. And I'd be damned if being a mom would get in my way.

It worked. He let me back in. Next stop was the financial aid department. Luckily, since I had never taken out a loan EVER, I got enough financial aid to finish my degree AND had some left over to pay a day care provider while I was in school. I was all ready to go!

I started school in September of 1997, and life was beautiful. I was losing the baby weight, I was leaving the basement, and I was getting smarter by the day. I was enjoying my classes, and for the first time, I was really grateful to be in college and learning subjects and things I loved. Grades were good, my husband had a steady job, and there seemed to be a light at the end of my depressing life's tunnel. Maybe when I graduated, we could save some money and get an apartment. Maybe I could even support myself AND the baby, and life could resume some sense of normalcy. Yes, it was all coming together.

And then, it happened.

I started to not feel so great, and I was tired all the time, so I took another pregnancy test, and guess what? I was pregnant again. And I was due three weeks after I was supposed to graduate. Why was this happening to me? This time it was a condom that had failed us. I cried and cried about my fate. My marriage had gotten to the point where we weren't even having sex but once every six weeks! I could barely stand the sight of him! We fought every day! How could this have even happened? Two children under the age of two! This was insane! I was supposed to graduate now eight months pregnant? I was going to have to study and take finals with a giant stomach in front of me?

The answer was a resounding HELL YES. That was exactly what I was going to do. Come hell or high water, through rain, snow, sleet, or sun, I was going to FUCKING graduate from college and get the HELL out of that basement. I could not let anything get in the way of that. It wasn't just about showing my daughter that she could do anything. At this point, it was about showing myself too.

Whether this was luck or just a little help from above, I don't know, but my last semester of college just consisted of credits I needed to fill in some gaps, so I took ceramics, choir, and yoga. I didn't need but one academic class, so there wasn't much to study for, and thank goodness because I had absolutely no energy or brain power to dedicate to much studying.

So yes, I wobbled my way around campus, stopping often for soft-serve ice cream from class to class. I got to a point where I couldn't sit straight in the desk anymore and had to inhabit two desks, one for my ass and one to write on. Sometimes the baby, my son, would kick me so hard that my textbook would fly into the air. But that last semester finally ended, and I waddled my giant body down the aisle to get my diploma, in my graduation robe and Birkenstocks, the only shoes that would fit my swollen feet. Two weeks later, my son Nate was born. I was a college graduate, and I was the mother of two. I was twenty-three years old, and life was just beginning.

Jessica Kupferman is a professional blogger, soon-to-be author, and speaker known for using her razor-sharp wit and personality to entertain the masses, mostly at her expense. She owns a digital marketing company called Badass Biz, where she helps small business owners and entrepreneurs strut their stuff online. To learn more about Jess, visit JessKupferman.com.

STRENGTH: IN NUMBERS OF TEARS
Sally Hope

It was a crisp, sunny day in February of 1995. I was fifteen years old, in the passenger's seat of my sister's maroon Mitsubishi, listening to the soundtrack of *Pulp Fiction*. The songs blasted out through the speakers as I watched the mountains whiz by. Eucalyptus trees swayed in the breeze to my right. Strawberry fields ahead. Blue skies and clouds above. In a lyric saying, "c'est la vie said the old folks, it goes to show you never can tell," I noticed the irony—since I was on the way to my dad's funeral.

"It's true," I thought. You never CAN tell. Anything. Especially not how life was going to turn out.

Eight months prior I was graduating eighth grade. I had a new boyfriend. I was entering high school as a cheerleader, and summer had just begun. Life, as it seemed, couldn't have been better. And then it happened—the phone call that changed everything.

"Your dad's been in an accident," said my stepmom over the phone.

"Well, is he OK?" I asked, figuring it was just his clumsiness again.

"Can I talk to your mom?"

I didn't know it at the time, but life, as I knew it, was over in that moment. My dad had gotten into a bicycle accident. Crashed into the wall at the bottom of the steep hill where he lived. And was a vegetable. My daddy. The one who taught me to throw a football. And detail a car. To dance the Charleston. And be polite. To tell a dirty joke. All of that was gone in one phone call. I didn't believe it at the time, but he would never return as that person. He left us in that moment.

Multiple hospital visits later, many months gone by, and I was in my childhood bedroom. But instead of two brass, twin-sized beds, one for me and one for my sister, my dad lay in the middle of the room in a hospital bed, doctor and Rabbi surrounding him, stepmom playing Enya on the CD player and rubbing him with lotion, Grandma curled in the corner crying, and my sister and I still. Silent. I watched as the day went on, as if I was an outside observer.

"This can't be real," I mused. One odd event after another. And then it was my turn. To say something. The end was here, no matter how much I denied it, and I was supposed to say something. The last thing. That would forever be my well-wishes to my daddy into another realm.

How on earth does a fifteen-year-old know what to say? In front of all those people? And so I just held his hand and said I loved him.

Within a few seconds, it was over. Still holding my hand, he passed on. Just like that. One minute here. Next minute gone. And I decided at that moment I wasn't ever going to cry about it. I wasn't going to let people feel bad for me. I was going to be strong.

And I was so "strong" that I completely shut off all of my emotions. I didn't let anyone in. I didn't cry. I went on as though everything was normal. I didn't want to be the weird one in high school whose dad had died. I wanted to be just like everyone else.

Inside I cried, "How could you do this to me?! How could you leave me?! Where did you go?? Why don't you love me enough to stay?" But I never let any of this bubble to the surface.

It wasn't until seventeen years later when it all came crashing down. All the things I had buried so deep inside came rushing to the surface in one fell swoop, and it overwhelmed me. I found myself sobbing on the floor over a boy I barely knew, asking the same questions of him: "How could you do this to me? Why don't you love me enough to stay?" I completely fell apart and realized that these emotions that were so overwhelming and so all-consuming had nothing to do with this new guy. That they were old wounds, never healed, just covered up. And that no matter how hard I tried, there is no such thing as denying emotions, and certainly, by trying I wasn't being as "strong" as I thought I was.

People tend to think that strength is something that can be measured by how much weight you can lift, or how little you cry, or how "tough" you appear to be. But to me, the strongest thing a person can do is allow themselves to feel what they're feeling. To be vulnerable. To look inside at tough emotions and invite them in. To cry when tears need to happen.

Completely falling apart was the strongest thing I ever did. Because it was real. Because it was true. And now I feel like I can move on without these hidden emotions hanging over my head, showing up in places where they don't belong.

So whatever it is in your life that you know, deep in your heart, needs to be done, whatever emotion you know you need to look at, do that. And don't look back. There are so many beautiful things ahead of you. Your life is waiting. And cry the tears. Each tear shed is a new opportunity waiting to happen. Take the lead.

Sally Hope is a blogger/love and life coach who loves hot-pink lipstick, crosswords, and cowboys. A former rock star, she is taking her show from the stage to the road by traveling around in an RV while coaching her clients to live the life of their dreams.

Her latest obsessions include country swing dancing, LOVE, chips and salsa, and adventuring. To learn more about Sally, visit her at SallyHope.com.

LET LOVE BE YOUR FUEL
Shenee Howard

What do YOU freakin' love?

I called it the boulevard of broken dreams.

It was a long stretch of highway full of empty stores and bored employees. Nothing to do. No one to help.

And it was my job to interview every. single. one.

I took a job working for one of those companies that creates listings for businesses in different cities, kind of like Yelp. I got a list of businesses every week, and I had to go to each one and interview them and take pictures of the building. I can't tell you what it is like to drive down a road and know you have to go to every business on that street.

Most of these places didn't really want to talk to me. Always some excuse about policies and rules, but secretly I knew that it might be from some type of embarrassment. Who wants the world to know how bad they are doing business-wise?

I felt like a vacuum cleaner salesman.

Most. Depressing. Job. Ever.

Especially since I was in the exact same boat. I had recently decided to quit the job market that decided to quit on me.

I was trying out "entrepreneurship" for size with very mixed results. My computer had just been stolen. I had to move back to my hometown.

I was flirting with depression.

One day I went into an exotic pet store. It was awesome. Brightly colored birds everywhere. Puppies. Lizards. Turtles. Neon fish.

It was also empty. Just like the others.

As soon as I walked in, a woman in her midfifties gave me a huge smile and welcomed me into her store. Smiles didn't happen much with the work I did.

She gave me the grand tour. I met the rabbits and the rats. They all had names.

She told me horror stories about the economy. She told me about getting another mortgage on her house so she could keep the store. She told me about her sick father and sister.

She loved to tell stories.

Finally, I asked her how she found the strength to take care of the animals, to try take care of her family, and to keep the store afloat.

Her answer was simple.

"I freaking love animals and I LOVE helping people find them. Love keeps me going."

I left with a new beta fish and a pep in my step.

"Love keeps me going."

She freakin' loves animals.

Since then, I have discovered that love is also a source of strength for me and my business.

I would be a dirty liar if I said things just started going awesome after that. I didn't magically make my first thousand or even my first hundred dollars, but I kept going.

It's that drive to do what you love.

LOVE.

It's almost a cliché word, so I struggle to use it here, but it's true. When you love something, you find strength that comes from somewhere else completely.

It's kind of like the mother who can lift the car off her kid.

I kept going because I knew without a shadow of the doubt that I loved what I was doing, even if I couldn't put words to it yet, even if it couldn't even buy me a box of macaroni and cheese.

Over the last two years, I have been cursed out by clients, have seen the numbers -212.00 in my account, and have crashed and burned more times than I can count.

Bu I freakin' love branding. And I love helping people discover their brands.

That is what I always say to myself when things start to suck. This is what keeps me going.

The store is still there, and I occasionally see cars out front.

Love continues to keep her afloat.

So, here is my question for you:

What do you freakin' love?

Let that be your fuel.

Shenee Howard is a brand engagement expert who teaches entrepreneurs and small businesses how to show up online. Shenee is also the founder of the digital programs Hot Brand

Action and Idea to Income. Her other loves: Ryan Gosling, The Backstreet Boys, superhero movie soundtracks, and movies with Keanu Reeves in a starring role. WHOAH. You can find her at HeyShenee.com.

THE SECRET GATEWAY TO STRENGTH
Tracy Matthews

Have you ever wondered why some people are gutted by their difficulties and why others actually catapult and thrive from their challenges? What makes one person strong in the face of adversity and another spiral into a sea of self-pity?

I have had an amazing life thus far. I really can't complain. I say this with a hint of a smile on my face because in certain people's "view" of a great life, mine probably isn't that "great" on paper. It's true. At times I have felt like a total mess.

You probably have those friends in your life who "on paper" have what appears to be an AMAZING life. However, they are constantly in a state of unhappiness, always looking for answers outside of themselves and they are complete and utter wrecks. Miserable.

As a multi-passionate entrepreneur, I have the blessing of wearing many hats in my life: a jewelry designer, a mentor, and a yoga instructor.

When I am wearing my yoga teaching hat, part of my practice is to start each class with a short theme or quote. I ask my students to reflect on how my words resonate with them. The themes that I choose are universal, such as dealing with fear and anger, staying present and focused on the breath, or dealing with setbacks and loss. While the topics I choose are usually something I sense the room needs, it often acts as a mirror in my own life.

In general, my students respond by taking the lesson and applying it to their own lives. It is not uncommon for a student to walk up to me after class and say, "That was exactly what I needed."

Now back to the question: Why is it that some people grow stronger and thrive in light of their challenges and others collapse and retreat in a sea of insecurity and shame?

Lately, I have really been reflecting on this. When I look back at my life thus far, I was handed some pretty BIG challenges: losses, setbacks, and struggles.

By the age of twenty-two, I had already dealt with the devastating and difficult divorce of my parents, the loss of my mother, and a severe case of body dysmorphia, anorexia and bulimia. By the age of thirty, my twelve-year relationship had shattered. I was humiliated by the infidelity of the man who I considered my "soul mate." By the age of thirty-eight, I shuttered my first jewelry business, filed for bankruptcy, and spent all of my savings trying to survive.

Maybe my life isn't full of the worst challenges ever. I haven't lost any children or limbs, I haven't suffered from any devastating illnesses, and I haven't been homeless. However, I have friends who haven't really had any major life events disrupt their lives, yet they still struggle and act weak.

I look at life this way: those things totally sucked, and in some cases, I still deal with the aftermath of my problems. However, I always knew that there was something better out there for me, whether it be a relationship, a new business, abundant financial success, vibrant health, and the list goes on. I am not insinuating that the grass is always greener. I am saying that if something doesn't work out, there is another open door waiting for me to walk through.

The Buddhists attribute suffering to attachment. I can't say that I am a completely detached person or that I didn't have anguish and suffering in my difficult moments. However, understanding my circumstances as a gateway to something better has really helped me move forward in my life and rise above my struggles with clarity, confidence, and strength.

So back to answering the question: What makes one person be strong regardless of any circumstance they face and another spiral into a sea of self-pity?

The difference between those who live in their power (the strong) and those who give it away (the self-pitiers) is simple. The strong ones know that even though things didn't work out in the way they expected, there is something better around the corner. They live life with a positive attitude. Their perception of their circumstances actually brings hope rather than despair.

By staying positive, abundance flows. By looking at your difficulties through a perceptive lens rather than a judgmental lens, you are able to learn from your challenges. When you have hope that things will get better, you will not be a slave or a victim to what life brings you. You will be a survivor, who is strong and resilient.

How will you learn from your challenges today?

Tracy Matthews is an eco-luxury jewelry designer who specializes in bespoke engagement rings, wedding bands, and special occasion jewelry. She is also a cofounder of Flourish & Thrive Academy, an online school dedicated to teaching jewelry designers how to be business savvy. In addition, Tracy is an avid yogi; she teaches several classes a week and practices every day to maintain her balance, peace, and awareness. To learn more about Tracy, visit TracyMatthews.com or FlourishThriveAcademy.com.

THE COURAGE TO BE ME
Andie Graff

From the time I was a little girl, all I ever wanted was to be married and be a mom. I'd never thought about courage until I realized I had it.

I married young without completing a college education, so I wasn't prepared for a "traditional" career, but I had done years of promotional and advertising modeling since I was fifteen years old and continued to do that in New York City and throughout the East Coast after I relocated there and got married.

My husband and I decided that I would be a housewife and stay-at-home mom because he was interested in continuing his education and pursuing an executive-level career. It was just as important to both of us that I be a wife and mother who raised the kids without working outside the home.

Our first daughter was born in December 1991, our son in October 1993, and our last daughter in March 1996. I was a very busy (courageous) stay-at-home mom! During the time I had my first daughter, my husband was pursuing his master's degree in business. He was in the medical equipment field and traveled extensively. He often worked all day and then traveled from our home in Bucks County, Pennsylvania, to St. Joseph's College in Brooklyn, New York. No easy feat!

Needless to say, I spent many years being "both" parents (courageously) while he furthered his education and continued to provide a very comfortable life for our growing family.

As expected, after receiving his MBA, he moved up the corporate ladder very quickly. In 1995 we were offered the opportunity to move to the West Coast so that he could assume a position of management with his company. We were very excited with this prospect because I was now expecting our third child and my parents were in Las Vegas, Nevada. I would have a support system in raising the kids, as he would be traveling more than ever.

We courageously moved to Las Vegas in February 1996, and my third glorious child arrived in March. We settled into what was a very busy and exciting time in our lives with a growing family and new, exciting career opportunities for him. Sadly, within months my father became ill and in 1997 passed away.

I continued to raise our children, and my husband continued to climb the ladder of success. Unfortunately, we had grown apart because of the endless amounts of time that he spent working on the road—usually three to five days every week—for what was now almost eighteen years. I suppose courage can be found in knowing when you're "successful enough" and remembering not to miss out on your life. I wonder if in hindsight he would have made a different choice.

All I can really remember of that time was waking up one day and realizing that I didn't want to be a Stepford wife anymore. A corporate wife's life is very stifled. Look a certain way, act a certain way, do this, do that. At forty I made the biggest decision I would ever make, ever. I decided to take my life back and find out who *I* really was.

He didn't want this; he wanted his old wife back, not this new rebel that had invaded her body. So after months and one last and very emotional argument, my husband did what most people in a desperate situation do: he tried to scare me. So he kindly pointed out that he didn't think I could ever survive without my "new car every two years, my endless credit cards, my big homes, and my various trips to Hawaii and other places on a biannual basis, etc." I was, after all, like my friends liked to call me "like a single parent with a great bank account."

As I stood there, I realized the only reasons he could find to remind me why I was making a huge mistake by leaving him were only about material belongings and money, and I felt he didn't know me at all. Did he think he bought me? If he did, I was returning myself.

YES! Of course I did enjoy all those things that his successful career so generously offered me. But I realized they did not and do not define WHO I AM. I will always be SO LUCKY TO BE ME! That thought BURNED in my heart and my soul.

We divorced in 2006, and after finalizing everything, I settled into my new life as a divorced mom with three kids, ages ten, twelve, and fourteen. The best part is I really liked who I was. I especially liked when I saw "old friends" who told me how much nicer and "softer" I was. Keeping up with the Joneses can make you hard. Well, I never forgot that statement that had burned into my heart. After a lot of thought and prayer, I decided to do something about it.

Now remember, I had no college degree or career to "fall back on." So getting a "job" would have been just that, a job. I felt a much bigger calling for me than that.

I knew it was an incredible risk, but I thought about what I wanted to do with those words and how I could use them not only to continue to emotionally support and encourage myself, but how I could use them as a message for my own children who had experienced the harshest of lifestyle changes. My children had a "privileged lifestyle," and that was now gone. I needed to teach them and remind them and myself that "things" don't make us who we are. WE do! Because suddenly those "things" are gone and we are still who we are.

The more I pondered this idea, the more it became a vision of the "mission" that I could create. I realized that what I had to say would resonate way beyond my children and myself. I realized that while I was searching for my own independence and empowering myself, I could do exactly the same for so many women out there—women who are feeling not good enough, not deserving of happiness, or, in my case, lost in a successful husband's shadow.

So I set out to design a logo for my new brand, but not just any logo: one that held meaning and represented what this line would be about. I thought about what I wanted "sltbm" to stand for. And that is how I created my logo.

"A CROWN because you are the queen of your life; a SHIELD to protect your heart, mind, and soul; and WINGS so you can soar and become anything your heart can dream."

I decided to create T-shirts with the new logo and "so lucky to b me" on them and test the market. I came up with what would become my "signature" quote that I still sell to this day, almost four years later as my number-one selling tee! The statement, "Because I am the one and only me; I am more than enough; say it, feel it, believe it" and SLTBM the tee and the movement was born!

That was in 2008. I found immediate success with my line in Las Vegas where I call home. I was a featured brand in numerous boutiques and specialty shops. Then the economy took a nosedive. At that point I had to decide what to do. So I pulled my entire inventory back in, as most of the small boutiques I was working with were now sadly closing their doors permanently. I took a much-needed break and focused on my children, enjoying what was left of their young years.

After a while I created a website and decided that the line would only be available via me, either online or when I attend various women's events, because I get to meet my beloved customers face-to-face and hear their astounding stories as to why this line and what I say are so meaningful to them. And the e-mails I receive tell me the stories of how my line and my messages have touched and continue to touch and encourage them in their own lives and those of the friends and family they have shared them with in magnificent ways.

Through very tough financial times and an uneasy world we live in, I have been able to continue this mission, to touch women where they need to be touched the most, and that is in the heart.

I never thought of myself as courageous until one day when that changed. I think of a conversation I had with my late mother. She was so much more than my mother; she was my best friend and my cheerleader. She was the most concerned about how I would "make it" without my husband. He took such good care of me, like a child. And as a mother, I see where that concern came from.

One day we were talking, enjoying a cup of coffee together, and she just looked at me and shook her head.

I asked, "What?"

She just smiled, tears in her eyes, and said, "I'm just so proud of you. As hard as it has been, you have never once complained, and instead of sitting around feeling sorry for yourself waiting for someone to take care of you, you're out there trying to make a difference for women everywhere. When I look at you, I am in awe of your courage."

I believe that's another reason I feel so lucky to be me. It did take courage to leave a comfortable life, to stand on my own two feet, and to be an example to my children. I know now that I am courageous, strong, and so lucky to be me. I also know it's never too late to figure out who you are.

Andie Graff is the founder and creator of the empowering apparel company called So Lucky To B Me. She believes every woman should put herself first and have the courage to be HERSELF, because you are more than enough. So Lucky To B Me has partnered with Stephen Baldwin and his daughters Hailey and Alaia as brand ambassadors for the line where a percentage of all the sales is donated to the Carol M. Baldwin Breast cancer research fund that Stephen runs in his mother's honor. To learn more about Andie and So Lucky To B Me, visit SoLuckyToBMe.com.

KINDLING
Casey Addinsall

She opened the door and tossed her keys in the blue dish, as usual. The sound echoed down the empty hall. It was so intensely quiet that she often thought she should get a cat. But when she finally made her way to the pet store, she realized she was less of a cat person and more a fish person.

And so she took home a red fighter. Now she and her fish, Finger, both feared to upset the silence.

She looked at her watch; it told her in no uncertain terms that she was late again. Great. Awesome even. Except, not. Late for what exactly, she could never figure, though the clock kept running miles ahead of where she thought she needed to be.

Staring down the hall, toward the kitchen, she wanted to take a step forward, but she was utterly exhausted. Her feet hurt, her head stung, and she could not move forward anymore. Her body would not transport her another step. She felt beat.

When and how she became so exhausted, she couldn't recall. Fax numbers, odd phrases offered to her, and song lyrics of songs from years ago had been committed to memory—but the source of this fatigue remained a mystery.

She supposed it didn't really matter. She just knew that she was in a fog that felt like it had extended an eon. And tonight, she'd had enough.

She dropped heavily to the floor; her body, handbag, and soul fell in a jumbled pile on the hardwood floorboards. She let her head fall into her hands as she exhaled heavily, "Fuck." A pocket of tension escaped her constricted frame in the gust of her breath.

She had forgotten why she was here in the first place. And now, she had barely an ounce of strength left and not the faintest inkling how she would get survive this space. "This is ludicrous," she thought, assessing the situation. Her body ached. She was hungry, and the only good Chinese place down the road closed about seven minutes ago.

Eggs on toast again, she supposed.

"Seriously, fuck." Another pocket of tension effused into the thick night encircling her, with it a burning tear made a dashing effort to assault her cheek. Another readied itself to tumble, and instead of thwarting their descent, this time she gave herself up to them.

"What am I even doing here?"

On the floor, and in life generally, she had disarmed her passion somewhere along the way and was running on other people's to-do lists. She couldn't remember making that stellar life choice, but acknowledged she must have at some point.

"OK, what is it that I have to do to get a break here? How can I fix this? Or make it go away? Or something." Her life had been swayed by other people's dreams. Her drive, her purpose…was unremembered. It was trifled when it should have been elevated.

"Help. Me."

Words she had not uttered this whole time. Stubbornness and misplaced pride had well concealed that notion long ago; she had instead manifested an impenetrable armor. Help was an alien concept, so much so that she wasn't entirely sure of whom she was posing this request. But there, on the floor in her hall, with her face still in her hands, she prayed to the ether.

"Please, help me."

Amid her personal chaos she relinquished, hoping like hell there would be some sort of response soon—because, quite honestly, she felt like an ass. An awkward, blubbering ass.

"Please, help me. I have no clue about what I'm doing, but you know that already, yeah? Well, I just worked it out. I'm not a freakin' super hero, and that blows—but I am only just holding a beat in my heart enough to keep going. Just…no strength left. I have no strength left. What do I need to do?"

And then she waited. And waited. Resolved not to move until her request had been answered. She was half expecting a serendipitous phone call, and she was open to hearing guiding voices.

She was not expecting the blazing cascade of white light that washed down over her, warming her from the inside out. It was a sensation like nothing she had ever known, like being thawed; but she hadn't even realized she was numb to start with.

"Well. That's new…really new."

She felt like she was being showered with diamond dust, not unlike that brooding guy from Twilight as he stepped into sunlight. She wondered if that's how it looked. As she stayed with the feeling, she felt a smack of serene calm descend as each wave of light embraced her every fiber.

She knew instinctually she was bearing witness to the kindling of her soul. And she was decidedly amused that her thoughts had adopted such lavishly descriptive language. She wasn't normally so cheesy and overblown, but right there, in the hallway, there she was, being kindled.

Fear. Love. Resentment. Dreams. Play. Value. Wisdom. Judgment. Drive. Limitation. Light. Trust. Knowledge. Assumption. Envy. Power. Intuition. Pride. Kindness…Strength.

They were all unearthed from the same place within her soul, but now she knew to harness her spirit to manifest the good within. She couldn't explain what the heck was happening, but she supposed it didn't matter. Her task was to explore it, enjoy it, and use it.

She felt that she wasn't alone.

She felt the shift in the air to possibility.

She closed her eyes, murmured "thank you."

She let the luster soak into the layers of her skin.

She lifted herself off of the floor and straightened up.

She caught a glimpse of herself in the mirror on the wall.

In that moment, she noticed that her reflection had a light all of its own…

Casey is a jubilation catalyst and creative muse at Sir Flamingo, where she engages feel-good nonsense all day long. Having walked under a lackluster rain cloud herself and come out a bundle of light, her mission is to encourage and inspire people everywhere to pimp their standards, do whatever it takes to get their cells dancing, and make a mark with their divine journey. "We're here for a good time, not a long time," she says, "so let's make it count." To learn more about Casey, visit SirFlamingo.com.

THE GIFT OF NOT ENOUGH
Cassandra Herbert

When you are struggling through the feeling of "not-enoughness," you're a rare person indeed if you can see it as a gift. In fact, for most people, gratitude for feeling "not enough" is quite a bizarre idea!

Ahh, but the feeling of not-enoughness isn't actually the gift. The strength and empowerment one develops over the years from transcending the feeling of being not enough—that is the beautiful gift.

Looking back over my life, I see that I started feeling as though I wasn't enough in fourth grade when I switched elementary schools. I am African American, and I went to a school in which the majority of students were Caucasian. Now I lived in suburbs, and most of the other African Americans in the school lived in the city. Being suburban like the Caucasian students and African American like the city students was a combination that left me on the outside of both groups. I felt as though I wasn't black enough nor white enough to be in either group. I would actually call myself gray.

During the first month of being in this new school, a couple of African American girls wanted to fight me. One of them said, "I call you out at 3:30 p.m. in the hallway." I knew that meant that they wanted to fight me at 3:30 p.m. I was terrified—I had never been in a fight in my life. I really didn't know what to do or why they wanted to have a fight with me. One of my friends said it was because they were jealous. Jealous? Jealous of what?

So at 3:30 p.m. I showed up. We went back and forth on who would make the first move, and then we pulled each other's hair. She punched my arm, and I punched her back. After the punch she ran away. I didn't know what to think. So I got on the bus and went home. The next day her friend called me out after school, pushed me down, and hit me. Before she could kick me, the bus came and we all ran to our buses.

I recall sitting on the bus, crying all the way home, not because she had hurt me, but because my spirit was crushed. I felt as though I wasn't liked by people of my own ethnicity, and I didn't know why.

To add to my social struggles, I felt I was not athletic enough in school. I had no hand-eye coordination, and during gym classes when we played team sports, I was the last one to be picked. In middle school and high school I wanted to try out for the field hockey team, but I was too afraid that I wouldn't be good enough.

Not only that, I also did not feel pretty enough. That awkward stage of adolescence that most of us go through seemed to last a long time for me. I was tall, skinny, and wore braces. Kids would say things like "You'll never get a boyfriend, 'cause bones are for dogs and meat is for boys." Wow, did this mess with my self-esteem!

To top it all off, I felt I was not enough when it came to academics. I wanted to be a part of the popular smart students' group, but they all seemed to get A's and I was struggling to get a B+.

Then, the change began…

One day I saw one of the "smart" girls give another "smart" girl" the answer to the test. That is when I realized that I was smart enough—smart enough to know better, not to cheat, and to study if I wanted a good grade.

A year later, I decided to try out for the field hockey team. It was something I really wanted to do, so I stepped beyond my feelings of not-enoughness, took the risk…and guess what, I made the team!

Now, I had to practice a lot because other girls had been playing for a couple of years. It was rough, because the coach wouldn't play me much, and this brought up a lot of feelings of inadequacy, which I did not like. So I started taking positive steps, continuing to practice and meeting with the coach, asking her to give me more playing time. I felt if I had more playing time I would become better. She was hesitant but agreed… and my playing improved, and I even got to start in a couple of games!

I only played field hockey for a season. I didn't try out the next year because I was in eleventh grade and had not become good enough to make the varsity team. I did not want to be an eleventh grader on the junior varsity team because that would trigger those feelings of not-enoughness.

By my senior year of high school, I felt as if I was finally being recognized for being enough. I was in the top 25 percent of my high school class, and I had many friends, both Caucasian and African American. In fact, the girl who beat me up in fourth grade was (and remains!) one of my closest friends. I even had a boyfriend.

Now I wish I could say that after all of this my feelings of not-enoughness went away…but no, they didn't. Instead, they were buried in my subconscious…and even as an adult, some of my decisions and drive to succeed have been driven by feelings of not being enough. I have learned to overcompensate for these feelings.

How has this pattern shown up in my life?

Wanting to learn more so I will never be judged for not knowing enough or being smart enough. I now have two bachelor's degrees and two master's degrees, as well as a number of certifications.

Wanting to be the best at my job. In all of my nursing jobs, I have volunteered for committees, have been the charge nurse, have been preceptor for new nurses, and I have led a number of educational workshops and presentations.

Wanting to be the best significant other—ever! In relationships I have been the planner and the one who gives and gives.

Wanting to do more and more so more people will like me and never think I am not enough. I have said yes to so many projects, activities, and groups that I'm practically a case study for Superwoman Syndrome. Even as I write this, I must take a deep breath because I've now exposed the not-enough feelings of Cassandra Herbert.

But, looking at all of these impacts, I see this is where the gift appears!

Despite my underlying feelings of not being enough, I have been able to show up and do all of these things. These experiences have enhanced my life in ways I'd never have known if I had allowed those feelings to paralyze me.

And do you know what else? My struggle to overcome those feelings has put me on the fast track of self-development. I have read numerous books and have attended lots of workshops on personal growth. As a result I have become more conscious of the not-enough feeling. I now sit and listen to my intuition before I say yes to a person or project. I recognize that people will still like me if I say no. I have been able to set boundaries and take time for myself.

Because I have had this struggle, I can be a more authentic and compassionate counselor: I am genuinely able to relate to women who feel they are not enough and assist them on a much deeper level than if I didn't have these feelings myself.

The feelings of not-enoughness have been a genuine gift in my life! I am truly grateful to those feelings for giving me the strength to accomplish all that I have done. By forcing me to grow, they have enriched my life and helped me to find my passion and purpose.

Cassandra Herbert is a holistic nurse psychotherapist, wellness educator, and speaker. She is the creator and owner of Just BEE Wellness and Zest and Harmony Counseling. In both of her businesses, she is very passionate about assisting women on releasing physical, mental, and spiritual blocks so they can have more energy and vibrancy in their lives. To learn more about Cassandra, visit JustBeeWellness.com and ZestAndHarmonyCounseling.com.

SEIZE THE MOMENT – THERE'S SO MUCH MORE TO LIFE THAN HAPPY ENDINGS

Cathy Presland

No one tells you how hard it's going to be look after your parents when they get old. One parent with Alzheimer's and one worn out by caring.

Things shift in levels. You ride along for a while, then next thing you know you're bringing in all their food and taking all the calls from their service providers. The doctor. The landlord. The carers. You manage for a while, but always knowing that another cliff edge might be just around the corner.

And the choices are so hard. It never seems the right time to progress into the next level of care. There isn't an ideal solution to caring for elderly parents it seems—only the "least bad" choice.

So it is has been with my dad this year. I would say it's been the worst summer that I can remember, but I'm holding tight to the idea that things happen for a reason. Yes, I've given up most of my days to spend time with him. Or to sort out emergency solutions. Or to advocate for his interests with the professionals. It's pretty exhausting!

But I try to see the lesson in all this. Is there a message for my own future? Or is it a reminder that work isn't really anything in the longer time and maybe it's better to spend time with family and friends? It's hard to see what that message might be in the midst of chaos.

My dad is the nicest man you could ever wish to meet—kind and generous and polite and always, always positive. And with Alzheimer's there's no faking it. Sometimes the worst traits of your personality rise to the surface. Sometimes the disease brings out characteristics you wouldn't wish on your worst enemy. Not with my dad. He's still the same lovely, positive, gentle person he's always been.

He's a man who's seen action. He enlisted as soon as he could in the war (as his generation calls it. There've been more wars since). He fought in North Africa and was behind the lines in Italy and France. He was evacuated at Dunkirk and almost lost his life when his ship was bombed. Saved, as he always tells the story with a smile on his face, in his "py-jamas" by a small fishing boat, part of the flotilla that came out in the dead of night to rescue the soldiers. What a farce it was, he relates, marching along the coast of France only to be sent back, marching the way they'd already come from. He smiles, though, remembering only the camaraderie and the friends he made.

With the Alzheimer's he spends most of his waking hours in those post-war years, when he was still a young man. Sometimes married and sometimes in the heady days of courtship. The most surreal conversations are the most fun—whether and how he's going to ask his now wife to marry him. Whether she's the one and what tactics he can employ to get her to say yes. It feels very strange to be giving your dad dating advice.

But as he gets older, he's become harder to care for. Not in his attitude. Just in his needs. He lost his sight ten years ago, and he lives mainly in darkness. It can make the world a very scary place if he's left alone, one of his therapists told us. Try to give him one-to-one support.

But one-to-one support is hard to manage, and the professionals say, "Oh, we can only intervene when there is a crisis." Apparently trying to avert a crisis isn't reason enough for intervention.

STRENGTH

After an increasingly tough few months, my mom's started to exhibit her own dementia. Or is it stress? Or just exhaustion. Who really knows. They say that caring can take a bigger toll on the carer. And so it has proved.

So we went through a few weeks of Mom phoning the emergency services every day and then them phoning me and me repeating each time that I can't be the one to say she doesn't need them. And her landlord calling me about the confused phone calls they get because "the hot water isn't working for her to make a cup of tea."

Yes, it's probably dementia talking, but at some level it's a cry for help. One that no one listens to. And when she is offered help, she won't take it. Total deadlock.

And with the burden of twenty-four-hour care for my lovely dad, she finally cracks. Is it relief or rock bottom that we've reached that "crisis" that everyone seems to have been waiting for?

But, nothing is ever all bad. Finally, we can get better support for my lovely dad—for the Alzheimer's but also for his visual needs. He is a man who now needs help washing and dressing. Who needs his food to be cut up and who needs someone around to know that he gets anxious in a dark environment. To know that he does better with bright lights and a colored cup. Please don't give him white bread sandwiches on a white plate because he can't see them. Let him keep what dignity he has by providing him with contrasting colors and someone he can laugh with.

So the last few weeks have been a blur of hospitals and care homes, driving around in an ever-increasing circle looking at yet more facilities. Maybe we should have been better prepared. Maybe we should have realized this is what it was coming to. Maybe I'VE been in denial about it? But, really, no one prepares you for this.

And in the midst of this, life doesn't stop. My family goes off on holiday without me, and my business is waiting for me to develop launch content for my new training program. Even the dog gets left home alone.

Everyone gets ignored.

For the boys I talk on Skype and vow never again to let them go off without me again.

For the business I go offline for a week and then decide on the spur of the moment to let some close connections into the course for free. I had no plan. Just the feeling that I'd rather share the content with a few people I knew would benefit, than it sit, being no use to anyone.

"Go get it," I said. "It's my gift to you. I want someone to take something good from this tough time."

And it's true that positive intentions flow back around. Unexpectedly, maybe. Unplanned, certainly. I know enough to know that doing good makes me feel good. But this goes beyond that. The students love the content. And they take action and start to get their books out there.

And the connections from it are wonderful. Like Ralph: "You've changed my life," he said. "Really, you have." Comments like this from these amazing people have uplifted me more than they will ever know.

And somehow that positive energy flows back to my dad. They don't know him or even know about his situation. But I know. And I know that somehow out of a bad situation, my spur-of-the-moment generosity has created more love in the world. I can't explain it, but it works.

And, no matter how bad things seem, even in the worst situation you can create moments of sheer happiness.

My boys spend afternoons with him in the remainder of the school holidays, time that is surprisingly calming despite the uncertainty of the circumstances. Despite the Alzheimer's, he knows who we are, and it's a respite for all of us just to sit and enjoy the sun with him, to reminisce about the old days and his old war-time buddies.

And he loves to be taken out. Such a difference from those last months at home when my mom kept him close, almost defensively trying to keep the carers away. We took him to the river on Saturday. A short walk and then an hour of hand-holding while we sat in the afternoon sunshine.

"Is it tea-time yet?" he says. "Will Dolly know where I am?" (his long-gone sister he hasn't seen for decades). "It's OK, Dad, she knows where you are." With his Alzheimer's he most often lives in the past. But he's present enough to know that he's happier around us. He knows we're important to him—people he loves and who love him.

So, whatever's going on around you, you can always create joyful moments. Live for them. Seize them with both hands and love them. The only time that matters is today.

Cathy Presland is an economist turned strategist who works with entrepreneurs who want to create a great business and a sustainable income from online training programs. Author of *Get Momentum Guide to Starting a Business,* she brings a unique combination of inspiration, motivation, and real, actionable strategies. Cathy's mission is to help you create a business you love so that you can be inspired to do the big stuff. You can get to know her at CathyPresland.com.

THE STRENGTH THAT COMES THROUGH DARK SPACES
Lisa Grace Byrne

After the birth of my first son, I could hardly talk about the experience. I didn't know how to share it, didn't know who to tell or even what to talk about.

Instantly, I catapulted into the terrain of new motherhood. Life submerged under a haze. I lost my orientation, and the world felt murky and confusing.

But what I do know is that something within me splintered.

One part of me could bond and love my little one. Could nurture and nurse. Could hold and rock and nuzzle and breathe in all the sweetness and goodness of his little being. One part of me reveled in the miracle of this experience and felt the joy-surges rise in unexpected moments of being with him.

Another part of me began to drift away. I was alternatively calm and present and then instantly racked with anxiety and overwhelm, processing layers of grief and trauma internally with no idea how to seek out help.

I was deeply depressed, in the depths of sleep-deprived neurosis that would give way to intense bouts of weeping at any moment.

One of my clearest memories was one of the lowest, most broken points of my journey.

About a week and a half after the birth of my son, my stitches hadn't come out from my episiotomy, and I was feeling pain in that area, so I thought I might have been infected. I made an appointment with my midwife (with whom I had a horrible experience with during the birth.)

I sat in her examination room waiting to see her, holding back tears and desperately trying to keep it together. I was naked underneath a simple paper covering. It was cold in her office. I was slightly shivering.

She entered and never once looked me in the eyes. She spoke into her chart. She told me to lie back and barely touched me. "Everything looks fine. Anything else?" she asked. I said no. She left and closed the door.

It must have taken me fifteen minutes to get myself composed from hysterically crying in order to dress and leave the building.

And it was that day that strength came to visit me.

By the time I reached my car, an otherworldly peace saturated my whole being.

This moment marked my journey (a long, winding journey) back to myself. In an instant I saw my pattern of handing over the care of my body, mind, and heart to people who were not worthy to have that level of access to me.

I entered motherhood with no maternal network. None of my close friends at that point had children.

I had no deep soul-sister friend network locally either. I had recently moved back to my home state and spent so many years living in other areas of the country that my close friends were simply not anywhere nearby.

And as I entered this new phase of my life, it became painfully obvious how distanced I felt emotionally with my mother. While my mother was always a doer and provider for my sister and me, I often grieved not knowing her deeply, not having access to her heart, and not feeling known by her throughout my life. Becoming a mother magnified these feelings and heaped another layer of intensity on my journey.

It is hard when you don't have a strong, loving, and emotionally connected network of support available to you. But strength rises when you would rather choose to walk the path alone for a while instead of handing over access to yourself to those not worthy.

I kept looking for strength to come swooping in on mighty horseback...but I've come to learn it often doesn't travel that way.

Strength comes on soft breezes, through dark spaces, and fits into the tiny cracks and fissures in your life.

As I drove home after that appointment, I was calmer than I had been for a long time. I had released the need to be well cared for by someone who was not able or available to do so. I began to protect my own inner, sacred core—a lesson I continue to learn how to do again and again.

I drove in my car and the world was flying by, and it was as though a veil had been lifted.

I went home and I held my baby. I offered my breast and fed this little child. I let in the strength that is perfected in weakness.

I softened around my broken places. I stopped judging the hard parts, and I began the long journey of loving all that is.

And loving all that is can simply be a wild and timid act of lifting up the lack, the less than, the needy, and the cracked places of your life as an offering—opening up a pathway where strength can come in and mend and make you whole again.

Lisa Grace Byrne, MPH CHHC, is building a worldwide community of healthy, strong, and vibrant mothers. She is an author, teacher, speaker, and founder of WellGrounded Life, which offers virtual courses and workshops for moms who want to restore their vitality and well-being. Visit her at www.WellGroundedLife.com.

STRENGTH IN THE TENDEREST PLACES
Grace Quantock

Strength was not something I was born with. It was not bequeathed to me in my DNA, nor floated into my crib as a fairy christening gift. I wasn't brought up to be a tower of tenacity and stamina.

To me, strength came as a circle. And it lives in the shape of a woman. In fact, of many women.

It is women who have helped me through the hardest times of my life.

The connections we make, forged in the dark nights when there seems no space for your soul, no hope, and no light coming. Bonds built then live onward, no matter what comes.

Wise women shared their power and learning with me. They taught me skills with the dowsing rods, how to read the cards, the meanings of the moon, and how to turn a cantrip to weave a charm.

When you have stood on the front lines facing mounted riot police. The name of the woman who pulled you from under the kicking mass that threatened to swallow you. The woman who got arrested with you so you wouldn't be alone in cells and scared. She is strength to me, and caring.

The circle, reaching out across the country. Five girls, all confined to bed. All desperately ill, but weaving from their beds, from their tender hearts, connections, cards, and caring that changed the world.

This circle was all I had to hold onto, my connection to the outside world; the women were my comrades and my fellow soldiers. Our bodies were the battleground and we fought with love. I write what I write now for all the girls who died and all the girls who didn't.

My first business was birthed from the piles of parcels and letters that flew between us. Knowing that not everyone is blessed to have such a circle, we built a business to send boxes of goodies to those hurting and in need of comfort. There is a handmade card in every box, just like the ones we sent back in the beginning.

I celebrated my twenty-first birthday with these girls; it was my first long-distance party, and we all wore princess hats with tumbling veils. My attic room was decorated as a palace (or as much as you can turn the servants' quarters of an eighteenth century townhouse into a palace).

These women listened to me, comforted me, needed me, and taught me how to have a full life without being able to lift my arms.

It can be easy to seem strong when we are standing tall, but what about when we are broken? There is strength in vulnerability, and I saw her split open, and I knew that in the pain, in the moment of breaking heart and breaking bones, there was true strength. Because in the pain was the hope and the trust that she would heal and grow strong again. To know that if it all falls there is something inside you that will pull you through as you start again, I see strength there.

It was a woman who held me through the birth of my book, teasing the tangles of ideas and spreading them out before me. We had a green sheet covered in Post-it notes pinned into chapters with dressmakers' pins. Every day we pulled it out, pins scattering, and turned the ideas into actions.

Strong women freed me from the confines of my mind. I was out of bed but stuck behind bars of old beliefs about my abilities. There are women out there changing the world from their stilettos and iPads 2s. Women in business are making beautiful changes, and every woman they empower and inspire leaves that place and goes on to help so many more. It is a secret, sweet sisterhood, and I am so grateful to have been sheltered by these women as I grew my wings.

Strength comes wrapped in airmail paper, in blue smudge ink, and is treasured. Letters, back and forth across the sea, between my best friend and me. We ink down our souls and figure out how to live, and after you didn't die, how to keep living.

Strength is not carrying on despite the pain; it isn't becoming hard and resisting. Becoming harder does not mean growing stronger. We are strongest when we feel the pain and choose to keep on loving, when we are bowed and aching but still wear body glitter, when we can't see the way forward but take the hand of the woman who walked this way before us and step out.

I am building circles still, a hundred thousand threads of golden gossamer, reaching out to women wellness warriors, blazing trails across the world. From my heart to yours, may you grow strong and have women to hold you as you do.

Grace Quantock is a sick chick turned wellness provocateur and healing trailblazer. She is an award-winning international wellness expert, motivational speaker, writer, and founder of Healing Boxes CIC. Connect with Grace and Turn Trail Blazer at GraceQuantock.com.

MY RECIPE FOR SUCCESS
Tracey Ceurvels

My daughter arrived on a sunny April day in 2008, almost a month earlier than her May due date. To say that I wasn't prepared for her is an understatement. I didn't have her crib, bureau, or her room set up. While I was in the hospital, my husband and parents raced to get it all done for our arrival home. Yet, even with the essentials in place, I wasn't prepared for the exhaustion that ensued. This little lovable creature needed me, all of me, all the time. I embraced my new role with the vigor of a new mom, even as my eyelids wanted to shut in the middle of the day or couldn't open during middle-of-the-night feedings. I'd spent my entire life without anyone needing me so, and admittedly it took some adjusting. As a new parent, I shed my former way of existing, like last year's spring garden now sprouting entirely different plants.

Fast-forward a few months. I was nestled into motherhood and my new routine. Not having had a "real job" in a few years, choosing instead to be a freelance writer, editor, and copywriter who worked both at home and in offices, I had carved out my own maternity leave, which basically meant if I wasn't in front of my computer I wasn't getting paid. Not only did I need to make an income, I also wanted to work: writing is a visceral part of me, and it was gnawing at me like a loud dream.

I remember a voice inside of me asking me what it would be like to write only what I wanted to and skip the writing I no longer enjoyed.

I remember asking myself how I could work for myself 100 percent.

I remember the same voice telling me that surely there was a way to marry my passions with making a living.

I remember a voice saying I wanted a new way of existing and earning money so that I could be there for my daughter and not leave her in the care of nannies.

Then an e-mail appeared in my inbox that seemed to be written for my eyes only. It was from a coach who promised a path to fulfill one's dreams, which is something I desired and couldn't figure out on my own. I hired her and together we crafted what would become my blog and business, The Busy Hedonist. It's a hub that encapsulates my passions: food, travel, and writing. I didn't know then my website would bring me the freedom I'd always desired.

For me, freedom means living life according to my own terms. It means designing each day according to my own desires. It means creating a career doing what I am good at, and doing only things I enjoy. It means making a living whether I'm glued to my MacAir or running around The Metropolitan Museum of Art with my daughter.

Since I am lover of great food, I call it my recipe for success. And since following that recipe, I've created my own personal version.

I pursue my passions of food, writing, and travel. I venture around the world in search of a great dish. I stand in my kitchen creating recipes for my busy food-loving readers at The Busy Hedonist. I dine out in NYC restaurants and discover unique ingredients and spices and cookbooks that home cooks will love and enjoy. I wrote a novel, and I'm now working on a screenplay and my own cookbook.

The adage "Do what you love and the money will follow" has rung true for me. What I do never feels like work. I'm focused on doing what I enjoy—all while making a living.

And you can do this too. To me, recipes are personal and you can create your own version for a successful and fulfilling life.

Tracey Ceurvels is a writer, journalist, food lover, and traveler who ventures around the world in search of a great dish. She teaches the art of travel writing, coaches writers, and inspires home cooks in the kitchen on her blog, *The Busy Hedonist*. Her articles about food and travel appear in *The Boston Globe*, The Gourmet Food Blog at Dean & Deluca, Hauteliving.com, and other publications. To learn more about Tracey or her app, NYC iFoodShop, visit TheBusyHedonist.com.

WHY IS BEING YOURSELF SO DAMN HARD
Molly Mahar

One of the toughest things you can do these days is "be yourself" in a world that wants you to be so many different things, all at the same time...

You hear, "Be sexy. Vulnerable. Good. Young. Successful. A survivor. Be dutiful. Creative. Loyal. Nice. A superwoman. Thin. Quiet. Rich. Be fashionable. Assertive. A homemaker. A businesswoman. Savvy. Connected. Be soft. Be strong."

You consume so many messages from others—from society, your community, your families—that tell you what is acceptable, desirable, or achievable that you can't hear the siren song within you—the song that screams with craving, melodious with individual choice, and laced with a booty-shaking beat.

That song gets quieted.

Instead, you wake up every morning with a heavy heart as you prepare do to battle with another day. You repeat the unspoken mantra of successful women: "Do it all and make it look easy. Do it all and make it look easy. Do it all and make it look easy."

You try to be all things to all people. To succeed. To measure up. To achieve.

Being yourself? Not even on your radar.

Until one day it is.

Without warning, that siren song of individuality plays full blast and nothing you do lowers the volume. You start hearing the cravings of your inner self. You start questioning the snide remarks of your inner critic who has been cackling with glee all these years of smallness and conformity. You start ignoring the expectations of others.

External measures of success, maps for the expected path, and the need to make others happy at your own expense start slowly fading away.

It's absurdly uncomfortable to start becoming yourself, but you'll arrive at the day when it's the only choice you have.

When you start standing up for yourself and your life, you'll get huge amounts of resistance from others. It's often disguised as thinly veiled friendly advice or assumptive motherly concern or backhanded compliments.

"A freelance writer? How amazing would that be? I don't know anyone who has pulled that off!"

"Moving to Brazil? How brave of you! Isn't that dangerous?"

"Oh gosh, I remember when I wanted to get a divorce. I finally realized that it just wasn't worth putting the kids through that."

You often start the unraveling of your staid social shell in small and symbolic gestures—dying your hair, getting a tattoo, or starting a blog to write with your real voice. You might progress to traveling on your own, quitting your job, breaking up with someone who "seemed perfect," or embarking on a dream that seems crazy to everyone else.

You will end up learning how to love yourself, truly and deeply, and through the messy, dark, and uncomfortable moments.

All of this "being yourself" may feel like a fight for your life—a battle for the ability to follow your heart in a society that doesn't celebrate those who stray off the path.

But let me tell you this, darling.

In being yourself, you're allowing yourself the ultimate honor. In finally tuning into your siren song, you're earning mad karmic soul points as the universe conspires to help you live your dreams.

You're saying, "I see you, Self, and I think your quirks, your ideas, your ways of engaging the world are beautiful. I'm not going to shove it down or shut you up any longer. I'm going to let you bubble to the surface in all your madness and glory.

"I'm going to let you dye your hair purple, or go to space camp, or live in the fire tower. I'm going to let you sell all your stuff so you can afford the tiny loft in East Village, or go back to school to get your MFA, or travel through Southeast Asia, or start that business. I'm going to let you homeschool your kids, or take a lover, or stand up to the injustice you've been enduring.

"I trust your intuition about people and opportunities.

"I want you to take giant leaps of faith and lean on others by asking for help. I will allow you to ignore the haters, to let the negative comments ping off your back, because you understand that you can't please everyone but that pleasing yourself is most important.

"You, Self, are strong enough to do all of this. You do not have to be everything to everyone all at the same time. You just have to be you."

Your strength is measured not in fighting or conflict or winning, but in remaining true to that inner voice and those crazy dreams. Your strength can be measured by putting the work in every day, by picking your own heart off the floor, and by running your own race.

Being yourself and allowing others the same grace is your measure of strength.

You do not need to "Do it all and make it look easy."

You do need to be you.

Flex those muscles. Listen deeply. Let go of external expectations—the "should," the "have-tos," and the "rules." Play your gorgeous siren song on repeat as you tackle showing up as yourself day in and day out.

Let it become easy. Trust in your strength.

I will do the same, soul sister. (The world be damned.)

Molly Mahar is a coach, speaker, writer, fierce love advocate, and joy enthusiast. She is the founder of Stratejoy, a positive corner of the Internet that provides thousands of women the strategies and inspiration to lead authentically joyful lives. Molly helps women in transition rediscover themselves through online courses, group coaching, and soul-stirring one-on-one work. Visit her at Stratejoy.com.

BREAKING DOWN THE WALLS
Amanda Krill

I've got walls. There I said it. I'm not strong. It's my walls.

I made it through adolescence with two lazy eyes with the help of my walls.

I've lost friends to cancer and a car accident, lost grandparents whom I held very dear, lost dreams, lost babies, lost love. I've spent money I didn't have (to the tune of $64,000) on credit cards I shouldn't have had and nearly lost my husband.

In my short life, I think I've lost more than my share. And I've always thought the walls I've put up around my heart are the only thing that kept me standing.

Thanks to my walls, I've weathered a lot of storms. And I've always thought that equaled strength.

Six years ago, I sat down with a calculator and my secret credit card bills. I went through and added them all up. Then I cried. How in the world did I let it get so out of control?

When I really, really thought about it, I realized a lot of my spending happened…get this…because of my walls.

I was unwilling to share my frustration with anyone. I was a stay-at-home mom of three very small (like all under three years old small) children. I was tired. I was angry. I felt like I didn't even exist anymore. My only job was to keep these kids clean and fed.

Now don't get me wrong—I adore these kids. And I wouldn't go back and not have them for the entire world. But—and this is a huge but—I felt both ashamed and afraid of the way I was feeling.

My walls were higher than ever. I felt like I couldn't tell anyone—especially my husband. He was already struggling in a job he hated. He was already overwhelmed from having three kids too. And he felt so far away that I didn't think it was a good idea to make things heavier than they already were by telling him I wasn't happy.

So I went shopping. A lot. I bought stupid stuff for the kids that they didn't need. I went crazy at Christmas, buying way more than anyone ever needed. I even put groceries on a credit card because I wanted to buy what I wanted rather than following a budget.

When I really think about it, the walls were what created some of my hardest struggles. They kept me from speaking my truth—and kept me from making myself vulnerable. Coming from a place of vulnerability is terrifying for me because I have delusions of strength, but the fact remains, in vulnerability is strength.

I realize now that it isn't my walls that have given me strength. It was me all along. The times that I've made it through my greatest trials, it's always been because I let the walls down and let myself out.

With this realization, I've also realized that strength comes in many shapes and sizes. The more I let my walls down, the more I see that people that I've never thought of as strong have their own strength. Even in situations that I know I would never make it through, they show strength that I know I don't have.

Strength is a woman loving her husband through his alcoholism and believing that he can change.

Strength is walking away when you know you can't change him.

Strength is getting up every day not knowing how you are going to feed your kids…but getting up anyway.

Strength is doing whatever you can do to put food in your kids' mouths.

Strength is leaving a job you hate and following your heart.

Strength is staying where you are and sticking it out while you nurture your dreams on the side.

Strength is standing up to the bully who won't let up.

Strength is quietly loving the bully and waiting for God to change their heart.

Strength is helping those who don't deserve it.

And strength is helping those who do.

We may not always feel it. And though sometimes you feel like you've got nothing left, you still get up every day and push through. That is strength.

Walking the road that God has put in front of you without fear because deep down you know that there are no mistakes is strength.

Letting yourself be vulnerable to other people is strength.

And most importantly, I've finally learned that tearing down the walls that have kept you safe for far too long is strength.

Amanda Krill is an intuitive web designer, branding coach, and marketing specialist. Her mission is to make over the Internet one website at a time. She is a Christian, a mom of three, and a wife who loves going to the movies, reading anything by C.S. Lewis or JRR Tolkien, and she is an avid fan of the Pittsburgh Pirates and the Chicago Bears. To learn more about Amanda, visit AmandaKrill.com.

TUNING THE MUSICAL INSTRUMENT OF YOU

Mahalia Michaels

Have you ever gotten to a place in your life where you knew that there was no going back to who or what you once were? Where it feels like you are standing at the edge of an alluring threshold, toes dangling, pants down and curious? Knowing that the only place to go or thing to do is jump headfirst into faith? That is how I felt after I healed the gaps in my brain, reunited and balanced my feminine and masculine energy, released my past traumas, and owned my sexual potency. This was when I began to shine and play my music. This is my birthright, and this is your birthright too!

Based on the rise in disease statistics, stress being the number one killer, it appears evident that we have a problem. Presently, much of the human race is surviving about 99 percent of the time in the sympathetic, hyper-arousal, adrenaline overdrive, fight-or-flight mode. We have forgotten to thrive in the parasympathetic, oxytocin-rich, trusting, loving, resting, digesting, cuddling, soothing, and nourishing mode. Did you know that you must be in a parasympathetic state in order to achieve an orgasm? This is why it feels so good to be making love. What if we tipped the scales over to our parasympathetic selves and invited more feminine softness into our lives more of the time? What if we maintained the ability to unite both ends of this hormonal smoothie in our brain, the likes of Master Trivedi, for bliss and omnipotent creation? What if this was how Master Jesus and Buddha did it? What if this was the recipe for infinite happiness, wellness, and success in all areas, including mental, emotional, physical, and spiritual? What if we all self-regulated our systems like this at the same time? What would our earth and her people be like then?

I was born a sparkling, innocent baby girl, full of love, sensuality, and passion for life. I was kindhearted, gentle, highly sensitive, and connected to the magical, spirit world, my Hunter/Edison genetics, and my intuitive, feminine, right-brained nature. Yet, at early development, my innocent being was shadowed with dark layers of fear, guilt, shame, self-doubt, and insecurity. You see, I was sexually traumatized at six years of age, soon followed by my first head injury. At the same time, a close family member began to bully me. As years passed and the bullying continued, I silently morphed into a biological soup for self-destruction. My ego mind and subconscious began a large cycle of pain and suffering. I became extremely competitive, utilizing my masculine energy and left brain for a false sense of protection and survival. Over time, I attracted six more head injuries, some serious concussions, causing me undiagnosed post-traumatic stress disorder (PTSD) and dysfunction. I was high functioning, yet my brain was divided with holes and gaps, my sexual fire was limp, and my heart was stuck in a prison of sadness. I moved every six months, having accumulating over sixty addresses. I could not hold a job, create financial stability, or attract healthy relationships. I began to stutter, I was nervous in public situations, and I had to wear glasses for my lazy eye. My breathing was short and strained, I had panic attacks, and I feared almost everything. I felt invisible and that my life was not worth living. I thought I was dealt a bad deck. I thought I was indeed a horrible, messed-up person, yet on some deeper level, I remained loving, forgiving, hopeful, and believing there must be more joy to this human experience.

My turning point happened during my seventh head injury. While speeding face first off of my bike into a huge rock, a miracle happened as my life flashed before my eyes. I could see parts of me living in cycles of pain, conflict, and torment. And, I could also see a caring, intelligent, genuine woman who wanted to be a better person, living a better life. I could see tiny sparkles in my heart, and this beam of dreams encouraged me. While lying grass-stained, shocked, broken, and tangled in the ditch, I boldly asked Spirit, "Please show me why I was put on this earth and how you want me to serve!"

A few weeks later and through a cycle of synchronistic events, Spirit answered in the form of a psycho-neurophysiologist. This doctor performed bloodless brain surgery and explained to me that I had the brain waves of a war veteran causing me a disability. He said that I had had this disability since my first childhood trauma. My brain had gone into a protective, repetitive shell. He asked if I would like to get unstuck off of the repeat cycle. As streams of hot tears rolled down my cheeks, I nodded yes and started my three-year journey of using sound harmonics to weave my brain and body back together. While hooked up to a computer that transmitted nourishing acoustics to my hungry brain, I also began to get in touch with my physical, mental, and emotional past. My traumas surfaced one by one, and as my strength grew, I eliminated their frequency. I absorbed any information I could about the brain, the effects of trauma, and PTSD that allowed me to clarify my disability and continue my path of resurrection. I learned that one small bump to the head can and will attract more bumps, just as traumatic, dramatic moments can and will repeat if nothing changes. It took me over one hundred various brainwave biofeedback and acoustical sound treatments to repair the holes, gaps, and neurosis in my brain. As I did, my original, feminine, intuitive, sensual nature returned.

As she returned, the fountain of my feminine sexuality was revealed. This is where the sacred, the mystical, and the alchemical magic of a woman thrives. Uniting with my divine feminine energy has allowed me to give back to Mother Earth in ways I could not have imagined before. "Why are we not taught this in school?" I ask myself. I feel it must be taught now in order to quench the lush Womb of Creation, emancipating people, especially women, to their birthright of pure love, freedom, joy, peace, innocence, wholeness, and oneness.

Sadly, there are millions of people suffering from these same visible and invisible injuries and who may not be aware of how to heal from these repetitive cycles. Imagine millions of innocent people stuck repeating trauma and drama! My book, *Sensual YOU*, was written to educate and illuminate people on this subject. It is resource-rich with diamond tools for both recovery and infinite happiness.

That being said, I invite you back to your sensual, oxytocin-rich, parasympathetic self. The one who is loving, orgasmic, and biologically blessed. The one who enjoys pleasure. The one who sparkles and shines. The one with beams of dreams, who knows there is so much more to this human dance. The one who is a naked alchemist.

To tune the musical instrument of YOU, start by #1. Falling madly in love with the wild, mysterious, divine feminine nature within and all around us. She is where our primal, sexual nature and power of creation resides and thrives. She offers the natural, organic, intuitive healing that is so greatly needed on our planet. She is pure, unconditional love. She always has been and she always will be. #2. Integrate and marry your inner masculine and feminine, left and right brain hemispheres, yin and yang. Unite the god and goddess, shiva and shakti of your understanding; bring them together to make love in the center of your mind. #3. Flood your brain and body with your feel-good hormone, oxytocin. This is achieved especially during orgasm. This is your personal loving, cuddling, bonding, and trusting neurotransmitter. Men and women both produce oxytocin. The more we share, care, and cuddle, the more we feel good and prosper.

This is where we pave a new path, heart, mind, body, and soul for a fresh, luminous life experience. The more musical wholeness and love that we see, feel, and be on the inside, the more harmonious heaven on earth we will see, feel, and be on the outside. Quantum science has proven that we are 99 percent energy and

1 percent matter. Is it possible then that we exist because this energy and this matter are making love? It is our birthright to feel good and SHINE! Now, imagine millions of innocent people awake, alive, and tuned to a nourishing and sensual musical symphony.

Naked: Raw, without ego, authentic, human, heart open, unplugged, and loving.

Alchemist: One who transmutes a common substance into something of great value.

Mahalia Michaels is a visionary, sound mystic, alchemist, author, dancer, international educator, and nurturing leader in the movement of self-love and actualization. She has practiced as a holistic health professional, educator, and loving guide for eighteen years. She is also the author, host, and founder of Sensual YOU, a book and play-shop designed to educate, illuminate, and activate sensual consciousness. To learn more about Mahalia, visit TheNakedAlchemist.com or Lummunocity.com.

WISDOM IS STRENGTH
Kimberely Arana

"Wisdom is Strength."

For our anniversary a few years back, my husband bought this amazing antique needlepoint sampler with these words. It shows the weight of time: brown and delicate, carefully preserved in a roughly fashioned old wooden frame. It holds court on the wall in our dining room, which is also the heart of the house. I homeschool, so my children and I spend many hours here, learning about the classic "Three R's" and what Russell Means calls the "Three L's": Look, Listen, and Learn. We share our meals, of course, and giggle and cry over the slow accumulation of life events, making memories. Every day at some point I look up at this ode to strength, meticulously crafted years ago by a local young woman, and it steels my heart for the years to come.

* * *

My eldest had always been "quirky" and a bit demanding. Seems like the first three years of her life she never slept, living completely off the vast love that she and I and her papa thrived on. Preferring more often to indulge in self-play rather than with other kids, I rationalized to myself she's a loner like her father. She was in turn intrigued and in awe of the world around her, and yet oddly disinterested and disengaged from the usual play of toddlers. She never cared for the social hen-pecking that young girls start up eventually. I took this as a sign that she had an instinctive wisdom and kindness, her amazingly innocent and sweet nature supporting this. It didn't occur to me it may also be because she literally couldn't understand it.

So, yes, I knew from the time she was born that she was different. Unusual. She is the utter opposite of what I would think of if you asked about "strength" and what it means to me. Delicate and wispy, there are times it seems she just hasn't fully landed here on earth yet. Sometimes I worry she might blow away with the harsh winds of modern life and we'll lose her forever.

Over time, it became clear that I was her anchor, and this frightened me. When she left the snug safety of our home and went off to school (just across the street), it become painfully obvious that she was not just quirky or unusual, but that something was "not right" (words used more than once since she was in preschool, with raised eyebrows and that pinched look of concern).

I can remember the very moment I realized that this was going to be lifelong challenge, not something we just needed to "get through" or that she would grow out of, the very moment when I first faced that my own years of struggle and challenges, my own definitions of strength, were about to become meaningless, the very moment when I have to admit that I finally, fully stepped into my role as her mother and owned this responsibility.

And in that moment, I was terrified by how weak I felt.

I had just come out of a brutal meeting with a school administration for issues regarding the care and teaching of our then second grade little girl. We had been going through a huge battle for almost two years, an intense hazing as we entered into the special needs machine of the public school system. I had started out trusting and naïve. We were now at a stage of being shocked, tired…and angry. We were being lied to, and my child was being mistreated. She was spiraling down into a chronic state of intense anxiety, unable to learn and afraid of her peers. We had many nights once again of no sleep; I would hold her tight as she quietly sobbed in my arms and asked me, "What's wrong with me, mama?"

On that night that is framed forever, much like the above adage, in my mind, I ran into another local mother there in the empty parking lot under the dim yellow lights; she was a real ballbuster and had a child of her own in this system. She was a seasoned fighter, this one. Standing there with keys in hand to unlock her car door, I started asking her questions. I was hoping for sage words, some kind thoughts and reassurance. Some evidence that I had been wrong about all the judgments I was harboring toward these adults at the school entrusted with my child. Instead, in an instant she changed my life, handing over my fighting orders and a battle cry:

"You better get ready, Mom! You've got a lifetime ahead of you fighting for your girl if you want her to get what she needs. You think it's bad here? It's bad all over with how these kids get pushed aside and forgotten. YOU'RE all she's got, Mama Bear! So you'd better pull those claws out and FIGHT for her."

You know those moments in your life when everything seems to come to a grinding halt with a realization that slaps you in the face? I still feel the crunching of my gut with those words, and just now the sting of tears arrive on cue, all over again. I knew this woman was right; I knew that it was my job to be Mama Bear. And I was so afraid I didn't have the power that I couldn't find the strength to do what I had to, to be what my daughter needed. To fight for her in ways I never felt others had for me.

I was terrified I would fail my child.

I went home and cried myself to sleep, my husband tenderly rubbing my back while I dreamt of all the battles ahead of me.

* * *

"Wisdom is Strength."

I'm relearning all the time, through my firstborn, not only what true strength means but also how it will serve her. It's not just about what you are physically capable of, just as our lovely sampler pays homage to. And it's not even what you are willing or able to fight for. (That's in the department of courage.)

In her life, and now in mine, it's about what you carry deep inside, what you listen to, and what you are willing to trust when nothing makes sense. For me, sometimes it's about knowing when is the right time to hold back the tears or to let them the flow…It's about trusting my inner wisdom and letting it lead, even when the room is dark and I have no idea where we're going. It's also about trusting my child's inner wisdom and helping her to do the same.

I used to associate strength with everything physical; I loved feeling physically strong and hated feeling small or weak. But I see now that having physical power has nothing to do with true strength. Strength comes from somewhere else, a place deep within that partners with the spark of life and a desire to thrive. And I worry—still do, if I'm being honest, even though she proves me wrong all the time—that my child will not have the inner strength she needs emotionally to navigate the challenges of life. The best way I can help her is to guide her toward listening to her own inner wisdom, to trust it and cooperate with it so that it grows strong and reliable, no matter the odds, so that someday, when Mama Bear isn't around, she has the strength to stand her ground by trusting her own inner wisdom.

Kimberely Arana teaches spiritual growth and personal well-being and is the founder of unshakablesoul.com. A natural intuitive, soul medium and initiated shamanic practitioner, she has over twenty years' experience in deep spiritual awareness and alternative healing. She holds a BA with honors from John F. Kennedy University—a pioneer in consciousness studies and holistic health—and is a graduate of the Northwest School of Botanical Studies/Professional Herbalist Program. To learn more about Kimberely, visit UnshakableSoul.com.

DANCING INTO JOY
Lela Barker

My soul drew inward as I sat with Cecilia's petite hand nestled inside my own. The cacophony of the world had gone silent; our surroundings blurred out of focus as I gently stroked her hand. The hue of her skin was so black that it appeared almost blue, her fingers short and stunted. Though I found solace in the warmth of her tender skin, I was reluctant to look anywhere other than our intertwined hands. Overwhelmed with waves of nausea, I listened closely as the translator repeated her story that day in the shade of a shea tree in the village of Otuke in northern Uganda.

The rebel soldiers of The Lord's Resistance Army had raided her village years ago, on the prowl for more children to take. More supplies to pillage. More women to torture. More havoc to wreak. Cecilia had narrowly escaped with her life, red rivers of blood seeping from a deep stab in her leg. All things considered, she counted herself lucky. Her daughter had been stabbed over and over again, left for dead in a pool of blood. A villager noticed her lungs drawing in shallow breaths the next morning as she lay in a field among the dead.

Streaks of warmth traced my cheeks. I could taste the saltiness as the streams rolled over my lips, hesitated for a moment, and escaped down my chin. My breaths were slow and deliberate as I battled a flash of heat that threatened my consciousness. My thumb mapped circles in her open palm as Cecilia spoke softly in the local dialect. I steadied my courage and lifted my head. The milky whites of her eyes were muddled by sorrow as she gazed off into the distance. When recounting the horror, it seemed easier for both of us to avoid eye contact. That soulful connection personalized the experience, and I feared the tsunami of emotion that it would inevitably unleash.

We carried on like that for a while, a gathering of women peering at imagined points of concentration far off in the distance as horrors were retold. A husband beaten so severely that he's permanently lame and blind. A nephew abducted; missing for seven years now, his fate unknown. A woman lost three bothers in a single day to rebel combat. Thatched roofs of village huts set ablaze as families slept peacefully inside. Monsters with semiautomatic machine guns standing just outside, ready to fire upon those who dared flee the flames licking at their feet.

Horrific tales of depravity poured from their lips, but no tears stained the cheeks of the women. I sensed that the reservoir of tears had long since been depleted, replaced with reluctant acceptance and finally, steely resolve.

Following a brief silence, one of the women rose to her feet rather suddenly and began to speak. Though I understood not a single syllable, there was a palpable strength in her tone. Others slowly rose and the sounds soon morphed into chant, which eventually evolved into melody. In unison—as if on cue—bare feet boldly struck the ground. Suddenly, the women erupted in dance.

Feet stomping. Tongues trilling. Hips swaying. Arms alternately reaching toward the sky and then retracting into claps. Jubilance!

These brave souls were fighting back against the evil that had come to roost in their quiet village. The cement walls of their homes still bore the scars of bullets. Their souls still bore the welts imposed by rape, torture, and loss. And yet they danced. With abandon. With genuine, unbridled joy. Though I was temporarily paralyzed by the juxtaposition of ecstasy and grief, Cecilia's broad smile and warm hands soon beckoned me to join them… feet stomping the bare earth, hands clapping in unison. Joy.

STRENGTH

We laughed together as they tried in vain to teach me the rhythmic African dances of their tribal lineage. Hearing the commotion, children ran to join us and soon undulated alongside us, giggling uncontrollably. Just moments ago, we were recounting their darkest days. Now? Now we were celebrating life.

As the day drew to a close, I embraced each woman, lingering for a moment in her arms and thanking them individually for the courage to share their stories with a complete stranger. Eventually, I crawled back into the truck to begin a long journey over rutted clay roads.

Back at my hotel and drained of emotion, I savored the comfort of the warm waters that poured over my body as I bathed in a bucket shower. Tucking myself in, I skillfully drew the mosquito net around my bed, imagining that it was a force field, protecting me from the atrocities I'd been exposed to that day.

My mind refused to be quieted as I struggled to process a vast range of emotions. How can they dance? How can these women who lived among evil, whose children have been snatched from their arms, who spent years in internal displacement camps brimming with disease but almost barren of food…how could they ever find joy again? Obviously, they have. I'd been blessed to witness their triumph for myself, but the mechanics of that process were lost on me.

As I lay there in darkness, I mediated on the bit of kismet that had brought me to Uganda. Earlier the same year, I'd been introduced to an American woman heading up an African nonprofit. They had recently expanded into shea butter production, and she approached me after hearing me speak about women's empowerment at a shea butter conference in Mali. We struck up a conversation, which blossomed into a friendship and eventually led me to this place.

You see, I own an international beauty company with distribution in more than one thousand spas across America, Europe, and the Middle East. My Bella Luccè® products have enjoyed a sell-out run on Shop At Home® television. The story of my company has been told in *Southern Living*, and my sugar scrubs and body crèmes have been featured in hundreds of glossy magazines. I've visited more than twenty countries on four continents to source exotic ingredients, attend press junkets, and develop proprietary treatments for some of the world's most iconic hotel properties. My passport bears the ink of a dozen Dubai entry stamps collected in less than thirty-six months. Pretty sexy stuff, eh?

You'd probably never suspect that eight years prior I was rationing food for myself and my two toddlers as I waited for the government to issue our monthly food stamp allowance. In 2002, I scooped up my two toddlers and walked away from a hopeless marriage without a dime to my name. I moved across the state to regroup and take refuge at my parents' home, deriving comfort in late-night chats with my mom over her famous chocolate pie.

Five years earlier, I had walked away from a full university scholarship at twenty-one years old after learning that I was simultaneously pregnant and battling cancer, neither of which had been in my master plan. At the ripe old age of twenty-six, I found myself broke, broken, and desperate. I'd never finished college, and now I was struggling to find any employer willing to take a gamble on a single mom with no marketable skills who was being dragged under by a tsunami of change.

So I pulled myself up by my bootstraps and created my own opportunity. Without the benefit of a bank loan, a college degree, or a sugar daddy, I founded a small business on a wing and a prayer. I battled through growing pains, a fledgling economy, the sting of jealousy from other women, and accounts gone bankrupt without settling the invoices they owed. I pushed past my own self-doubt and stared down the feeling of being a "fraud" because I didn't have a fancy business degree. I pressed onward despite the weariness spawned by an Atlas-worthy balancing act, juggling home, career, motherhood, and personal fulfillment.

And now I lay silent in a Ugandan village ten thousand miles from home, pondering how women who have faced adversity overcome their challenges to find joy in their existence.

And I realize that I, too, have come through a similar process. Thankfully, my children are healthy and still with me. I have a comfortable home with all the luxuries provided by my Western lifestyle. I sleep well at night without fear of my personal security. My troubles certainly aren't of the same caliber as my African friends, but we all have a boogeyman. We've all experienced sorrow and mourning. Mourning marriages, loved ones, freedom, financial security, health, missed opportunities…Pick your poison, but every one of us has been immersed in sorrow at one time or another.

That day in Uganda I learned the inherent value of the joy that comes from triumphing over adversity and evil. The importance of women coming together to share their experiences and support one another. The wisdom of dancing through sorrow.

I carry the spirit of those African women with me in all of my endeavors. When I feel lost, weary, or broken, I remove my shoes, strike the ground with my feet, and remind myself to dance into joy.

Ten years ago, Lela Barker was a broke and broken single mother living in her parents' spare bedroom. Today, she's the founder and CEO of Bella Luccè, a wildly successful international beauty company; the executive director of a Moroccan-based nonprofit; and president of Lucky Break, a small business consulting firm empowering creative entrepreneurs. Blessed with an innate business sense, she's succeeded on her own terms without the benefit of an investor, sugar daddy, or college degree. To learn more about Lela, visit LelaBarker.com.

SISTERHOOD OF STRENGTH
Jessika Hepburn

Always, always, for my mother.

The most courageous acts of extraordinary strength go unwitnessed and uncelebrated every single day. Our true heroes don't show up on the news, have fancy slick websites, or a bank account full of zeros. Bear witness to the strong-hearted sisters whose struggles go unseen, because if a woman cries out in the darkness and there is no one there to hear her, she is still weeping.

Witness the strength of the mother as she crawls out of bed after two hours of sleep to cradle her baby and pulls, from somewhere deep in her gut, the tenderness to whisper words of hope into those tiny ears. She doesn't feel hopeful; her heart is a pile of broken shiny bits that she is piecing back together, and her loneliness pokes constant holes in her heart, yet she reaches inside to find some speck of joy and breathe life into it. Day after day she puts her children to bed only to hit the books, until the sun peeks through her window and it's time to get the kids dressed for school.

Witness the strength of the advocate as she stands up into the silence to call out injustice, not once or twice, but every single time it slaps her in the face. She is the dark face in the white room, the *other*, the lone fist raised. She armors herself in conviction and steps out to be a voice for the unheard in a thousand little ways no one will thank her for. She's at city hall asking why the only community center is being shut down, taking on school administrations to include children with disabilities, and working for the rights of sex trade workers in our cities. Her passion for change makes her seem invulnerable, so she goes home to her apartment and falls silently, completely apart, then puts on her breastplate and goes back into the battle.

Witness the strength of the survivor as she swims up fierce dark rivers of the heart. All alone she becomes her own lifeline and pulls herself to shore, but she can't find moorage, the bank is slippery, and she is adrift. No Cinderella happy ending for the battered girl as she claws her way back to herself to become her own prince. She knows there are things so terrible they can strip everything from you and leave you raw and broken. Yet she pulls from somewhere the strength to believe she will one day face her own reflection unencumbered and free.

A moment for all those mamas who gather their hopes around them like superhero cloaks and put one foot in front of the other on the road to a better life. A moment for all the women who speak out into silence in the hopes we will join our voices with theirs. A moment for all those who have been broken by others and who are on the journey back to wholeness.

I witnessed these stories of strength as my mama fought her way through my childhood. Five foot nothing of African-Cherokee-Jew, she was a natural force of pure mama-love. As a young single mother with no emotional or physical supports, she kept us afloat while always making room in our lifeboat for others. She rebuilt herself after a past filled with abuse and horror stories but refused to be a victim, trying to teach me about my own beauty while working to see her own. When my racist grade four teacher told me I was stupid and tore up my work because he hated the color of her skin, instead of backing down because he was well-connected and up for the vice principal position, she held him up to the light and lost him his job and reputation in the community. When my Aunt Lizzie put a gun in her mouth and took her life just before my twelfth birthday, my mama held us together and moved across the country to make a new start. When I took out my anger on the world at her, and on myself, she never stopped fighting for me or believing in my potential for greatness. Throughout it all she took herself from unemployable and undereducated to an award-winning journalist with an honors degree in philosophy all entirely, heartbreakingly alone.

Nothing has made me appreciate my mother's struggle like having daughters of my own. She birthed me hard and cold in an unfriendly hospital surrounded by judgment, all so that one day I could bring my girls into the world with her arms around me, my love behind, midwives in front, surrounded in a circle of support. Years of banging against the injustices of the world, trying to make it see some sense or failing that, bandage up some of its more painful messes, left my mama without the resources to keep shining, and she has been swimming hard upstream against her own dark rivers this year. I try to give her back the gift she has given me every day of my life—the knowledge that I am not, and have never been, alone. Now it is my turn to hold her with my strong arms as she births a new life for herself, the relationship shifting as we mother together now, moving from strength to strength.

The sad thing about strength is that it isn't infinite; you can use it all up and not realize you've run dry until you call on it for backup and find yourself drained of resiliency. The only thing that fuels strength is to be witnessed and celebrated by others who have been there. So when you see your sister struggling, reach out and hold her tight. Hug her with the fierce love you can only give to another woman who is standing where you have been and looking up. Let's work together so that when we cry out in the darkness there are arms to hold us safe and keep us in the light.

Jessika Hepburn has dedicated her life to the transformational power of community. She believes two hands can make the world more beautiful, four hands can start a revolution of goodness, and a hundred hands can be an unstoppable force. Through her work as editor and leader of the Oh My! Handmade community, she has created a space where the diverse creative entrepreneurs of the world can connect to build the work of their dreams, figure out how put food in the fridge, and find a big hug when things don't go as planned (and they never go as planned). Visit her at OhMyHandmade.com.

THE WAR AGAINST MYSELF
Kimberly Riggins

There is always one event, a time, that marks you forever.

There's no other way to say it.

Being raped turned my world on its head.

I will never forget that moment.

It almost feels like it was yesterday. I can still feel the tear-stained mascara running down my face.

It was late. I was tired. Everyone else was sleeping—something I should have been doing.

But instead I was arguing with my boyfriend, who happened to be as high as a kite.

At one point, he shoved me and I felt the cold door of the refrigerator against my back. I was infuriated.

And then I heard *those words*.

"I love you and I'm sorry. I have no idea why I did that."

I fell for his apology. And I followed him into another room where we could "talk" some more. But, within minutes, I found myself pinned underneath him, pushing and pulling to get away, trying to scream but unable to make a sound.

By the time I broke free from his relentless grasp, the damage was done. He left abruptly and I sat there alone, my pants around my knees and blood on my underwear—my face flushed with anger and shame.

How could this have happened to ME?

I locked myself in the bathroom, sat on the toilet, and cried and cried until I had no more tears left. When I finally stood up and looked at myself in the mirror, I was filled with disgust and self-hatred. I felt as though the Kimberly I knew was gone—her dignity smashed into a million tiny pieces.

"Who are you?" I asked.

And the voice that spoke back to me said, "Your worst nightmare, you stupid bitch."

For the first time in my life, I was no longer that girl who had her shit together. I was an ugly, fat, undesirable loser who deserved everything that was coming to her.

Bring on the artillery. There is going to be a war. A war against myself.

* * *

The loathing and tormenting went on for quite few years following that day.

I was relentless, constantly reminding myself of how weak I was or how stupid I'd been for putting myself in that situation to begin with.

The shame was painstakingly suffocating.

But rather than reach out for help, I punished myself some more.

At this point, I was starving my body daily, overworking it (exercising six hours a day) until I could barely physically move, and sleep depriving myself till I no longer could cognitively function.

I was a mess.

It wasn't until I hit rock bottom that my epiphany revealed itself.

I was lying on the cold tile floor, too tired to move, crying a river of tears—wondering how the hell I got here.

What am I supposed to do?

I found my answer.

I stood up, dusted myself off, and picked up the phone.

"Mom. Dad. I'm coming home."

* * *

It took unbelievable strength to let go of my shame. To stop hating myself and to find peace.

It certainly wasn't easy. It took a hospital stay, at least six different therapists, and many years of deep, transformational work.

But I was determined to thrive. And I never gave up.

* * *

Today I rely on that strength to persevere through life's hurdles. It has helped me pave my way through the world and has allowed me to freely share my gifts and passions with all of you.

In many ways, my strength has been my saving grace. I'm really not sure where I would be without it.

So look within yourself and find where your strength lives. And tap into it today.

You'll be amazed at its infinite wisdom and power.

Kimberly Riggins is a body image and self-love expert. She is also the author of the transformational book, *Love Your Naked Ass*, creator of the wildly successful self-love program The Ravishing Renegade, a dark chocolate lover, and a self-proclaimed wine connoisseur. Kimberly's mission is to brazenly inspire you to ditch your bullshit and own your worth so you can step out into the world as the bold, powerful woman you were meant to be. To learn more about Kimberly, visit KimberlyRiggins.com.

ACKNOWLEDGMENTS

Taking on a project like this is no easy feat. I have so many people to be grateful for…

In fact, I would like to give thanks to everyone in my life for your undying support, love, and encouragement. Even in the darkest of days, your support has always helped me see the light. My heart explodes with love for all of you.

There are a few people who played an intricate part to making this book and project come together that I believe deserve to be recognized.

Amanda Krill, you took on this project with gusto and turned the website for The Watch Her Thrive Project into a masterpiece. Thank you for recognizing that this project would be so much bigger than I imagined. Your willingness to offer your help and my knowing I can count on our friendship means the world to me.

Lucinda Kinch, for bringing the book cover to life. You truly captured the essence of a thriving woman and turned it into a beautiful piece of art. Your ability to see my vision is uncanny and I am honored to know you.

Bianca Filoteo, for taking my script and turning it into a powerful, riveting video. You have a gift. Thank you for being as passionate about this project as I am.

Nikki Groom, your ability to string my words together so eloquently is a godsend. You have saved me hours of valuable time and infused so much power and soul into my words.

Erica Kelly, for believing in my mission and for volunteering your writing expertise. Whenever I found myself frustrated or overwhelmed with my words, you were there to help me refine them. Thank you for helping me get out of my own way.

Erin Giles, for helping me bring my vision into a reality. It would have taken me years to figure this out on my own. With your class, I found the courage to step forward and "do good" regardless of my circumstances.

The Watch Her Thrive Sponsors, without your generous donations, this book would have never been published. I am eternally grateful for your support.

Finally, I would like to express my deepest thanks to all the contributing authors. Without your amazing stories, this book wouldn't exist. Thank you for being so raw, honest, and open. You have impacted me in such profound ways. I am truly blessed to know each one of you.

ABOUT THE WATCH HER THRIVE PROJECT

The Watch Her Thrive Project is more than a movement. It's a revolution and a catalyst for women to rise from the ashes of devastating domestic abuse and rape.

Every nine seconds in the US, a woman is assaulted or beaten. And one out of every six American women will be the victim of rape in her lifetime.

It's statistics like this that bring your struggles into perspective. You see, I'm all too familiar with adversity. In my younger years, I survived rape and an eating disorder. And as an adult, I was forced to face bankruptcy, foreclosure, and beginning my life all over again from scratch.

But I beat the odds. I bounced back.

Sadly, not all women are so fortunate. In fact, one in three women who are victims of murder are killed by an existing or former partner.

These are devastating statistics. But there is hope. I created The Watch Her Thrive Project to give those women who feel like they have no way out the resources, support, and opportunities they need to thrive.

ABOUT FOUNDER KIMBERLY RIGGINS

Kimberly Riggins is an intuitive changemaker, wealth warrior and self-love expert who understands all too well how to face adversity. As a young adult, she suffered from a rape and an eating disorder. As an adult, she had to face bankruptcy, foreclosure, and had to start her life all over again from scratch.

The one thing she learned through her own struggles is that there are so many other people in the world who have it much worse than she did.

She bounced back and is beating the odds but knows that it is in part because she had access to resources, support, and opportunities.

She also understands that for other women to beat their own odds they need resources, support, and opportunity. She created The Watch Her Thrive Project to give those women who feel like they have no way out a space to grow and an opportunity to thrive.

HOW YOU CAN HELP

Make A Donation

Donating as little as ten dollars (the price of a few Starbucks coffees) will help provide women in need with a stipend that they can use for whatever they need most—basic necessities such as food and shelter, school fees for her children, or investment into income-generating activities. To make a donation, go to WatchHerThrive.com/Donate.

Share the Message

The Watch Her Thrive Project can be found on social media.
Facebook: www.facebook.com/TheWatchHerThriveProject
Twitter: www.twitter.com/KimberlyRiggins
Pinterest: www.pinterest.com/KimberlyRiggins/The-Watch-Her-Thrive-Project

www.ingramcontent.com/pod-product-compliance
Lightning Source LLC
Chambersburg PA
CBHW060104170426
43198CB000108/766